D1467087

EMERGENCY DISPUTES
AND NATIONAL POLICY

INDUSTRIAL RELATIONS RESEARCH ASSOCIATION

•

PUBLICATION NO. 15

•

(The previous books in this series were published by the Association, in Madison, Wisconsin, with one exception—No. 11, Manpower in the United States, published by Harper & Brothers, New York.)

EMERGENCY DISPUTES
AND NATIONAL POLICY

EDITORIAL BOARD

Irving Bernstein

University of California, Los Angeles

Harold L. Enarson

Western Interstate Commission
for Higher Education

R. W. Fleming

University of Illinois

HARPER & BROTHERS PUBLISHERS

NEW YORK

Main   Emergency disputes and
HD   national policy.
5324
.I5   (331.89 In2)

EMERGENCY DISPUTES AND NATIONAL POLICY

Copyright, 1955, by Harper & Brothers ©
Printed in the United States of America

All rights in this book are reserved.
No part of the book may be used or reproduced
in any manner whatsoever without written per-
mission except in the case of brief quotations
embodied in critical articles and reviews. For
information address Harper & Brothers
49 East 33rd Street, New York 16, N. Y.

FIRST EDITION

K - E

Library of Congress catalog card number: 55-11400 ..

BARD COLLEGE LIBRARY
ANNANDALE-ON-HUDSON, N.Y.

CONTENTS

Introduction

v

PART III

WHAT ARE THE ELEMENTS OF A NATIONAL POLICY?

APPENDIXES

INTRODUCTION

The strike is the most dramatic form that labor-management relations take. A nationwide and industry-wide stoppage in a basic industry may do more than capture the imagination; it may also shut off goods or services vital to the health and safety of millions of people. This, in essence, is the national emergency dispute issue.

Like most great policy questions in a democratic society, it is more readily framed than resolved. This is because the emergency problem provides an arena for a set of irreconcilable convictions that most reasonable Americans share. In the great stoppage in a key industry we find the union insisting upon its right to strike, the employer insisting upon his right to run his business without government regimentation, and the community insisting upon its right to an uninterrupted flow of goods or services necessary to the public health and safety. Admittedly, there are no pat answers. Policy must be shaped out of conflicting values and imperfect knowledge.

The present national policy, set forth in Title II of the Taft-Hartley Act of 1947, stems from the strike wave following World War II. There is probably no provision of this controversial statute so universally criticized as that dealing with emergencies. Yet the critics can agree only upon what they dislike; their affirmative proposals run the gamut from nothing at all to compulsory arbitration.

This is the axis upon which the present volume revolves. In question form it may be framed in this fashion: what does the interested legislator and citizen need to know in order to shape a national policy for emergency disputes? This fundamental query divides itself logically into the three subquestions that form the main sections of the book: (1) what is a national emergency dispute? (2) what is the Taft-Hartley experience? and (3) what are the elements of a national policy?

Given this focus, it has been necessary to devote only incidental attention to two important areas of investigation. They are the experience with transportation disputes under the Railway Labor Act and that with public utility stoppages under the state compulsory arbitration statutes. The basis for these decisions is editorial and casts no slight upon the inherent significance of strikes in the railroad and public utility industries. In fact, one could argue with cogency that emergencies are more likely to occur here than in the industries covered by Title II.

A product of many hands, like the present one, inevitably suffers a loss of unity. The editors were fully conscious of this when they set about their task. Hence the author of each chapter was assigned little more than his title and was instructed to develop his analysis as he saw fit. As a consequence, there is a certain amount of disagreement and a lesser amount of overlap among chapters. Both might have been avoided by a rigid editorial policy, but the cost would have been the destruction of the symposium. The editors, like good shoppers, preferred to pay a lower price for a better product.

As a result of this policy the volume has no concluding chapter. Instead, the editors have elected to set forth here in the introduction several ideas that tend to run through the authors' analyses. This generalizing is undertaken with the warning that some of the authors may not share all of these views.

The first point of emphasis is the multisided character of the great strike. It is at the same time an exercise in *economics* affecting, among other things, the volume of output in the struck industry and industries that depend upon it, the level of consumption, and the income to the firm and the workers; in *politics* reflecting the relationship between union and employers with the President, members of Congress, and, sometimes, the courts; in *the government of private organizations* relating to the authority of negotiators and the degree of internal cohesion within the union as well as the employer group; in *public opinion* stemming from the attitudes of the principal media and their manipulation by the contestants; and, often, in *military policy* mirroring the stage of the nation's foreign relations.

The risk in an analysis of important stoppages is oversimplification, stressing one factor to the exclusion of others. The firm may look only at its profit prospects, the senator facing re-election only at his constituency, the dissident union faction only at its quest for power, the newspaper editorial writer only at his deep-rooted prejudices, and the Pentagon only at the shortage of a military item. Public policy, however, calls for a balancing of all considerations.

To the complexities of many-sidedness must be added a second generalization, that there are sharp differences in impact among strikes in the same industry as well as among strikes in different industries. A steel stoppage in a period of military mobilization is far more dangerous than one of identical duration in peacetime. The effects of a coal strike are more slowly realized than those of a rail walkout because the fuel can be stored and the service cannot.

These subtleties suggest the third point, namely, that policy must be fitted to the particular strike. The officers charged with its shaping must possess, in the hackneyed phrase, an arsenal of weapons. One does not shoot ducks with a howitzer. Enabling legislation, therefore, should afford the President flexibility.

These complexities, in the fourth place, make it clear that there is no "solution" to the national emergency strike problem. The human mind has a tendency to simplify the real world. In periods when the nation's dispute load rises sharply, this propensity takes form in plans to eliminate strikes. In this area gadgetry will not work. In fact, any single scheme is likely to do more harm than good. To the extent that these plans stem from foreign experience, furthermore, they reflect economies and collective bargaining systems much less complicated and interrelated than ours.

This leads to the fifth point, that the main charge against Title II of Taft-Hartley is not that it is wrong but rather that it is ineffective. In many important strikes the President has elected not to invoke its procedures, and even when he has, they seem to have had little influence on the outcome one way or the other. Both the prophets of disaster and of salvation have been proved incorrect.

A sixth generalization is that the whole problem of the national emergency has been exaggerated in the public and legislative minds. This is understandable in the historical context out of which Title II grew. The fact, however, is that the statute was passed too late to deal with the great strike wave of 1945-1946, but, rather, has been in effect during a much quieter period. The time has come to examine the problem realistically. Excepting wartime, of course, it seems clear that the number of industries with an emergency potential is limited and that only a few strikes even in those industries have actually produced national emergencies. Further, despite a widespread conviction to the contrary, these stoppages create no challenge to the sovereignty of the state. Reason, however, does not necessarily determine what people think; we may have an unrealistic policy willy-nilly.

This tendency to exaggerate must be qualified by a seventh point, namely, that the low incidence of national emergencies reflects the current stage of economic and bargaining organization. In fact, there are now few vital industries with complete union organization and industry-wide bargaining. It is possible that their number will grow in the next generation with the secular expansion of the labor movement and the integration of bargaining structures. That is, the emergency problem may be more significant in the future than it is today.

Eighth, governmental intervention in a major dispute must be executive action. For a variety of reasons Congress is incapable of dealing with these cases except in a broad enabling fashion. The courts, obviously, can handle only narrow aspects of them. The often-phrased question—how shall we keep disputes out of the White House?—reflects, therefore, a fundamental misunderstanding of government. The President and his agents have no alternative but to express concern over the effects of a prolonged strike in a basic industry. In fact, failure to take affirmative action may be as much an act of intervention as a positive step. In some disputes the government is always present at the bargaining table—in fact or in effect.

Finally, the most significant factor giving edge to the emergency problem is foreign relations. International pressures have profound influence upon domestic affairs—the level of business activity, the state of the First Amendment, and the impact of strikes. Big war, little war, cold war, peace—each provides a different vantage point for evaluating a strike. There is a direct relationship between international tension and the public risks in a work stoppage. A national emergency policy geared to peace does not work in war, and the other way around. The removal of the causes of international friction would do more than anything else to minimize the disaster context within which the public tends to view emergency strikes.

A special word of gratitude must be expressed for editorial work done on the manuscript by Mrs. Barbara Dennis, Editor, Institute of Labor and Industrial Relations, University of Illinois, and by Mrs. Anne P. Cook, Editor, Institute of Industrial Relations, University of California, Los Angeles.

IRVING BERNSTEIN
University of California, Los Angeles

HAROLD L. ENARSON
Western Interstate Commission for Higher Education

R. W. FLEMING
University of Illinois

PART I

WHAT IS A NATIONAL EMERGENCY DISPUTE?

Discussion of the national emergency strike must begin by finding out what it is. Hence Chapter I is an essay in economic definition, framing criteria and drawing borders about those industries and bargaining relationships that have an emergency potential. In Chapter II the economic impact of historic strikes in these critical areas is examined to determine the frequency of emergency. The problem, however, goes far beyond economics. By turning an intense light upon a particular case—the 1952 steel strike—Chapter III illuminates the political and public opinion sides of the national emergency. Chapter IV furthers understanding by disposing of a widely held misconception: that a great strike is a challenge to the sovereignty of the state.

AN ECONOMIC DEFINITION OF

THE NATIONAL EMERGENCY DISPUTE

BY GEORGE H. HILDEBRAND

University of California, Los Angeles

THE PROBLEM

The concept of national emergency disputes gained popular currency during the second world war, when uninterrupted production became a social imperative.[1] With the great strike wave of 1945-1946, the public was forcefully made aware of the new-found power of organized labor, and the emergency concept acquired broad usage even in peacetime. Under the impetus of this crisis in labor-management relations, the idea next found statutory expression in Title II of the Labor-Management Relations Act of 1947. This section of the law is elastic, contemplating a wide variety of industries whose disputes conceivably could be held to be national emergencies, providing that all or a "substantial part" of the industry is either threatened by a stoppage or has one already in progress, and that the President and a court of competent jurisdiction believe that the dispute will "imperil the national health and safety."

It is axiomatic that fundamental legislation should not be enacted in times of crisis, when dispassionate reflection and exhaustive study are not possible. Nonetheless, this provision of the Taft-Hartley Act

---

[1] The concept of national emergency disputes was first applied to the railroads, in a legislative history that goes back to the Arbitration Act of 1888. It was also implicit in the no-strike-no-lockout pledge of the first world war.

3

does rest upon the sound principle that there exists a class of disputes in which the rights of the parties to resort to unlimited economic warfare may have to be subordinated to the claims of the public to continued production.

There is little disagreement with this principle itself. However, there is also little disagreement with a second principle, that the freedom to engage in strikes or lockouts is an essential ingredient of collective bargaining, which in turn is considered desirable national policy. Yet it must be patent that instances can occur when the two principles will conflict with each other. This, in essence, is the problem of national emergency strikes. Under what conditions can the rights of the public to continued production be said to override the rights of the parties to shut down production? If there is a class of national emergency disputes, what are their common characteristics? When is major federal intervention reasonably justified, and when is it not? Can we get beyond the arbitrary and unreflective principle that intervention should occur when public opinion demands it?

Obviously, a decision that a specific dispute involves a national emergency will depend upon the point of view of those who make that decision and of those who support it.

Public opinion, for example, is likely to regard any nationwide strike as a crisis demanding immediate and perhaps drastic government action, even if the losses are demonstrably insignificant either to the economy or even to the national safety. Conflict on this scale seems formidable to the public eye, because it is newsworthy and usually well publicized in melodramatic terms. Public opinion is likely to be undiscriminating, hence to subject responsible public officials to unreasonable pressures for precipitate action.

Moreover, there can be reasonable differences among dispassionate observers regarding the need for intervention—differences that stem from diverse points of departure. For example, the present chapter looks at the emergency problem from an economic point of view. That is to say, it proceeds from a group of criteria whose purpose is to emphasize the range and character of the economic losses involved, as a basis for judging whether a dispute should be considered a national emergency. Clearly, the economic standard is not the only reasonable one to apply. Legal, political, and military considerations are also likely to be involved.[2]

Yet whatever the standard, it seems crucial to a free industrial order that drastic federal intervention in these disputes ought to be minimized, to be used only when clearly justified by some reasonable principle. If so, we can hardly be content with reliance upon public opinion alone as the ultimate standard of reference. The success of democratic government rests upon the possibility of rational agreement and consent, upon the predominance of reason over passion. If reason is to prevail, we shall require carefully formulated standards for intervention. This, indeed, is the best guarantee that public opinion itself can be intelligently developed, rather than passively accepted on the doctrine that might makes right.

THE INFLUENCE OF FOREIGN RELATIONS

In the formulation of economic criteria for defining the national emergency dispute, it must be admitted at the outset that the range of such disputes will depend in part upon the foreign relations of the United States. Foreign relations set the scope and urgency of the defense requirements of the nation. In this way they directly affect the industries and component products that have to be considered essential from the emergency standpoint.

Concerning foreign relations, there are three main possibilities: actual warfare, in which this nation is engaged; cold war, in which the threat of open warfare is ever present in varying but always marked degree; and generally peaceful relations, where tensions will exist but the likelihood of open or veiled conflict is small.

In actual warfare, public opinion will no doubt dictate a policy of general strike prevention. For local wars of the Korean type, the policy would probably be more flexible than if the nation were

[2] There already exists some literature on this problem: Irving Bernstein and Hugh G. Lovell, "Are Coal Strikes National Emergencies?" *Industrial and Labor Relations Review*, 6 (April 1953), pp. 352-367; Neil W. Chamberlain and Jane Metzger Schilling, *The Impact of Strikes* (New York: Harper, 1954); Orme W. Phelps, "Public Policy in Labor Disputes: The Crisis of 1946," *Journal of Political Economy*, LV (June 1947), pp. 189-211; Sumner H. Slichter, *The Challenge of Industrial Relations: Trade Unions, Management, and the Public Interest* (Ithaca, New York: Cornell University Press, 1947), pp. 149-167; and Edgar L. Warren, "Thirty-Six Years of National Emergency Strikes," *Industrial and Labor Relations Review*, 5 (October 1951), pp. 3-19.

engaged in direct conflict with a major power. Nonetheless, war as such would vastly extend the scope of stoppages constituting national emergencies, and for good reason. In wartime the economy is geared to a single end, and public opinion is not likely to tolerate precise rational discriminations between activities that are actually essential and those that are not.

By contrast, if international relations were so peaceful that there were no real threats to what this country considers its vital interests, the range of possible emergencies would become much narrower, with its limits dictated by other considerations.

This leaves the case of cold war, the one now actually prevailing. Official policy is based upon the proposition that armed strength, backed by unimpeded technological progress in armament, is a requisite though not exclusive means for prevention of aggression. Taken as a datum, this means that there are certain types of production whose continued and uninterrupted flow is imperative for national safety. The intercontinental bomber is one such product. Fissionable materials for military use are another. Strikes involving vitally important defense products, for which there are no close substitutes, would thus fall into the national emergency class. Indeed, this could be the case even if only a single producer of some specialized kind of armament or material were concerned.

ECONOMIC CRITERIA FOR DETERMINING NATIONAL EMERGENCY STRIKES

Given, then, an international environment of cold war, what criteria ought to be satisfied to warrant a responsible judgment that on economic grounds some particular dispute constitutes a national emergency? There are four, all of which are necessary and no one of which alone would be sufficient:

1. The impacts of the dispute must be national rather than purely local.

2. The product or service must be essential, in the sense that its use cannot be dispensed with or postponed without quickly and seriously impairing the safety or health of the whole nation.

3. The dispute must embrace all or a substantial part of the industry.

4. The emergency must be imminent or actual, rather than an

ultimate prospect if the stoppage were to last an indefinitely long period.[3]

1. *The impacts of the dispute must be national.*

All strikes involve economic losses. For these losses to be national, they must be broadly diffused over the whole country, and not concentrated upon producers and users in a particular local or intraregional area. In other words, an emergency can be *national* only when its impacts are nationwide.

Two classes of disputes meet this criterion: (1) where the firms produce for a national market; or (2) where the firms turn out a service or product for the federal government and the item is urgently required for national defense. For purposes of the criterion, it makes no difference whether the firms themselves are geographically concentrated or diffused. What is important is that the impacts of a strike can be felt over the whole country, in the form of lost supplies to users, lost markets to suppliers, and lost incomes through direct and indirect shutdowns. Clearly these losses must be significant and widespread if drastic federal intervention in disputes is to be employed with wisdom and hence sparingly.

Industries that serve national markets obviously qualify—basic steel production and nationwide railroad service providing strong instances.[4] Producers of urgently required defense goods, such as intercontinental bombers, stand on a different footing: though here, too, the impacts of a strike would be nationwide, strictly speaking, these firms do not serve a national market. Instead, their market has a single buyer, the federal government, acting for the whole people in providing for the external safety of the nation. On this basis, a stoppage in production of high-priority defense goods would also have nationwide impacts.

Some confusion may arise between national marketing and national use of certain products. For instance, electric power is

[3] These criteria differ somewhat from those proposed in Chapter II, p. 25.

[4] Some national market industries have increasingly become regionally decentralized, for example, basic steel and meat packing. Decentralization means that an increasing part of production may be for regional and local account, in superficial similarity to electric power. Yet the comparison with power must fail, for there remains considerable crosshauling in steel and meat packing, and the principal producers are organized on a branch plant basis, with centralized policy making. Therefore they still serve a national market.

nationally used, but it is produced and sold in local markets, not national ones. For this reason power strikes do not jeopardize the health or safety of the people as a whole, granting the gravity of the local emergencies they may entail.[5]

Although nationwide impacts are an essential condition for national emergency disputes, they are not a sufficient basis for declaring that a national emergency actually exists. Pianos, organs, wallpaper, and pottery are all products turned out by industries that serve national markets. However, these products are obviously not essential to the immediate health or safety of the population. Clearly, then, the essentiality of the product or service must also be considered in determining national emergency disputes.

2. *The product must be essential.*

From the economic standpoint, "essential" is a term to be viewed with some suspicion, because all commodities are substitutes for one another in some degree. Indeed, one of the most impressive features of the American economy is its enormous and probably increasing flexibility in providing substitutes. However, substitution usually requires time, while the essence of an emergency is its urgency. Accordingly, there are certain goods and services that have strategic importance for the economy, and so may be considered essential in this sense.

They fall into three classes: (1) products and services that are essential to the external and internal safety of the people; (2) products and services indispensable to the immediate health and safety of final consumers; and (3) products and services whose continued production is essential to a sustained flow of real and money income to much of the population.

The first category includes those defense goods that are vital to national security under conditions of cold war. Admittedly, there are practical difficulties in gauging this kind of essentiality, for ultimately it rests upon professional military opinion, which is usually inclined to take a sweeping view of the urgency question.

---

[5] Of course, if a joint strike embracing electrical utility firms throughout the country ever were to occur, the impacts would become national, as in the national market case. This possibility seems too remote now for serious consideration, for there is little incentive to extend the area of a strike beyond the effective area of the product market. Hence strikes in industries serving local markets are likely to remain local.

The internal safety of the whole population is a joint responsibility of the federal and local governments. The services of local government would not figure in the emergency strike problem, because they concern local populations alone. At the federal level, there are many essential services, among them the armed forces, the intelligence agencies, the courts, the Post Office, and others. On grounds of essentiality, the federal services would qualify for potential emergency status. However, as we shall see later, the likelihood of strikes involving federal employees is small.

The second dimension of essentiality concerns products and services indispensable to final consumers. To qualify as essential in this sense, the product or service would have to be such that interruption of its flow would have prompt and serious impact upon the health and safety of final consumers. Neglecting the other emergency criteria for a moment, examples would be medical and hospital care, utility services (gas, light, water, local transit, telegraphic and telephonic communications), gasoline, foodstuffs, and intercity passenger transport. To these we would also have to add transportation for bringing certain of these goods to accessible markets. In some of these instances storage is impossible (electric current is an intangible, and households lack facilities for keeping stocks of water or gas), or it is impracticable on a large scale (it is costly to lay in large stocks of foodstuffs).

To be essential to final consumers, consumption of the product cannot long be deferred (one cannot long postpone eating) or dispensed with altogether (water has indispensable household uses). Most of the items suggested are services. Durable consumers' goods may be disregarded because their purchase can be postponed without hardship. Regarding the services, it must be recognized that freight transportation is the most ubiquitous of the group. Its role is vital for the geographic distribution of intermediate goods requisite to the production of essential final goods. For example, bituminous coal is an intermediate good, yielding almost half of our electric energy. Transportation is vital to its effective use. In addition, freight transport is equally vital for the distribution of essential final goods. Although it is inconceivable under present circumstances that a strike in the food-producing industry could cut off all foodstuffs, given the broad possibilities for substitution here, by contrast a transport strike could effectively cripple deliveries of foodstuffs to consumer markets, since substitution possibilities are so much more restricted in transportation.

However, merely to explore the question of essentiality for final consumers is to indicate its narrow bearing upon the problem of national emergency strikes. For nearly the entire list of such essentials involves goods or services that are produced for local or regional markets. Within the foodstuffs, this would include vegetables, milk and dairy products, most canned and packaged goods. Retail meats might represent an exception. Admittedly, there would be serious local hardships if any consumer essentials were cut off by strike, but it could not be said that the result would be a national emergency. The only obvious exceptions would be long-distance telephonic and telegraphic communications, railroad service, and bituminous coal, all of which involve national markets.[6]

There remains the third distinct basis for essentiality: a product or service may be essential to the continued employment and income-earning capacities of much of the population. This may be termed the income aspect of essentiality.[7] It means that certain products and services may be so ubiquitously used in further economic production that the cutting off of any one of them could seriously impair output generally and, through this, reduce the incomes of many people throughout the nation. Durable producers' goods (plant and equipment) can be excluded here, because their acquisition can usually be deferred for some time without adversely affecting current production.

In a general way, production in an industrial society advances through a series of technological stages, beginning with the products of farm, forest, and mine, then proceeding by further transformations into basic raw materials such as primary steel or aluminum, after which subsequent fabrications yield semifinished and

---

[6] It is noteworthy that at the time of the great strike wave of 1945-1946, when for understandable reasons the notion of national emergencies was being loosely applied, many of the dramatic instances cited involved local production for local markets, for example, gas in Milwaukee, electric power in Pittsburgh, local trucking, tugboats, and elevators in New York City. Yet with the possible exception of local trucking and tugboats in New York City, which could have interstate significance, none of these strikes constituted a genuine national emergency, even granting the seriousness of their local impacts.

[7] This element has been thoroughly developed by Chamberlain and Schilling, *op. cit.*, pp. 32-36, 245-248.

then finished products that are ultimately distributed to final consumers or industry users. In the earlier stages prior to fabrication, the commodities take the form of relatively homogeneous raw materials, consumed by a broad group of fabricating industries. The raw materials stage is thus far more critical for income essentiality, because the impact when production is cut off is more sweeping. Hence certain raw materials industries are particularly important from the standpoint of essentiality and potential emergency status.

Two observations are now in order. First, certain services are broadly used throughout the whole technological range, among them railway transport, electric energy, and telephonic and telegraphic communications. A nationwide stoppage of any of these services, therefore, would have an immediate, cumulative, and serious impact upon almost all branches of the economy, having the character of a national emergency by cutting off production generally, reducing the incomes of much of the population through enforced shutdowns, and so imperiling its health and safety. Lest this danger be overemphasized, it must be recalled that electric power is most unlikely to be cut off throughout the nation, while telephone and telegraph services are close substitutes, unlikely to be simultaneously suspended. This leaves the railroads in a highly strategic category, where public opinion has always rightly placed them.

Second, certain commodities in the technological sequence are more "basic" than others, because they are indispensable either to many types of further production at the later stages, or to the production of ubiquitously used services at all stages, such as electric power or railway service. Among these primary commodities would be basic steel, bituminous coal, petroleum and its products, and important nonferrous metals such as aluminum, lead, copper, and zinc. If the supply of any of these raw materials were cut off for a long enough period, there would follow widespread derivative impacts upon production as a whole. Here too a national emergency conceivably could arise.[8]

[8] Direct-user industries would be affected; also dependent industries (indirect users) requiring the products of direct-user industries; also intermediate and final distributors; and wholesalers and retailers supplying other commodities to final consumers whose incomes have been reduced. In basic steel this sequence of shocks would be particularly severe. On the question of dependent third parties, see Chamberlain and Schilling, op. cit., pp. 22-39.

To conclude, then, the more ubiquitous the use of a product or service in general production, or the more basic a commodity for further production, the greater will be the potential of the industry producing it for creating national emergencies.

3. *The dispute must involve all or a substantial part of the industry.*

It is easy to exaggerate the vulnerability of the economy by concentrating exclusively upon the essentiality of certain highly strategic, national-market industries. For one thing, the likelihood that a dispute would close down all or a substantial part of an industry depends upon bargaining circumstances that are relatively rare. For another, the shutdown of an essential product (not service) industry would have to last a relatively long period of time, well beyond what has been the usual experience in the past, for stockpiles to approach exhaustion and widespread derivative closures to occur.

Regarding the industry coverage of the dispute, the first requisite for a possible emergency is that the workers must be highly organized; in other words, that there be no substantial nonunion component which could continue to supply the market.[9] With the possible exception of telephone service, this probably holds true for all essential product or service industries supplying national markets.

However, the emergency potential of an industry also depends upon the kind of bargaining system in effect. There are four main situations in which this potential is likely to be high: (1) the employers bargain through an industry-wide association; or (2) the employers bargain separately with a single union but contract expirations and negotiations are approximately concurrent; or (3) there are separate company negotiations and multiple unions, but expirations and negotiations are concurrent and common strategies are followed; or (4) there are separate company-wide negotiations

---

[9] "Highly organized" would suggest that 60 per cent or more of the employees belonged to unions, which would hold for railroads, bituminous and anthracite coal, telegraphs, metal mining, basic steel, and primary nonferrous metal production. "Extent of Collective Bargaining and Union Recognition, 1946," *Monthly Labor Review*, 64 (May 1947), p. 766. The 60 per cent rule loses force where the products of firms in the industry are highly differentiated, as in military aircraft. Here the best approach would be to consider each firm an "industry," since its product has only remote substitutes within the class.

but some one firm is the dominant producer, supplying, say, at least 60 per cent of a relatively homogeneous product.[10] If no one of these characteristics describes the bargaining system of the industry, a dispute is most unlikely to close it down entirely or even in substantial part, and no nationally significant losses either to final consumers or of incomes generally would occur.

4. *The emergency must be actual or imminent, and not merely a remote prospect.*

The closure of any nationally essential industry must ultimately have highly ramified derivative impacts. Clearly, however, any real emergency must be immediate and tangible, and not merely an ultimate grim prospect. Recognition of this is essential if indiscriminate government intervention into a broad range of basic national industries is to be avoided. Obviously, widespread government strike control is something to be shunned by all those who prefer voluntarism in industrial relations. Fortunately, a realistic view of the emergency problem points clearly to the conclusion that sweeping strike control is not necessary.

Distinction must initially be made between essential industries yielding services and those yielding tangible products. Since services cannot be stored, shutdowns of national-service industries have immediate and rapidly cumulative impacts on users.[11] In this category we would include railway freight and passenger service. Railway services account for over half of the total ton-miles of intercity freight. If cut off by strike, large losses could quickly be sustained by producers and final consumers, since large-scale substitution of other carriers is impossible within the short period of time encompassed by an emergency. Here, then, the linkage between an actual

[10] In the basic raw materials group, primary aluminum has the Aluminum Company of America as the leading producer, but its capacity in 1949 was only 49 per cent of the industry total at the primary stage. U. S. Department of the Interior, Bureau of Mines, *Minerals Yearbook 1949* (1951), p. 113. For the others, concentration ratios of the portion of total value product or of value added in industry production by the four largest firms indicate no clear dominance. *Report of the Federal Trade Commission on Changes in Concentration in Manufacturing* (1954), pp. 138-147. In the field of highly differentiated essential defense products, single-firm dominance makes for high emergency potential under collective bargaining.

[11] Railway services in a sense can be "stored" through anticipatory shipments, though hardly on a significant scale.

emergency and the onset of a strike is very close, so close that the emergency could be said to occur at almost the moment the walkout begins.

By contrast, the linkage is by no means so close in the tangible product industries. These products are stored in inventories that normally allow continued production without replenishment for considerable periods of time. Further, inventories can usually be built up when a general stoppage is anticipated, unless the supplier industry is already working close to practical capacity. In some cases, primary copper, for example, imports are an important supplemental source. In addition, it is common for industrial users to impose self-rationing as a means of stretching inventories to stave off complete shutdowns. Also there are some situations where interproduct substitutions are feasible. Thus in the bituminous coal strikes, railroads formed emergency pools of diesel engine power and by using it intensively they were able to reduce their dependence upon coal-burning equipment.

Together, these offsets mean that the diffusion of effects from a shutdown in some branch of essential raw materials production will be delayed, usually for a lengthy period. Ordinarily, this delay will provide adequate time to permit pressures to bear in favor of a settlement, well before any needed intervention under emergency powers. However, there can be exceptions, and here arises the problem of determining when an emergency becomes actual or imminent.

It seems safe to say that no simple rule can be devised to serve as a warning that a genuine emergency is impending. Certainly the mere existence even of an industry-wide strike in basic steel production would not automatically constitute a national emergency, although such would surely be the case with a national railroad strike. Yet if a steel strike were to last long enough, it would have widespread crippling effects.[12] The real difficulty in devising a warning signal is that the appearance of an emergency depends in no unique way upon the passage of clock time. Time is clearly involved, but the relation between strike length and an actual emergency differs among industries and, indeed, among strikes even in the same industry. User stockpiles and rates of raw material con-

---

[12] For illustration, see Irving Bernstein's account of the 1952 basic steel strike, in Chapter II of this volume, p. 38.

sumption differ from one strike to another, because the relationship depends upon variables that undergo change—seasonal movements in production, general business fluctuations, and numerous erratic influences. Thus Chamberlain and Schilling found that a forty-day bituminous coal strike in the spring of 1946 scored over-all losses that were not much higher than those from a sixteen-day bituminous strike in the fall of 1946. Also, the two-day national railroad strike in May 1946, caused general losses by the end of the first day that were as large as those registered for the twenty-eight-day basic steel strike in January and February of that year.[13]

To sum up, large-scale strikes and national emergencies occur simultaneously in an essential service industry such as the railroads. However, in the tangible product industries a large-scale strike is not automatically a national emergency. The onset of such an emergency must be gauged by informed judgment, according to the facts of the case.[14] Among these facts would be the stockpiles available to important user industries, the availability of imports as substitute sources for these users, the current rates of raw materials consumption by these users, the scale of actual or impending shutdowns of industries either supplying the struck industry or using its product, and the essentiality of the struck product, or of derivative products that incorporate it, for military items deemed essential to national defense.

WHICH INDUSTRIES NOW HAVE A HIGH EMERGENCY POTENTIAL?

With the use of the four criteria, it is now possible to draw up a list of industries where strikes have a high potential for creating national emergencies. All of these industries supply a product or service that is either nationally marketed or is sold to the federal government for purposes of national defense. In all cases the product or service is essential to final consumers, or to the production of income generally, or to national defense. All the industries have

[13] Chamberlain and Schilling, *op. cit.* The calculations of these authors indicate that losses from the basic steel strikes began to mount rapidly after the thirtieth day.

[14] Here it appears that the preference for rules over administrative discretion must be disregarded, for it seems safe to conclude that no workable rule can be written. However, rules have a vital place in governing the procedures for intervention in emergencies.

a bargaining structure likely to bring about a substantial or complete shutdown in the event of a strike. And for all of them the link between the occurrence of a strike and the onset of a national emergency is sufficiently close to be more than a remote possibility. Obviously this list will exclude several essential products or services, simply because the industries in question fail to meet all four criteria together.[15]

Industries with High Emergency Potential

Critical defense products
Mining, smelting, and refining
   of fissionable metals
Railroads
Bituminous coal mining
Basic steel products

Admittedly, the category of critical defense products is a miscellaneous one and not a true "industry" because of the highly differentiated nature of the products. It would include, for example, specialized types of essential military aircraft, where each firm may be viewed as an "industry" in itself; manufacture of fission products and of various new weapons; and possibly production of certain electronic devices. Clearly, not all defense goods are of high urgency. Further, it must be acknowledged that the question of what items are of high urgency is not easy to resolve and cannot be examined here.

If fission products are considered essential, one should also include the mining and primary producing industries that turn out the metallic raw materials themselves, for example, cobalt, lithium, uranium, and zirconium. Rather sparse information indicates that there are few firms in each of these fields. Where they are organized by unions, they probably should be classed in the dominant producer group, which means that strikes in separate concerns are likely to impair total production seriously. Doubtless stockpiles are an offset, so that the link between a strike and an emergency involves some slack as to time.

Clearly railroad services belong on the list. They are essential to final consumers, to the production of incomes, and to national

---

[15] This list may be compared with that proposed in Chapter II, pp. 28-29.

defense. Bargaining is industry-wide and a strike would promptly generate a national emergency. However, strikes involving single railroad companies alone would not fall into the emergency category, for their impacts would mainly be local, and substitute rail and motor transport services usually would be available.

Bituminous coal (including lignite) must be on the list because of its many vital uses, for example, in the production of coke and of electric power, or as a still important locomotive fuel. Also, bargaining is industry-wide. However, stockpiling and self-rationing are important offsets, and therefore a bituminous coal strike would have to last relatively long to create an emergency.

The basic steel products group embraces domestic iron-ore mining, blast furnace production, steelworks and rolling mills (where plates, sheets, strips, rods, bars, tubing, and some forgings are turned out), and electrometallurgical steels (ferro-alloys). This group is an indispensable supplier for many secondary manufacturing industries. The firms are integrated technically, and with one major exception are completely organized at all stages of production, mainly by the United Steelworkers. Although formal bargaining is company-by-company, the traditional leadership of United States Steel and the simultaneity of contract expirations mean that strikes are likely to be industry-wide. Moreover, in basic steel a national emergency would probably develop with greater rapidity than in bituminous coal, if past experience is any guide. Again, however, product storability would delay impacts well beyond their appearance in a national railroad strike.[16]

On the basis of this list of industries with high emergency potentials, which labor unions accordingly acquire strategic importance?

In the category of critical defense products, the two most important unions in aircraft production are the United Automobile Workers (UAW), CIO, and the Machinists (IAM), AFL. In the manufacture of electronic equipment, the two leading organizations

[16] With the exceptions of critical defense products and mining of fissionable metals, the industry classifications here employed were all taken from Executive Office of the President, Bureau of the Budget, *Standard Industrial Classification Manual*, Vol. I, *Manufacturing Industries*, Pt. 1, "Titles and Descriptions of Industries" (1945), and Vol. II, *Nonmanufacturing Industries* (1942), prepared by the Technical Committee on Industrial Classification, Division of Statistical Standards. All industries referred to belong to the "four-digit" group, identified by principal product.

are the International Union of Electrical Workers (IUE), CIO, and the United Electrical Workers (UE), independent. For the principal atomic energy installations, AFL employees are represented by the Atomic Trades and Labor Council, affiliated with the Metal Trades Department, and CIO employees by the United Gas, Coke & Chemical Workers of America. The IAM has also recently entered the industry. In the mining and smelting of fissionable metals, the principal though by no means dominant union is the Mine, Mill & Smelter Workers, independent. However, labor representation in nonferrous metals mining and refining is complex and currently is undergoing some change.

On the railroads, the traditional craft structure has been maintained and so there is a large number of strongly situated organizations. These fall into two main groups, the operating brotherhoods and the traffic groups affiliated with the Railway Labor Executives' Association. The former group includes the Engineers (BLE), the Firemen (BLF), the Conductors (ORC), and the Trainmen (BRT) —all of which are independents. The traffic group embraces the Switchmen's Union, AFL; the Yardmasters, independent; the Train Dispatchers, independent; the Telegraphers, AFL; and the Signalmen, AFL. There are several other crafts for clerical, backshop, and maintenance-of-way work, but none has the strategic power of those referred to above.

Bituminous coal mining is, of course, almost completely organized by the United Mine Workers (UAW), independent. In basic steel, the United Steelworkers (USA), CIO, are clearly dominant at all stages of production.

ESSENTIAL NATIONAL INDUSTRIES NOW HAVING LITTLE OR NO EMERGENCY POTENTIAL

There are, admittedly, many other industries that are immediately essential to the safety and health of the nation. Yet all of them fall outside the category of high-potential emergency status, because they fail to meet one or more of the four jointly necessary criteria.

Among this group, for example, wholesale meat packing ranks high, but its collective bargaining system is still sufficiently decentralized to make a substantial industry-wide strike rather unlikely. Long-distance telephone and telegraph services fail to qualify because each is a close substitute for the other and collective bargaining is independent for each field. Crude petroleum production and petroleum refining can be eliminated because unionism is still weak at the crude production level and collective bargaining is decentralized in refining, making a substantial shutdown improbable at either stage.

In the nonferrous metals group, copper, lead, zinc, and aluminum ore mining all have decentralized collective bargaining, while substitution through imports is highly significant. These judgments also hold for smelting and refining of primary copper, lead, and zinc. In primary aluminum production, bargaining is company-by-company, with rival unions and independent negotiations, again making industry-wide strikes improbable.

The main output of lumber depends upon the logging industry and upon general sawmills and planing mills. Here again imports are important, and in addition collective bargaining is decentralized on an area basis, with rival unionism.

Excluding the railroads, emergency potential is low in the transportation group. Common carrier air transport has separate company bargaining. Substitution is therefore possible for all principal routes, though the carriers are jointly vulnerable to strikes by ground crews. Ocean-borne transportation (including longshoring) in all its industry categories—foreign, noncontiguous, intercoastal, and coastwise—has regional bargaining. Furthermore, intercoastal and coastwise water transport has close substitutes in rail and motor truck services. Long-distance motor trucking has rail and water substitutes. Water, truck, and rail transport together are organized by separate unions, having separate negotiations. Petroleum and gasoline pipelines for technical reasons are almost invulnerable to successful stoppages, and here too the bargaining structure is so decentralized that a substantial shutdown of the main interregional services is not now possible.

There remain the services of the federal government. Although their essentiality is high, their emergency potential today is negligible. Strikes against the government are already forbidden by law, which deprives strikers of their civil service status, and in any case union organization is weak among government employees.

CONCLUSIONS

The general approach used here for the classification of national emergency disputes rests upon a distinction between losses that are nationwide and those that are locally concentrated, and between losses that are immediate and acute and those that are remote and modest. These distinctions are essential if the problem presented by these disputes is to be seen in realistic perspective. It is for this reason that market area, essentiality, range of probable shutdown, and closeness of the tie between a shutdown and the appearance of a genuine crisis have been emphasized. They have been emphasized separately and collectively. All of them must be present for an industry to have high emergency potential.

The state of foreign relations exerts an independent bearing upon the emergency problem. If the present cold war were to yield to a valid and respectable condition of coexistence, one could expect that the categories of critical defense goods and of fissionable metals and their products would become much less urgent. Accordingly, these industries would lose their present high emergency potentials. By contrast, open warfare would drastically increase the scope of the whole emergency problem.

Final consumers have a considerable range of essentials and there is no doubt that they are vulnerable to strikes. Relative to the national emergency problem, however, final consumers turn out to have a surprisingly small role. Most of their essential goods and services are produced for local or intraregional markets whose radii are too small to make them sources of possible national emergencies. Certainly this would be the case for medical and hospital care, utility services, and foodstuffs excluding meats. And though meat and gasoline are produced for markets of much wider geographical scope, the collective bargaining structures in these industries are currently too decentralized to bring about national emergencies. For final consumers, therefore, the national emergency problem is limited to the railroads.

Turning to industrial consumers, we have distinguished producers' goods according to their time structure. First, there is railroad service, which is not storable and which is ubiquitously used. Here vulnerability to strikes is high. Second, there are the principal raw materials. These are essential to continued production by the fabricating industries. Though stockpiles provide an interval between a raw materials strike and the appearance of a national emergency, and usually this interval is sufficient to settle most strikes, still the principal raw materials industries loom large for the national emergency problem. In contrast, the machine-fabricating industries do not, because the continued production of durable producers' goods is not, in the short run, essential to continued production as a whole.

Yet in the raw materials group only the bituminous coal and basic steel industries now have high emergency potentials. The reason is that both industries are vulnerable to nationwide shutdowns, because their bargaining systems are so highly centralized. All the others drop out of the high-potential category because their present bargaining structures are too decentralized to make a substantial or total strike likely at this time.

This survey of the problem of national emergency disputes is thus tinctured with some optimism, for it suggests that under present conditions both the range and frequency of such strikes are actually quite small. Hence it is well to inject a note of caution at this point.

In most of the essential national product industries whose emergency potential today turns out to be low or negligible under the criteria employed, the principal reason for the verdict is the decentralized nature of their systems of collective bargaining. That is, the bargaining is at most on a company-by-company basis, there is no dominant producer, and for various reasons a common strategy involving the whole industry has either proved unsuccessful or has not even been attempted. This is clearly true for wholesale meat packing; long distance communications; crude petroleum production and petroleum refining; mining, smelting, and refining of primary nonferrous metals; timber and lumber; and common carrier air and water transportation.

Centralization of collective bargaining could eventually develop in these industries along some one of several possible lines: formal industry-wide bargaining, mergers of rival unions, common-front strategies by rival unions, industry-wide strategy where one union is dominant, or concentration of output in a single dominant firm. If centralization were to occur in some form in the future, the emergency potentials of these industries would certainly rise, perhaps thrusting them into the currently critical group.[17] To illustrate, if the longshore unions on the Atlantic, Gulf, and Pacific coasts were either to merge or to adopt a common-front strategy, shipping strikes would then become nationwide. Given the importance of international trade, potential emergencies here would become much more likely.

Thus the question depends upon how one views the strength of centralizing tendencies in collective bargaining in these industries. Although the problem cannot be explored here, centralization of some type seems a likely prospect on a possibly important scale. If so, then the problem of national emergency strikes may grow over the years, even though it is still likely to fall well short of the panic dimensions envisaged in 1946.

Another necessary qualification concerns that borderland of interstate strikes in essential industries, strikes that are not actually "national" in their impacts though neither are they purely "local." Examples would include regional systems of electric power production and distribution, ocean transportation between the American mainland and Alaska and Hawaii, and interstate trucking of foodstuffs and other essentials into major centers such as New York City. Strikes in these instances are likely to threaten promptly the health and safety of relatively large populations. If for legal reasons the problems cannot be adequately met by local authorities, they might well constitute a special kind of emergency and as such perhaps become a responsibility of the federal government.

Despite these qualifications, optimism about the relatively small dimensions of the problem of national emergency strikes still seems warranted for the present period—and not only because the range of probable cases is now so small. In addition, stockpiles, substitutes, and imports provide rather broadly available means for delay or even relief so far as the actual occurrence of national emergencies is concerned. Delay provides time for the forces of public opinion to exert pressure for settlement, as well as opportunity for the parties to reach agreement before the last extremity is attained.

---

[17] Paradoxically, there is another tendency at work, running counter to centralization of bargaining—continued development of substitutes in the economy, which tends to reduce the essentiality of given products through time.

Save for the unusual circumstances invoked by inflation and the release of war-imposed tensions during 1945-1946, voluntarily negotiated settlements prior to the point of real emergency have been the rule and not the exception. If this continues to be so, the problem of national strike control will not seriously threaten the present system of voluntary bargaining within the calculable future.

THE ECONOMIC IMPACT OF STRIKES

IN KEY INDUSTRIES

BY IRVING BERNSTEIN

University of California, Los Angeles

The great strike in a critical industry is many-sided. It is at once an exercise in politics, in law, in history, in military policy, in public opinion (and myth making), as well as in economics. This chapter will deal only with the last. It may offer useful estimates of the economic impact of big strikes; it will tell us virtually nothing of the behavior of politicians, judges, secretaries of defense, or the public. It is possible to demonstrate that a stoppage has no serious effect upon the nation's health or safety in the face of a precisely opposite conclusion by government officials and the public.

When the lens is focused upon economic impact, the resulting image is reduced in scale. There is a common tendency to exaggerate both the number of industries and the number of strikes that produce national emergencies. The industries with an emergency potential are severely limited and the incidence of great stoppages in those industries is equally restricted.

The concept of national emergency is inherently gross rather than refined. If the word "national" has any meaning as applied to strikes, it presumably connotes some approach to an economy-wide impact. By definition, therefore, stoppages in industries with local or regional markets are excluded. The result is that the majority of operations directly affecting health or safety are removed from consideration—electric light and power, heat, gas, water, police, fire control, sewage disposal, hospitals, medical service, milk distribution, and local transit. Similarly, the word "emergency" does not suggest a delicate pat; if a strike has an "emergency" impact it must by definition hit the public hard.

Since the purpose of this volume is to treat great strikes from the viewpoint of policy, it is necessary to come to some conclusion, however tentative, on whether or not they are national emergencies. This requires a working definition of the term "national emergency." Three economic tests will be applied: first, the strike must have an actual as distinguished from a potential effect; second, it must impose hardship rather than inconvenience; and finally, its impact must be national rather than local. To be described as a national emergency, a walkout must fulfill all three criteria. Strikes will be classed according to these standards in three groups: clearly nonemergency, marginal nonemergency, and emergency.[1]

In wartime these tests are of no use. Then the economic impact upon the public is irrelevant; the only meaningful standard is the successful prosecution of the war. Under the pressures of conflict, the government tends to regard virtually all strikes as contrary to the national interest. During World War II, for example, the National War Labor Board asserted jurisdiction over a dispute involving the Brooklyn YMCA in face of the facts that the "Y" was not in interstate commerce, that the State Labor Relations Act exempted charitable institutions, and that a strike could hardly impede the war effort.[2]

The defense industry in peacetime is equally unamenable to application of these criteria. Assume, by way of illustration, a hypothetical strike in late 1954 at the plant of a manufacturer of equipment necessary for a new plutonium-producing installation of the Atomic Energy Commission. To decide whether this stoppage constituted a national emergency, one would have to answer at least

---

[1] This definition is carried over from Irving Bernstein and Hugh G. Lovell, "Are Coal Strikes National Emergencies?" *Industrial and Labor Relations Review*, 6 (April 1953), p. 353. For a related but somewhat different definition, see Chapter I, p. 6.

[2] *Termination Report of the National War Labor Board*, Vol. I, pp. 33-34. The Board proceeded on the theory that strikes are contagious, and therefore sought to eliminate all of them.

the following questions: What share of the output would go to peaceful as opposed to weapons production? What would be the impact of delay upon weapons delivery? What was the existing stock of weapons available to the United States and its allies as well as the best intelligence estimate of the supply possessed by possible enemies? What was the prospect of war? Obviously, these questions could be answered, if anywhere, only at the highest level in the executive branch of the government.

The conclusion is inescapable that the problems of measuring the impact of strikes in wartime as well as of stoppages in defense industries in peacetime can be disposed of here only by avoidance.

In estimating the emergency impact of important strikes, reliance will be placed upon both statistical and nonquantitative data. The former consist of weekly (where available) and monthly series for those industries which constitute the principal suppliers to and consumers of the struck industry, as well as general economic indicators that suggest the effects upon the whole economy. In the interest of brevity and readability, statistical material will be kept to the indispensable minimum. The nonstatistical information consists of reports published in the *New York Times*, supplemented in the case of the 1946 rail strike by several other sources. Selection, following the criteria, is confined to actual effects. All the strikes analyzed have occurred since World War II.[3]

Before proceeding to examine the strikes themselves, it is neces-

[3] The method, in other words, is essentially that set out in the article by Dr. Lovell and myself already referred to. Since its publication, another essay in measurement has appeared: Neil W. Chamberlain and Jane Metzger Schilling, *The Impact of Strikes* (New York: Harper, 1954). Although this is not the place to review this ambitious undertaking in detail, the fact that its method is not employed calls for explanation. Its first shortcoming in light of the present purpose is its failure to establish criteria of national emergency, to fix a point at which strikes in general or specifically constitute emergencies. The end product is merely an array of big stoppages ranked quantitatively by the authors' estimates of their impact upon the public. The second difficulty stems from the attempt to quantify in the absence of firm data. Chamberlain and Schilling ask all the pertinent questions and answer every one even when the result is no more than an informed hunch. Here many fewer questions will be asked but their answers will be reasonably precise. Both methods, clearly, leave something to be desired, one for trying to do too much and the other for doing too little. A really satisfying study would require a team of field researchers to examine exhaustively the effects of a particular strike while it was in progress.

BARD COLLEGE LIBRARY
ANNANDALE-ON-HUDSON, N.Y.

sary to filter out those industries in which national emergency stoppages might occur.

THE POTENTIAL INDUSTRIES

Industries differ markedly in their importance to the community. There is, however, little point in drawing attention to extreme differences, say, between costume jewelry and railway transportation. In a complex, integrated economy like ours, industries must be arrayed along a continuum of essentiality with only minor differences separating those that adjoin. Hence any dividing line drawn between products or services that are indispensable and those that are not is necessarily arbitrary. The decision must be in part a reflex of the decider's prejudices, and not all reasonable men would agree.

There are, obviously, a large number of industries that are essential. In many cases a cessation of output over a sufficiently long period would create a crisis that satisfied the criteria of national emergency. Table 1, which deals only with highly unionized industries, contains a list of twenty-six. The critical question, however, is which of these industries have this potential as a result of a strike, given the historic stage of economic and collective bargaining development that presently exists in the United States. If an industry is to qualify, it seems reasonable to insist that the following tests should be satisfied:

1. The industry must be highly unionized.
2. Its product or service must be essential.
3. It must have a national product market.
4. Its employees must be represented by a single labor organization, by several unions whose strike policies are coordinated, or by one or more craft organizations with power to shut down the industry.
5. Bargaining must be on an industry-wide basis in fact or in effect.
6. The collective bargaining agreements in the industry must expire on the same date.

Failure to meet any one of these tests removes an industry from the potential emergency group. That is, a strike could not become a national emergency if only a fraction of the employees were organized, if the product or service was nonessential, if the market was

TABLE I. POTENTIAL NATIONAL EMERGENCY INDUSTRIES

Highly Unionized Industries	Essential Product or Service	National Market	Single or Coordinated Unions	Industry-wide Bargaining	Uniform Contract Expiration Date
Actors and musicians	Agricultural equipment	Agricultural equipment	Airline pilots	Coal mining	Coal mining
Agricultural equipment	Aircraft and parts	Aircraft and parts	Automobiles and parts	Railroads	Railroads
Aircraft and parts	Airline pilots and mechanics	Airline pilots and mechanics	Coal mining	Steel, basic	Steel, basic
Airline pilots and mechanics	Aluminum	Aluminum	Meat packing		
Aluminum	Atomic energy	Atomic energy	Railroads		
Atomic energy	Automobiles and parts	Automobiles and parts	Rubber		
Automobiles and parts	Bus and streetcar, local	Coal mining	Steel, basic		
Book and job printing and publishing	Canning and preserving foods	Electric machinery			
Breweries	Cement	Longshoring			
Bus and streetcar, local	Coal mining	Machinery, except agricultural and electric			
Canning and preserving foods	Construction	Maritime			
Carpets and rugs, wool	Electric machinery	Meat packing			
Cement	Longshoring	Nonferrous metals and products			
Clocks and watches	Machinery, except agricultural and electric	Petroleum refining			
Clothing, men's	Maritime	Railroad equipment			
Clothing, women's	Meat packing	Railroads			
Coal mining	Nonferrous metals and products	Rubber			
Coal products	Petroleum refining	Shipbuilding			
Construction	Railroad equipment	Steel, basic			
Dyeing and finishing, textiles		Sugar			

Electric machinery
Furs and garments
Glass and glassware
Gloves, leather
Leather tanning
Longshoring
Machinery, except agricultural and electric
Maritime
Meat packing
Metal mining
Millinery and hats
Motion-picture production
Newspaper printing and publishing
Nonferrous metals and products
Paper and pulp
Petroleum refining
Radio technicians
Railroad equipment
Railroads
Rayon yarn
Rubber
Shipbuilding
Steel, basic
Steel products
Sugar
Telegraph
Telephone
Theater stagehands, motion-picture operators
Tobacco
Trucking, local and intercity
Woolen and worsted textiles

Railroads
Rubber
Shipbuilding
Steel, basic
Sugar
Telephone
Trucking, local and intercity

Telephone

local or regional, if unions competed rather than cooperated, if bargaining was on a company-by-company basis, or if the contracts expired at different times.[4]

Table 1 is an effort to apply these tests to the American economy, filtering through at each step those industries that qualify. The base group is taken from the most recent Bureau of Labor Statistics study of the extent of collective bargaining.[5] All industries with 60 per cent or more of their wage earners under union agreement in 1946 are listed in the first column. To this group have been added telephones and atomic energy, both of which have probably reached the 60 per cent level since 1946. Essentiality is liberally defined, with the result that several marginal industries have been classed as essential.

The group of highly unionized industries totals fifty-one. When they are sifted through a loose screen of essentiality, twenty-six remain. This number is reduced to twenty-one by the national market test. It is then cut sharply to seven by insistence on a single union or coordinated unions. The two last steps, industry-wide bargaining and uniformity of expiration dates, leave the same three industries: coal mining, basic steel, and railroads. Even with these, however, a certain amount of stretching is necessary. Although the coal negotiations are conducted on a national basis, the agreements are regional and it is not wholly outside the realm of possibility that one region might split off. In the railroad industry, of course, the contracts are by craft and even within the operating group there is the possibility of disagreement. In the great 1946 strike, for example, only the engineers and trainmen went out. The nature of the industry, however, permits any one of the operating brotherhoods to stop the trains. In steel there is technically no industry-wide bargaining, although the employers tend to stick together. However, it is possible, as in 1949, for the union to shake one of the basic steel companies loose from the others.

One industry that failed to pass the tests, meat packing, came so close as to call for a word of explanation. Approximately half the

[4] For a different approach yielding identical results (excepting defense industries), see Chapter I, pp. 15-16.

[5] "Extent of Collective Bargaining and Union Recognition, 1946," *Monthly Labor Review*, 64 (May 1947), p. 766.

nation's meat is supplied by the Big Four packers. While they are solidly unionized, membership is divided among three organizations —the CIO packinghouse workers (71 per cent), the AFL meat cutters (17 per cent), and the Swift independent (12 per cent). The CIO and the AFL have demonstrated some capacity to cooperate, but hardly in all cases.[6] The packers, too, tend to integrate policies, but probably not to the same extent as in steel. The contracts, of course, are signed individually by each company although they expire on the same date. These facts emphasize the borderline character of meat packing. It seems more reasonable to exclude this industry from the emergency potential category because the Big Four provide only half the supply, other foods can be substituted for meat, and there exists a good deal of division on both sides of the table.[7]

Hence examination of strike effects will be confined to three industries: coal, steel, and railroads.

BITUMINOUS COAL

Between V-J Day and the end of 1954, a span of nine years, there were four nationwide bituminous coal strikes, an average of about one every two years. All of them appeared in the first half of the period: April 1-May 29, 1946 (interrupted by a two-week truce beginning May 11); November 20-December 7, 1946; March 15-April 12, 1948; and February 19, 1949-March 4, 1950 (broken at several points by work resumption). There has been no stoppage since early 1950. This concentration, doubtless, reflects a fundamental shift in the market for coal. Prior to 1951 demand was brisk and the miners could gain by striking; since that time the market has declined drastically and there has been little to achieve by stopping work.

Coal strikes, except under extraordinary demand conditions, have

[6] It is interesting that the first interunion dispute to go to arbitration under the AFL-CIO no-raiding agreement involved these two organizations at the Swift plant in Moultrie, Georgia. The arbitrator, David L. Cole, awarded in favor of the CIO. By failing to withdraw a representation petition from the NLRB, the meat cutters in effect repudiated the decision and, in winning the election, gained representation rights. Bureau of National Affairs, *Daily Labor Report*, October 20, 1954, p. A-9.

[7] Mr. David Dolnick, Director of Research for the Amalgamated Meat Cutters, was helpful in supplying this information.

little impact upon the economy because of the critical problem of oversupply.[8] In effect, a strike is an inescapable layoff by another name. This can be demonstrated generally and crudely by comparing output in strike and nonstrike years. Average annual production in the four years between 1946 and 1954 in which stoppages occurred was 521 million short tons as compared with 491 million in the five strike-free years. In other words, average output when the mine workers shut down the pits actually *exceeded* that in years when they did not do so by some 30 million tons, or about 6 per cent.

It is worth noting that all but one of the four stoppages to be considered are the three worst that have taken place in the thirty-five years since the post-World War I inflation. Two were in 1946, reflecting the unusual demand conditions following the termination of the second world war, and the other was the unique endurance contest of 1949-1950.

Since these four strikes have been examined in detail elsewhere,[9] only the conclusions will be presented here. The first 1946 stoppage had a serious impact upon the economy after the first month. Residents of some localities, especially in Illinois, endured hardship for a short time and millions of others were inconvenienced. This strike falls in the middle group of marginal nonemergencies.

Coming on the heels of this walkout and during the winter, the second stoppage in late 1946 probably had a more severe impact than any other coal strike of modern times. It is likely that most of the people of the United States suffered some inconvenience, and genuine hardship existed in a few communities. The return to work came at the critical moment, putting this strike, like its predecessor, in the class of marginal nonemergencies.

The 1948 walkout had only sporadic effects and must be considered as clearly nonemergency in character.

The 1949-1950 marathon had only a minor impact upon the public in its first twelve months. Serious local shortages developed in the last few weeks and the final settlement came as hardship

[8] A recent study has reaffirmed this conclusion: C. Lawrence Christenson, "The Theory of the Offset Factor: The Impact of Labor Disputes upon Coal Production," *American Economic Review*, XLIII (September 1953), pp. 513-547.

[9] Bernstein and Lovell, *loc. cit.*, pp. 361-365.

appeared in some localities. Like the 1946 strikes, this one falls in the area of marginal nonemergency.

STEEL

The steel industry differs sharply from bituminous coal in having a much less aggravated overcapacity problem. During most of the period 1946-1954, in fact, steel operated at or near its maximum output levels. For this reason, if no other, one would expect that a strike in steel would have a greater public impact than one in coal. Since the end of World War II the steelworkers' union has shut down the entire basic steel industry (excepting one medium-sized independently organized firm) on three occasions: January 21 to the end of February and early March 1946; October 1 to mid-November 1949; and June 2 to July 24, 1952.

At the statistical level it is possible to examine the impact of a steel strike from three points of view: suppliers to the steel industry, leading consumers of its products, and the economy as a whole. The supply side is suggested by series for bituminous coal (weekly), iron ore (monthly), and freight carloadings (weekly). Consumption is indicated by series for those industries which take in excess of 5 per cent of steel output: motor vehicles (weekly), construction (monthly), metal cans (monthly), freight carloadings (weekly), and machine tools (monthly).[10] The general impact is suggested in part by all the series already mentioned as well as by three others that appear weekly: insured unemployment, department store sales, and electric power. Weekly data, where they are available, are naturally selected over monthly data.[11]

The 1946 strike significantly affected steel production in six weeks. Taking average weekly output in the six weeks preceding the walkout as a base, the decline in the first four strike weeks was

[10] Consumption by industry market was averaged for the five years, 1947-1951, with these results: automotive, 17.8 per cent; construction, 12.1 per cent; containers, 8.4 per cent; rail transportation, 7.3 per cent; and machinery, industrial equipment, and tools, 5.1 per cent. American Iron & Steel Institute, *Annual Statistical Report, 1951* (New York: American Iron & Steel Institute, 1952), p. 61.

[11] All weekly data upon which this and succeeding analyses are based are derived from statistics published in the *Weekly Supplement* to the *Survey of Current Business* of the Department of Commerce; monthly from the *Survey* itself.

97 per cent, in the fifth 81 per cent, and in the last 28 per cent.

This severe curtailment in steel production appears to have had little or no effect upon two of the major suppliers, coal and railways, and to have had a sharp impact upon the third, iron ore. If the six-week average preceding the strike is taken as a base of 100, in no week of the stoppage did bituminous coal output fall below 106. In fact, it varied only slightly between that figure and a top of 112. It seems that the coal operators were either able to continue sales at a high level to the steel companies or to alternative purchasers or were accumulating stocks in anticipation of the coal strike that commenced a month after the steel strike ended. The situation of the railways was similar. Using the same base, freight carloadings never fell below 100, and ranged between 102 and 113. The picture in iron ore differed markedly, stemming, no doubt, from the fact that the steelworkers represented the ore miners and called them out on strike. Here it makes little sense to use the same base period analysis because the ore ports are frozen in January and February when the stoppage occurred. If we compare January-February ore shipments in 1946 with average shipments in those two months in 1944, 1945, 1947, and 1948, we find that they declined 52 per cent. There seems little point, however, in classifying strikers as part of the "public" in measuring the impact of a stoppage.

The effects on consumption are somewhat difficult to measure because data for the most important consuming industry, automobiles, were not published in early 1946, and three of the four remaining series are monthly. It may be noted, however, that the steel stoppage was contemporaneous with the much longer General Motors strike, so that the volume of automotive demand was sharply curtailed at that time. The four other series evidence no impact. Construction activity mounted steadily month by month both during and after the steel strike. Carloadings, as already noted, were completely insensitive. Machine tools—selected as suggestive of the machinery group—revealed no significant fluctuations. In the case of metal cans, there was a marked decline in output in February. This, however, is the seasonal pattern and the drop in 1946 was typical of what occurred in the two preceding and the two following years.

All the data heretofore discussed taken together leave the impression that the impact of the 1946 steel strike on the economy as a whole was not great. This is confirmed by an examination of three other weekly series. The volume of claims filed for unemployment compensation, presumably, would reflect a severe steel shortage in industries that depend directly or indirectly upon that material, although it would not be influenced by strikers who were out of work. The claims load did, in fact, reach a level in the strike weeks modestly higher than the average for the preceding six weeks. No particular significance can be attached to this fact, however, since January and February are typically high months of unemployment, and volume reached the strike level two weeks before the steelworkers walked out. It does not seem unreasonable to conclude that any impact the strike may have had was not in excess of 100,000 persons, or substantially less than 1 per cent of the insured labor force. The weekly movements of both department store sales and electric power production suggest a virtually complete indifference to the steel stoppage.

The *New York Times'* coverage of the strike confirms the statistical analysis: the steel stoppage did not have a severe impact upon the economy. On the twelfth day of the walkout the *Times* reported 66,000 workers laid off in the nation, almost half of them employees of the Ford Motor Co. For the rest, there were 8,200 coal miners, 6,000 railway workers in the Pittsburgh district, and 15,000 in various industries. On the twenty-fourth day the paper made a survey of the effects in the New York metropolitan area and found them minimal. The only closed operation was the Ford assembly plant at Edgewater, N. J., while the Hills Bros. coffee plant had been shut down for three days because of a temporary shortage of containers. The Civilian Production Administration's local office noted no unusual rise in applications for steel allocations under its emergency program. Warehouse stocks, though down by one third, provided a margin of safety on most items. Certain industrial operations reported no effects: the two largest aircraft producers on Long Island, the Todd Shipyard in Brooklyn, a major typewriter concern, and Singer Sewing Machine in New Jersey.

In summary, the 1946 steel strike had little effect upon suppliers (if we except the striking ore miners), upon consumption, and upon the economy as a whole. In the absence of a showing of substantial hardship, it must be classed as clearly outside the emergency category.

The steel strike of 1949 had a far sharper economic impact. It significantly curtailed steel production in seven weeks. Using the average of the previous six weeks as a base, output fell 90 per cent in the first five weeks of the stoppage, 75 per cent in the sixth, and 33 per cent in the seventh. The problem of measuring impact is complicated by the fact that the coal miners were out for seven weeks commencing September 19, that is, two weeks before the steel strike began. Hence it is difficult to isolate the source of a particular fluctuation as between coal and steel.

On the supplier side, bituminous production fell to an extremely low level. Here it seems reasonable to attribute the cause almost entirely to the coal strike rather than to a diminution in demand from the steel industry. With respect to the rails, we may estimate the effects of the steel stoppage as having been roughly in the magnitude of 10 per cent. That is, using the average of the three nonholiday weeks preceding the coal strike as a base, carloadings fell 10 per cent during the first two coal strike weeks and 20 per cent during the five weeks in which both stoppages were running. Iron ore shipments were severely curtailed in October and November, again reflecting the fact that the ore miners joined the strike.

Consumption was also seriously affected, notably in the case of motor vehicles. If we take average output for the preceding six weeks as a base, automobile production slid slowly for four weeks to a maximum decline of 7 per cent. In the fifth week it dropped sharply to 20 per cent below the prestrike level and held that pace for three weeks until the end of the strike. The most devastating period, however, was still to come. In the two weeks following the walkout output fell by one half. In the third week it reached bottom, 67 per cent below the base period average. Even thereafter recovery came slowly. Construction activity declined modestly in the second month of the strike and continued to do so for three additional months. Since this was the winter slow season, it seems reasonable to allocate the responsibility primarily to factors other than the steel strike. Carloadings, as already noted, declined in the neighborhood of 10 per cent because of the steel stoppage. Machine tool shipments lost 10 per cent in the first month but proceeded to recover almost all of it in the second. Since month-to-month fluctuations are highly erratic, there is no basis for a refined decision. The base period analysis is not appropriate for metal cans because of sharp seasonal factors. A comparison of the decline from the August peak to November in 1949 with the average for the two preceding and two following years reveals a greater drop of 10 per cent in the strike year.

The general indicators, as might be expected, show lesser effects, with the possible exception of insured unemployment. This series, which had been declining steadily for six weeks prior to the strike, reversed its direction and began a steady climb. By the last week of the stoppage more than 300,000 had been added to the unemployment compensation rolls. A peak of over half a million new persons was reached two weeks later. Although seasonal layoffs in agriculture, construction, lumbering, and apparel affected these totals, secondary effects of the steel strike unquestionably had an impact. Department store sales, by contrast, appear to have been wholly insensitive. Similarly, electric power production declined only slightly, about 1 per cent during each of the first six weeks of the stoppage.

The serious impact suggested by the statistical analysis gathers detail in the *New York Times'* reports. Railroad workers began to be laid off within three days of the outbreak of the strike on October 1, 1949. By the fifth, Packard and Briggs Body in Detroit had temporarily furloughed 13,000 employees. The McCormick Works of International Harvester notified 3,500 on October 14 that their services were not needed. Willys-Overland in Toledo shut down its final assembly for a week commencing the fifteenth. At about the same time railway car builders began to curtail production to stretch stocks. For the same purpose General Motors went on a four-day week at its truck and bus plant in Pontiac, Michigan, in mid-October. General Electric laid off 7,500 at Erie, Pennsylvania, on October 18. The following day the Steel Shipping Container Institute announced that thirty-seven container manufacturers, employing 8,000, had suspended work. On the twenty-third, construction of rocket-testing stands at the guided missile center in New Mexico halted. The following day Kaiser-Frazer closed down. At the end of the month the Hotpoint Division of General Electric furloughed 5,000 in Chicago. Meanwhile, General Motors extended the four-day week to several other operations and by the end of the month closed three plants, two Chevrolet and one Fisher Body, in Flint, Michigan, making 17,000 idle.

In November the situation took a turn for the worse. Effects on auto suppliers became evident with the layoff of 3,500 at Electric Autolite in Cincinnati on the fourth. On the same day Chrysler dropped 35,000 from its Dodge, DeSoto, and Chrysler operations. Hudson on the sixth furloughed 14,000. At about this time the bedding industry, notably Simmons, reported reduced shipments. By the end of the month the *Times* reported temporary idleness for an estimated 250,000 automobile workers.

In summary, the 1949 steel strike, with an assist from the contemporaneous coal stoppage, had a sharp impact upon the economy. A number of industries experienced a moderate reduction in operations. The most severe effects by far appeared in the automotive industry, and the bulk of unemployment was concentrated in such towns as Detroit, Flint, and Pontiac. This may have been mitigated in part by the fact that model changeovers came at just about this time. Since hardship appears to have been limited to a few communities, it seems proper to classify this stoppage as a marginal nonemergency.

The mounting intensity of the steel strikes reached a climax in the great conflict of June 2-July 24, 1952, which significantly cut production in nine weeks. Taking average output in the preceding six weeks as a base, the steel series fell 57 per cent in the first, in the neighborhood of 85 per cent in the next seven, and 53 per cent in the last week.

The impact upon suppliers was substantial. Coal shipments were affected at once and were below the prestrike level in all but one strike week. In the worst week output fell 31 per cent below the average for the six weeks prior to the strike and the decline for the period as a whole averaged 13 per cent. Carloadings suffered markedly, dropping gradually to a low point 40 per cent below the prestrike level in the fifth week and averaging a decline of 17 per cent for all strike weeks. Iron ore, as usual, virtually ceased to move.

The consumer effects followed a familiar but this time a more aggravated pattern, the automobile business taking the brunt of the steel shortage. Car manufacturers succeeded in holding at the level of the six weeks preceding the strike for four weeks. In the fifth, however, output plummeted 31 per cent and then dropped steadily to a disastrous 84 per cent low in the final strike week. The next two weeks were only a little better. By the third week following the stoppage 88 per cent of prestrike output had been recovered. Construction activity appears to have been insensitive, mounting steadily month by month during the summer. Carloadings sustained a serious decline. Machine tool shipments in June exceeded the four-month prestrike average by 10 per cent, but in July fell 14 per cent below that level. Since recovery was rapid following the walk-out, it seems safe to attribute the July losses to the steel shortage. Metal can shipments, despite a great contemporary hue and cry, rose markedly and in conformity with the seasonal pattern both during and after the strike. Taking the four months prior to the stoppage as a base, shipments rose 25 per cent in June, 59 per cent in July, and 75 per cent at the August peak. This was managed by channeling the output of Weirton Steel, the only operating producer, into cans in order to save the perishable food pack.

The impact upon the general indicators appears to have been greater than in the case of any previous walkout with which we have dealt. Insured unemployment rose by almost exactly 400,000 between the week preceding and the eighth week of the strike. Though this appears on its face to be less than in 1949, the reverse seasonal factors make it a good deal worse. The 1952 strike, rather than occurring as seasonal unemployment rose, took place in June and July when agriculture, construction, and lumbering were hiring people from the jobless rolls. Although it is impossible to be precise about the volume of insured unemployment stemming from the steel strike, it does not seem unreasonable to suggest a figure of at least half a million. Department store sales, too, reflected the effects, notably in the second month. In the fifth through eighth weeks of the strike, sales were about 25 per cent under the prestrike average. Though this is partly explained by the normal summer lag, an examination of seasonally adjusted data leaves little doubt that the walkout was an important factor. Electric power production, as usual, revealed a marked insensitivity to the stoppage.

The *New York Times'* coverage is so voluminous as to require some breakdown by industry. To deal first with suppliers: On July 14 it was reported that more than 50,000 coal miners were thrown out of work. The impact on the rails was evident as early as June 4 when the New York Central let 8,000 go, the Pennsylvania following two days later with 9,000. In mid-month the Association of Railroads estimated lost revenue at a rate of $5 million per week. As of July 9, the Baltimore & Ohio had been forced to make 10,619 employees idle. By the middle of July an estimated 100,000 rail workers were out of jobs. The stoppage of iron mining in the Great Lakes district resulted in an estimated loss of 25 million tons of ore, approximately one-third of which was marked for winter stockpiling.

The impact on consumption was at least as severe. The automobile industry evidenced effects at the end of June, notably in a layoff of 27,500 by Ford and 38,000 by General Motors. On July 3 the GM truck and coach division in Pontiac began to furlough 5,200. On the same day two Akron tire companies ran out of steel rims and 1,000 workers lost their jobs. In mid-July Willys-Overland released 8,500 in Toledo and the Budd Co. furloughed over 10,000, many in its body division. At the same time Ford virtually closed the River Rouge plant, affecting 72,000, and Chrysler laid off 55,000 on the fourteenth. Meanwhile, Briggs Body had let out 15,000 and Briggs Mfg. 16,000. As the strike ended, Buick and Ford announced new curtailments affecting 33,500. Even as late as mid-August Ford declared that eighteen of its nineteen assembly plants were shut down.

The situation in construction, of course, was more favorable. In early July the *Times* reported a shortage of steel window frames as slowing down a hospital in New York City and an apartment project in Brooklyn. On August 1 the New York City building program was estimated to have been set back two to three months. The railroad equipment industry was more seriously affected. By June 26 one freight car assembly line was down and several other stoppages were imminent. As the strike ended, American Locomotive reported plans to lay off 5,000 in Schenectady, and Pullman-Standard announced a terminal freight car delivery. There were numerous statements, particularly from California, that a potential shortage of cans might cause the loss of the summer fruit and vegetable pack, but, as already noted, this did not occur. The agricultural equipment industry suffered heavily from the strike. At the end of June, International Harvester laid off 3,000 in Springfield, Ohio. In mid-July, John Deere furloughed 2,000 at three of its plants. By the twenty-fifth, Caterpillar Tractor had cut its force by 18,000 and Harvester by 44,000. The impact was felt in a variety of other industries. In mid-June Lincoln Electric in Cleveland began to curtail electrode production. On the twenty-fourth, the Petroleum Administration for Defense ceased giving priority to wildcat oil drilling. By June 28, Midland Steel Products had stopped operations in Cleveland. In the middle of July, layoffs were in effect at Westinghouse Electric in East Pittsburgh, at American Radiator & Standard Sanitary in Louisville, and in several General Electric plants. At the same time river barge lines reported heavy losses in traffic. *Iron Age* announced at the end of July that those depending on coke oven by-products, notably the chemical industry, were hard hit.

The aggregate secondary employment effects are impossible to measure precisely. The *Times* reported two widely differing estimates at the end of the strike: 450,000 and 1,400,000. Taking these guesses in conjunction with the insured unemployment figures, it appears reasonable to say that somewhere between 750,000 and 1,000,000 persons suffered some loss of working time as a consequence of the steel strike.

This 1952 stoppage differed markedly from those in 1946 and 1949 in that it occurred when the United States was engaged in an international conflict. Hence it is necessary to note the impact upon the war program. On June 18 the mortar shell line at Lempco Products in Cleveland shut down. John R. Steelman, acting head of the Office of Defense Mobilization, reported on July 3 that aircraft deliveries were beginning to be affected because of shortages of landing gear and other parts. As of approximately that date one military truck line had been halted. Ford's production of bazooka rockets stopped on July 11. The Army's largest shell plant, operated by Chevrolet in St. Louis, closed on July 22. In early August the Kingsbury ordnance plant near Michigan City was forced onto a four-day week. After the strike Steelman informed President Truman that it would take a year to offset the effects of the shortage on defense production. Secretary of Defense Lovett reported failure to meet delivery schedules on the following items: a plant that should have shipped 130 artillery pieces in July actually sent out 35; artillery shell deliveries were off by one-fourth; two yards producing naval barges did not meet their schedules; only 25 per cent of expected shipments of heavy diesel tractors arrived; and rocket output fell behind by one third.

In view of the widespread hardship effects upon suppliers, consumers, employment, and the defense program, it seems appropriate to class the 1952 steel strike as a national emergency.

RAILROADS

The railroad industry differs from both coal and steel in providing a service which cannot be stored. Hence the public impact of a rail strike is virtually immediate. The railway unions, therefore, are most reluctant to engage in a nationwide stoppage; in fact, the action of the engineers and trainmen of May 23-25, 1946 is the only walkout national in scope that the operating crafts have ever called.

Members of the two unions quit work at 4:00 P.M. in each time zone on the twenty-third and stayed out for forty-eight hours. The labor organizations permitted operation of trains carrying milk, troops, and hospitalized servicemen as well as trains of the already seized Illinois Central. Nevertheless, by the second day, according to the Railroad Association, freight traffic was 1 per cent of normal and passenger volume was even lower.

Since the strike was so short, the statistical analysis employed for the other industries is not applicable. Rather, it is necessary to rely on press reports—the *New York Times*, the *Los Angeles Times*, and those summarized by Chamberlain and Schilling from the former as well as from the New York *Herald-Tribune*.[12]

The strike disrupted long-distance passenger traffic all over the United States. As it went into effect, there were scenes of confusion and jostling to catch final trains, while travelers were stranded in many cities. Reports were published of people living in stalled Pullmans in the midwest and of servicemen's wives with babes in their arms staying in Los Angeles' Union Station. Airline and bus facilities were swamped and incapable of meeting the abnormal demand. The Navy canceled leave for its personnel excepting emergencies.

The impact upon commuters was equally severe. Of close to half a million such persons who entered New York City daily by rail,

[12] Chamberlain and Schilling, *op. cit.*, pp. 149-159.

about four-fifths reached home before 4:00 P.M. on the twenty-third; the remainder, however, either arrived late or spent the night in town. On the following day heavy auto and bus traffic produced serious congestion at the bridge and tunnel approaches to Manhattan as well as for parking facilities. In Los Angeles the situation was worse because of a concurrent transit strike, since the 1,500,000 persons who relied on public transportation daily had no such facilities whatever. A consequence was an enormous increase in private car, taxi, and limousine use, resulting in the worst traffic snarl in the city's history. In Washington, D.C., taxi drivers were reported to be hauling a passenger to New York for $80 and meals.

The effects upon freight were devastating. The government at once established priorities to limit shipment to most essential items. In the face of vanishing traffic, the railways laid off large numbers of nonstriking employees. The steel industry, already hobbled by the coal strike, suffered heavily. United States Steel virtually ceased operating; Jones & Laughlin closed at Pittsburgh and shut three-fourths of its Aliquippa works; and Bethlehem stopped entirely except for one plant. Those bituminous mines that were working were severely affected and heavy layoffs fell upon the anthracite mines. Reports of sharp curtailments came from General Motors, Nash-Kelvinator, Studebaker, and John Deere. A shortage of newsprint caused about a dozen metropolitan newspapers to eliminate advertising. Home builders in Los Angeles complained bitterly of short materials.

The strike left large numbers of freight cars containing livestock and perishable food stranded across the nation. California agriculture was especially hard hit. The Salinas lettuce crop, loading at a rate of 200 to 250 cars daily, was halted with a reported loss of $200,000 per day. The Stockton-Lodi cherry crop was similarly affected, though on a lesser scale. In Kern County 8,000 potato harvest laborers were furloughed, as were 4,000 citrus workers in Orange County. The Holly Sugar Co. in Santa Ana closed on the twenty-fifth. Poultry and cattle were reportedly sent to early slaughter because of a shortage of feed. The Western Growers' Association estimated the loss to California and Arizona agriculture at a rate of $450,000 per day, while Governor Earl Warren wired the President concerning a "tremendous loss of foodstuffs now occurring."

The Post Office embargoed all mail excepting first class and air mail weighing 16 oz. or less. UNRRA relief shipments were disrupted. Activity in the Port of New York ground to a halt. The New England governors, whose states imported 75 per cent of their food, met to adopt emergency measures; Connecticut reportedly was without beef, pork, lamb, veal, or bacon. Disorganization of metropolitan facilities was widespread: Harry Bridges, for example, could not find a hotel room in Los Angeles.

These reports, which could be multiplied several times over, leave no doubt that the 1946 rail strike was a national emergency. One can only wonder what might have happened if it had continued for another three or four days.

CONCLUSIONS

Only three of fifty-one highly unionized industries in the United States have a national emergency potential: coal, steel, and railroads. In the nine years following World War II there was a total of eight nationwide strikes in these industries—four in coal, three in steel, and one in railways. By applying the criteria of a national emergency (national impact, actual effects, and a showing of widespread hardship), two of the eight (one steel and one railroad) were emergencies, four (three coal and one steel) were serious but failed to satisfy the criteria, and two (one coal and one steel) caused little public inconvenience. The results leave little doubt that the national emergency problem, in so far as it is economic in character, has been much exaggerated.

The period in question, 1946-1954, was unusual in that it included demobilization following the greatest conflict in our history and the economic stresses of the Korean War. Both significantly influenced the incidence and severity of strikes. Hence it is no coincidence that the two emergencies occurred in 1946 and 1952 and that two of the four near-emergencies came in the former year. This suggests that the historic phase of the American economy is critical in giving an edge to the problem. A time of strain lowers the threshold of emergency. During a great war there is no slack at all; in a period of mobilization, reconversion, or during a secondary war there is a little; with peace there is a great deal.

Slack is a function of the complex, interdependent economy in which we live. This economic system, to use a poetic image, is a seamless web, and cutting a single strand, with rare exceptions, neither destroys nor impairs the whole. The interrelationships among industries are long-run in character; in the short run it is normally possible for an industry to live on its stocks, to defer its consumption, to find alternative sources of supply. Week-to-week and month-to-month fluctuations in an industry's output are influenced far more by cyclical and seasonal factors than they are by strikes in other industries upon which it depends.

What, then, is the significance of these conclusions for public policy? First, the wide divergencies in impact among strikes in different industries and among those within the same industry suggest that a national emergency policy must maximize flexibility. That is, a rigid statutory definition of emergency is more likely to provoke than to prevent trouble. A second point is that the officials who handle big strikes should be sophisticated in collective bargaining and should have reliable sources of information concerning public impact. On the latter there is evidence that the reporting in the past has been both inadequate and colored. The President, clearly, should have some means of measuring the impact of a large strike factually and currently. Finally, the emergency problem appears to be more closely related to war—including economic mobilization and reconversion—and defense industry than to the peacetime activities of the American economy. Hence policy should discriminate between these stages and industries.

In closing it is necessary to revert to the note upon which this chapter opened: the great strike in a basic industry is only in part an economic phenomenon. Economic analysis, therefore, can make only a limited contribution either to our understanding or to the shaping of public policy.

· III ·

THE POLITICS OF AN EMERGENCY DISPUTE:

STEEL, 1952*

BY HAROLD L. ENARSON
Western Interstate Commission for Higher Education

There is a deep disquiet about government intervention in emergency labor disputes. The general feeling is that presidential intervention has frequently been premature and ineffective. Shutdowns in basic industries have not been prevented. Indeed, federal intervention has sometimes complicated a dispute and prolonged a stoppage. This discontent finds expression among university economists who, discounting the severity of the *emergency* in past "emergency disputes," insist that federal intervention should be shaped primarily by abstract, formal economic tests, presumably developed or at least applied by political eunuchs.

Prescriptions for the handling of emergency disputes are many. Some advocate a rigid hands-off policy. Others argue for detailed economic definitions of emergency or for new patterns of presidential or even congressional intervention. Still others believe that the Taft-Hartley emergency procedures are sufficient. Within the labor relations fraternity, it is fashionable to urge restraint on the federal government, call for "maximum flexibility"—whatever that may mean—and proclaim that presidential intervention is "political," as if it could possibly be anything else!

* The writer was employed at the White House on the staff of John R. Steelman from 1950 to 1952, and was a "participant-observer" during the many months when the steel dispute was the "albatross" of 1600 Pennsylvania Avenue.

46

What have we learned from past government intervention in emergency disputes to guide public policy in the future?

First, some kind of intervention, at one stage or another, is unavoidable. Emergency disputes cannot be wished away. Certain disputes go to the heart of the economy and of the national defense. They generate pressures for intervention which no elected government dares to ignore. The endurance of the parties exceeds the capacity of government to take a strike in certain key industries. Thus one or both of the parties can force intervention.

Second, intervention reflects the public antagonism to stoppages which threaten a national emergency. Government will seek to *prevent* an emergency from developing. The dominant pressures will always be for early, perhaps premature, intervention. Government must anticipate what may happen and act accordingly. It cannot await that precise moment when the experts have concluded that the stoppage is intolerable.

Third, in key industries the *possibility* of government intervention has a significant impact on the bargaining environment. Expectations of what the government may do become part of the total expectations which determine the strategy of the parties. Government is the silent partner in the bargaining process of our basic industries. The law of emergency disputes, the state of the economy and of public opinion, the balance of forces in the political system—these and other considerations are the inescapable concern of bargainers in what might be called the "emergency-prone" industries.

Fourth, intervention complicates a dispute since it substitutes three-way for two-way relationships; collective bargaining gives way to tripartite negotiation. Labor and management devise strategy in anticipation of the strategy of government—and vice versa. The disputants seek to mobilize support within the White House and the Congress. Traditional collective bargaining issues tend to be submerged by political conflicts, and the positions of the parties reflect their alignments within the political community rather than customary economic valuations. Bargainers may assume the role of political ideologists.

Fifth, intervention must be timed and shaped to take into account the prevailing attitudes of the country and of the Congress. Presidential power is bounded by the Congress, the courts, and public opinion—by the consent of the political community. In few areas of our national life does the President have so little actual legal power in the face of such large responsibilities and exaggerated public expectations. Since presidential intervention is primarily a matter of moral leadership, the battle for public support is crucial. Traditional conflicts between President and Congress make the latter a natural "redoubt" for either labor or management, whichever feels disadvantaged in the scramble for support at the White House.

Sixth, intervention is increasingly dictated by the dangers to the economy and to the defense program: by the coercions incident to a hostile world. As long as the cold war persists, emergency disputes will tend to be defined in terms of the defense program. The executive measures the dangers and determines the next steps to be taken. But Congress, the courts, the country, and, above all, the participants in the dispute will determine whether such intervention succeeds.

Seventh, intervention is severely handicapped if the extent of the emergency is exaggerated. The government "cries wolf" at its peril. The penalty of exaggeration is disbelief. The point needs no elaboration.

Finally, government intervention in emergency disputes is preeminently the responsibility of the President. "Keeping labor disputes out of the White House," though a laudable goal, is not always possible. The President carries a burden he cannot shift. In emergency disputes, people look to the President as a center of initiative and responsibility. As chief executive he is also chief mediator and protector of the peace. He is expected to "do something," to produce a settlement no matter how complicated the issues or intransigent the parties. Nor can he push responsibility upon a reluctant Congress.

If these observations suggest that the "politics" of an emergency dispute dominates its character and provides an indispensable key to understanding, that is exactly what is intended. In this connection, politics may be quickly defined. Politics is coterminous with government and with public policy.[1] The politics of an emergency

---

[1] The politics versus economics approach has its limitations. As E. S. Mason has suggested, "In the realm of public policy, there are no economic problems, no political problems; there are merely problems." Preface by E. S. Mason *in* C. J. Friedrich and J. K. Galbraith, eds., *Public Policy: A Yearbook of the Graduate School of Public Administration* (Cambridge: Harvard University

labor dispute deals, therefore, with the intricate maneuvers and interaction of persons and groups as they move in, against, and through the labyrinth of government.[2]

The steel dispute of 1952 is perhaps the outstanding example of the dominance of political considerations in an emergency dispute. It serves admirably to illustrate the observations made above. Its politics was anything but simple.[3] Underlying the controversy were the pressures of groups, the momentum of institutions, and the force of ideas and ideals. The steelworkers' union sought a wage increase; the industry resisted a wage increase and fought to safeguard its wage-price relationship, and the government tried to stabilize both wages and prices while maintaining uninterrupted production and free collective bargaining. These conflicting objectives precipitated the breakdown in collective bargaining, a wage-price controversy, and finally a battle between the President and both Congress and court, prolonging and intensifying the dispute.

The strike which was "unthinkable" for so much as a single day— which reportedly threatened the physical security of our troops in

---

Press, 1953). Analysis of the collective action of groups is the "stuff" of both politics and economics, of Mill's long-lost "political economy." The institutional economics of John R. Commons is paralleled by the group politics of Arthur Bentley.

[2] Politics is a chunk of life. Its outward machinery is the schoolboy's triumvirate—executive, legislature, and judiciary—and the infiltrating political party and pressure group. Its forms are laws, regulations, policies, decisions. Its function is the fashioning of tolerable compromises out of the conflict of persons and parties, interests and institutions. Its "stuff" is the hopes, faiths, fears, and expectations of people. From these, loyalties are generated, myths are shaped, programs are developed, and support is mobilized in the legislature and the voting booth.

[3] To many, the "politics" of the steel dispute was transparent. Those who believed that President Truman made a "deal" with Philip Murray are matched by those who saw the steel companies' "refusal to bargain" as a conspiracy to force up prices, wreck economic controls, and discredit a Democratic President. Partisan suspicion is always a comforting substitute for hard thought and the search for evidence. In any great controversy, much action takes place in what Walter Lippmann has called the "unseen environment." Facts and experience which cannot be directly apprehended must be imagined. Actors and spectators alike saw only fragments of the play. For drama it was—excellent drama, providing conflict, suspense, denouement, and a plot whose progression no one could have guessed, least of all the participants who moved on and off the public stage.

Korea—persisted for fifty-three days. Before the strike was ended the stabilization program was damaged beyond hope of repair; the mobilization program was disrupted; the President and the Congress were embroiled in a bitter struggle; a constitutional crisis had developed; the Taft-Hartley Act assumed new prominence as a campaign issue; 1,200,000 steelworkers had lost an average of $600 each; and the nation had lost 20 million tons of badly needed steel, as well as some of its faith in collective bargaining and in government intervention.

ROOTS OF CONTROVERSY

The steel dispute had deep roots. It was enmeshed in the struggles over the Taft-Hartley Act, the alternative emergency machinery of the Defense Production Act of 1950, and the collapse and reconstitution of the Wage Stabilization Board.

The emergency provisions of Taft-Hartley precipitated a running conflict between the President and the Congress and between labor and management. Management, supported by majorities in the Congress, hoped the emergency provisions could curb the President, blunt the power of unions, and protect the nation from "national emergency" disputes. Unions professed to see the emergency provisions as a backward step to the hated "government by injunction." After 1948 President Truman used the emergency provisions of Taft-Hartley sparingly and reluctantly, much preferring the use of *ad hoc* fact-finding boards. Experience reinforced political predisposition. Taft-Hartley boards of inquiry generally proved to be hopelessly handicapped because they were forbidden to make recommendations. Fact-finding boards were flexible; they could mediate, make recommendations, report—suit their strategy to the case. The thinking of the White House was reflected in the establishment of the Steel Industry Board of 1949. The logic was this: why should an injunction be used if the parties would *voluntarily* agree to postpone a stoppage?

This approach placed President Truman squarely at loggerheads with the Congress and with management. The White House was severely criticized for "by-passing" Taft-Hartley, despite the historic recognition that in labor disputes as in other matters the President may seek advice where he chooses. To the protagonists *in steel*, Taft-Hartley was a sensitive nerve.[4]

With the Korean War, Congress imposed price and wage controls and, in Title V of the Defense Production Act of 1950, authorized the President to hold labor-management conferences preparatory to establishing "effective procedures for the settlement of labor disputes affecting the national defense." Plainly the architects of this provision were treading familiar ground. They envisioned a state of national emergency where high-level conferences of labor and management would develop agreed methods of finally resolving critical labor disputes—in short, a new "War Labor Board" backed by a no-strike-no-lockout pledge.[5] Title V posed more questions than it solved. If a new labor board were established, would it be a substitute for the emergency provisions? Were the emergency provisions in fact being mothballed for the duration?[6] Could some defense disputes be handled under Taft-Hartley while others were assigned to a new defense labor dispute agency? Would it be possible for the government to maintain at the same time two systems for handling emergency disputes without inviting chaos? These were questions the Congress blithely ignored when it stipulated that, in setting up the new disputes machinery, nothing be done "inconsistent with" the Taft-Hartley Act.

Not until the President reconstituted the Wage Stabilization Board with power to investigate both economic and noneconomic issues in disputes threatening the defense program did these questions come into sharp focus for the Congress—and for the protagonists in steel.

The Wage Stabilization Board was barely launched when on

[4] See Frederick H. Harbison and Robert C. Spencer, "The Politics of Collective Bargaining: The Postwar Record in Steel," *American Political Science Review*, XLVIII (September 1954), pp. 705-720.

[5] Title V was hurriedly drafted one Saturday afternoon by a team from the National Security Resources Board and the White House, and was forwarded informally to the Senate as an administration request. Slight revisions were made by the Congress.

[6] The emergency provisions, as Sylvester Garrett and Charles Gregory pointed out, were devised for a peacetime economy and were wholly inadequate to meet the wartime need for machinery which provides a high degree of finality. See comments in *Proceedings of Third Annual Meeting* (Chicago: Industrial Relations Research Association, December 1950), pp. 14-34.

February 16, 1951, Regulation 6, the so-called "catch-up" formula (equalizing wages with increases in the cost of living), precipitated the mass resignation of the labor members.[7] Efforts to reconstitute the Board quickly ran into the problem of handling labor disputes in the defense emergency. Industry argued that the emergency provisions of Taft-Hartley were adequate and that the Title V provisions should not be implemented. Labor argued for a "War Labor Board" type of operation, with disputes in defense plants resolved by the same tripartite agency charged with wage stabilization.[8]

Compromising the issue proved difficult. Labor members had to be brought back on the Board, but on terms which would not alienate the industry members. In five weeks Stabilization Administrator Eric Johnston held some seventy-three meetings with top-level business and labor representatives, but without success. A new forum for negotiations was imperative. On March 15, 1951, the President established the National Advisory Board on Mobilization Policy as a framework for new, high-level negotiations.[9] On April 17 the Advisory Board recommended—industry members dissenting—that the WSB be empowered to accept labor disputes "threatening the progress of national defense" and to make fair and equitable recommendations for settlement. Four days later the recommendation was put into effect.[10]

[7] There were also deeper causes. Labor felt that price controls were soft, that its participation in the mobilization program was too limited. See Thomas Holland's "Chapter on the Earlier Period of the Wage Stabilization Board" submitted to the WSB History Project (Government Archives).

[8] The dominant attitude within the White House was that some system for handling labor disputes must be developed. However, it was felt that a formal Title V labor-management conference would surely fail and that a public failure to achieve consensus would only sharpen antagonisms. In the unlikely event that such a conference developed an agreed system for "finally deciding" labor disputes, the nation would be saddled prematurely with a system which by its very nature would wear well only for a brief period and hence ought to be reserved for a possibly greater emergency in the future.

[9] A similar board, also composed of four members each from industry, labor, agriculture, and the public, had been useful in World War II in resolving basic conflicts of interest between major pressure blocs.

[10] Executive Order 10161, April 21, 1951. The disputes functions were not, as commonly thought, premised on Title V, but rather on the President's general power to seek advice where he chooses. The Justice Department held that no "agreement" within the meaning of Title V had been reached, either by Johnston in his many conferences or by the President in his discussions with the Advisory Board. Legally, the disputes role of WSB was in the tradition of the

The reconstitution of the WSB sharpened old antagonisms. Plainly, management regarded the new machinery, which combined disputes authority with wage stabilization, with deep distrust.

It was against this background that steel negotiations opened in the fall of 1951.

THE STEEL CASE GETS UNDER WAY

The steel dispute was predestined for the Board. Wage and price control made government intervention virtually certain. Collective bargaining formalities began November 30 and promptly reached an impasse. The "failure of mediation" soon followed. Conciliation Director Ching reported to the White House that bargaining was hopelessly deadlocked since the employers had insisted that "there would have to be relief from the price angle for any wage concessions that were made."[11]

The price issue obviously complicated the dispute. To the steel industry an agreement with government on price relief was the indispensable precondition of a wage bargain. This made for a complex of bargaining relationships involving three groups (union, management, government) and two kinds of issues (wages and prices). No one was sure just how a wage settlement and a price settlement could be worked out simultaneously. The formal machinery of government offered no encouragement and indeed raised hurdles. Price increases were not granted in anticipation of wage increases, nor was there any disposition on the part of government to tie price increases to wage increases. For the most part, wages and prices were in separate compartments. True, the Economic Stabilization Agency was a "single agency," as required by law, but it developed into a third agency providing an occasional umbrella of control and protection for two independent and largely isolated

---

Steel Industry Board of 1949 and similar fact-finding and recommendatory bodies going back to the turn of the century. See testimony before the Lucas Committee: *Dispute Functions of Wage Stabilization Board*, Subcommittee of House Committee on Education and Labor, 82d Cong., 1st sess. (1951). During the summer of 1951 the House defeated (217-113) the Lucas amendment stripping WSB of disputes authority.

[11] *New York Times*, December 21, 1951. In mid-November, Benjamin Fairless of U. S. Steel had stated publicly that the wage issue "probably cannot be determined by collective bargaining and will apparently have to be decided finally in Washington." *New York Times*, November 15, 1951.

"bureaucracies," the Wage Stabilization Board and the Office of Price Stabilization.

As the December 31 contract expiration date approached, the union, the steel industry, and the stabilization agencies maneuvered for advantage. Philip Murray talked of the callousness of steel employers; the industry paraded its faith in stabilization by arguing there should be no wage increase and no price increase; Mobilization Director Charles Wilson and his colleagues boldly laid down the law. The government, said Wilson, would not be stampeded into abandoning its wage-price controls. Nor would it, said Stabilization Administrator Roger Putnam, permit the steel companies to raise prices to compensate for any wage increase; the steel companies are "bargaining with their own money . . . ; as calamitous as a steel strike might be, ruining our stabilization program would be worse."[12] Thus the battle for public opinion was joined.

On December 22 President Truman certified the steel dispute to the WSB for fair and equitable recommendations for settlement.[13] "Losses in steel production," said the President, "would have an immediate and crippling effect on mobilization schedules. . . . The machinery of the Wage Stabilization Board offers a practical substitute for a test of economic strength."

The steel dispute was widely recognized as the test of the disputes machinery and of stabilization. Pressures within the union made it necessary for the steelworkers to push hard for a large wage boost and the union shop. The union determined to put all its energies into the wage case, hoping that the WSB recommendations would improve its bargaining position. The steel industry resolved to resist

[12] New York Times, December 15, 1951.
[13] The steel companies alleged a "deal" between Murray and the President. In a telephone conversation with Murray the President is reported as saying, "If you willingly and voluntarily agree to a suspension of the strike, I believe you need have no fear of . . . Taft-Hartley." (The Steel Labor Case of 1952, a booklet prepared by the steel companies.) There was such a telephone conversation but no "deal." Murray was by no means reconciled to letting the dispute go to the WSB. The contract expired December 31; Murray barred a consideration of any government plea until a special union convention, set for January 3, could consider it. This looked like either noncooperation or a senseless gesture of protest, and the President promptly ordered the staff to "draw up the Taft-Hartley papers." The President spoke plainly; the union must accept the WSB procedure or face Taft-Hartley. Only after receiving Murray's personal assurances that the union would voluntarily cooperate did the President agree to use the WSB procedure rather than Taft-Hartley.

wage increases, particularly increases forced upon it by government. Moreover, the industry was determined that any wage increase should be matched by a proportionate price increase. Neither party exhibited any enthusiasm for the sacrifice of economic objectives or advantage. The makings of a crisis were at hand.

On January 7, 1952, the WSB began the "steel case." A panel appointed to sift the facts and issues discovered a tangle, together with an intransigence which made agreement on even minor issues virtually impossible.[14] The battle of the press releases began. Steel company presidents charged that wage demands were outrageously high and no wage increase could possibly be granted without a compensating price increase. The union claimed that the steel companies were joined in a ruthless conspiracy to block rightful wage increases. "Dope" stories issued from industry, union, and government spokesmen. "Leaks" from OPS told the story of steel profits, measured current profits against the OPS industry-earnings standard and the Capehart amendment, and rejected steel's case for a price increase before it was ever presented.[15]

Even as the industry and the union made their respective cases on wages to the Wage Stabilization Board, the industry began its persistent campaign to storm the citadels of price stabilization. It felt that the government would talk tough, as in 1946, but when the chips were down would prefer labor peace to a disastrous strike.[16] Its

[14] Murray spoke of the "arrant, blatant, obvious hypocrisy" of the steel industry in opposing any wage increase. The industry said a wage increase in steel would "unleash new forces of inflation." In a nationwide broadcast Ben Moreell of Jones & Laughlin Steel charged that if the union's demands (put at 54 cents) were met, steel earnings would be "wiped out."

[15] The earnings standard permitted price increases if profits for an entire industry fell below 85 per cent of the three best years 1946-1949, thus limiting cost absorption. The Capehart amendment permitted sellers to recover cost increases incurred from the date of the Korean War to July 26, 1951, thus allowing a complete pass-through of wage increases in violation of basic principles of price control. The amendment grew out of the Westinghouse Company's predicament; Westinghouse granted a wage increase subsequent to its competitor and found itself disadvantaged by the cutoff date, which blocked a pass-through of cost increases. The steel industry steadfastly refused the increases it was entitled to under Capehart, presumably because it wanted to prove that wage increases required price increases.

[16] The final price settlement in 1946 was negotiated between the industry and OWMR Director John W. Snyder in the course of a nationwide steel shutdown in which the wage issue was no longer in dispute. Rereading the 1946 experience it is hard to believe we learn much from history. See John Dunlop, "The

trump card, which it hoped to obscure, was its power to hold out on a wage settlement until its price demands were met. The industry therefore sought constantly to stress the union shop as *the* major issue in dispute. It also camouflaged the drive for price concessions as a demand for "equal treatment"—for "matching" or "compensatory" price increases.[17] Amid the complications of wage-price policy, "Capehart adjustments," and the earnings standard, the industry's plea was simple and attractive, obviously and unarguably fair to the man in the street. Did not wages affect costs and costs affect prices? Was it not inevitable that a wage increase must mean a price increase? The steel industry thought it bad enough to take an imposed wage settlement, but intolerable to allow government to dictate the translation of wage changes into price changes.

The Wage Stabilization Board was unable to meet the initial deadline of February 23 and two extensions were worked out, the union accepting Chairman Nathan Feinsinger's request for a delay of the strike until April 8 (April 4 plus ninety-six hours' notice). In return the Board promised the parties that it would bend every effort to complete its recommendations by March 20. The March 20 deadline intensified the pressure. Time, used carelessly at the outset, was now treasured. During round-the-clock sessions the public members searched for a settlement formula which could be fitted within the stabilization program. On the labor side they met unyielding pressure for substantially higher wages and a strong union-

Decontrol of Wages and Prices," *in* Colston Warne, *Labor in Postwar America* (Brooklyn: Remsen Press, 1949).

[17] Stabilization officials thought the argument for a "compensatory" increase wholly specious and pointed out that tying individual wage decisions to price decisions, and vice versa, would make any consistent policy in either field impossible. As OPS Director DiSalle told the CIO convention on November 5, 1951, "If wage increases are granted only where employers can absorb them without price increases and denied where price increases would be required, all equity disappears from the wage policy. Actually, if excessive wage increases are granted in industries where employers can absorb, it is impossible to prevent similar wage increases in other industries where employers may be unable to absorb." *New York Times*, November 6, 1951. By the same token, if wage increases were "passed through" into price increases, no consistent or equitable price policy would be possible. There is considerable evidence that the steel industry has timed its price increases to coincide with the conclusion of labor negotiations to cement in the public mind the conviction that wage increases are the principal cause of price increases.

shop recommendation; the internal politics of the CIO decreed that Philip Murray as president of the CIO get for the steelworkers a wage boost equal to if not greater than the General Motors-United Auto Workers contract already approved by the Board. The politics of the steel industry apparently dictated that the Board not be used for mediation efforts. Preservation of the industry's bargaining position required that the industry members of the Board be a dissenting minority. This left the public members isolated and alone. Convinced that a steel strike must be avoided, they bargained with labor in their search for a solution satisfactory to labor and (hopefully) acceptable to industry. Tripartitism was put to a hard test.[18]

On March 19, after two days and nights of intense negotiation and jugglery, the Board reached a public-labor majority recommendation, industry bitterly dissenting. The majority recommended generous wage and fringe benefits and negotiation of some form of union-shop clause by the parties. The "package"—12½ cents plus an additional 2½ cents at six- and twelve-month intervals and 8½ cents in fringe benefits—was quickly put at 26 cents by the press. The "26-cent package" looked outrageously large to many, including President Truman and key staff members then on vacation in Key West and without the full text for twenty-four hours. (The "26-cent package" was deceptive—as if eggs were advertised at 90 cents a dozen, or steak at $1.50 a pound, without pointing out that one meant a dozen and a half eggs and a pound and a half of steak. Eggs are customarily priced by the dozen, and labor contracts by the year!) For 1952 the recommended wage adjustment averaged 13¾ cents an hour.

The union promptly accepted the recommendations, barely able to conceal its pleasure; the industry as promptly rejected them, making no effort to hide its displeasure. To Wilson, the recommendations on their face seemed excessive, signaling a major break in the stabilization line. Chairman Feinsinger's assertion that the final recommendations were substantially in line with the proposals earlier

[18] Within the fraternity of labor experts and the tradition of tripartitism, the mark of true excellence is tripartite unanimity; failure to achieve at least a majority recommendation means abject failure. Hindsight suggests that a public member recommendation, standing alone, might have been appropriate. Critical analysis of the creed of "tripartitism" is long overdue.

discussed with Wilson—indeed more conservative—did little to blunt Wilson's sense of betrayal.[19] For at no time had a 26-cent package ever been discussed. As director of the mobilization program, vested with sweeping authority, Wilson felt a responsibility for the stabilization program which he was helpless to exercise.

MOBILIZATION CRISIS

In the rush of events following the decision, all thought of renewed bargaining was discarded. After conferring with steel industry representatives in New York, Wilson flew to Key West to meet with the President; he returned Monday evening March 24 with "a plan" for resolving the steel controversy. Whatever the "plan" was—and Wilson and President Truman's memories differ— it was never formally unveiled. Under the insistent prodding of reporters at Washington's National Airport, Wilson broke his silence. "If the WSB recommendations become final," said the nation's mobilization chief, "it would have a tremendous effect on the stabilization plan of the country and would lead to . . . inflation, to a very serious degree."[20] In Aspen, Colorado, Feinsinger, when asked for comment, said, "I don't believe Mr. Wilson could possibly have been quoted correctly," and promptly took the next plane for Washington to save the WSB from the fate of repudiation which Wilson had artlessly posed. Wilson's subsequent public statement, that his "personal view" of the recommendations need not affect the situation, was of no avail. Even before Wilson could get in touch with Murray,

[19] Feinsinger had earlier "touched base" with his superiors in ESA and with Wilson, Director of ODM, indicating the bent of the Board's thinking. However, the exact terms of the WSB recommendations were not divulged to anyone, including the White House, prior to the formal vote and the public release of the decision. For all the elaborate hierarchy of bosses, the WSB proved to be virtually autonomous. General wage policies were "reviewed" by the Economic Stabilization Administrator but frequently after the fact. The Board negotiated policies with ESA, never really recognizing ESA's authority. As a tripartite organization, the Board was a forum for bargaining on national wage policies. The argument for sovereignty is that if labor and management representatives are to win the consent of their clientele, they must have power and not be mere executors of policies developed elsewhere. In dispute cases, neither ESA nor ODM had policy control, though the Board was bound by existing wage policies and standards.

[20] New York Times, March 25, 1952.

the union chief's bitter reactions had made such a meeting impossible.[21]

The labor dispute was all but forgotten. "Official Washington," said the *Wall Street Journal*, "is in an uproar."[22]

Wilson tried without success to mobilize his stabilization team behind him. His "plan" was to ram through a price increase, regardless of existing price standards, presumably with the backing of the President. OPS Director Arnall was incredulous and suggested that on an issue as basic as this he would like to hear such instructions from the President's own lips. Wilson therefore requested an appointment with the President.

Meanwhile the White House began an agonizing reappraisal. The conflict between Wilson and the Board could not be mediated. One had to be supported, the other repudiated. Stabilization officials were adamant. Wilson's proposed pass-through was regarded as the end of price control. Not only did the steel industry reject any cost absorption whatever but it insisted on an increase in excess of the wage cost. Moreover, Wilson's price offer was regarded as setting the minimum, not the maximum, which the industry would extract. The wage recommendations looked high, though not necessarily fatal to wage control. To support Wilson on wages meant precipitating the breakup of the Board, a strike, and the end of labor participation in wage control and hence of wage control itself. To support Wilson on prices meant yielding the whole of price stabilization to the steel industry and in all likelihood precipitating the resignation of Arnall. The White House made a reluctant choice. The WSB recommendation had to stand; Wilson's "give-away" to the steel industry had to be blocked, even at the risk of losing Wilson. Moral

[21] Said Murray, "Mr. Wilson does not know the issues; he does not understand them, and his only knowledge of the issues comes from the steel corporation executives who summoned him to New York for a hasty briefing session—no constructive purpose could be served by attendance at a meeting with Mr. Wilson. . . . No self-respecting union would consent to bring any dispute before the Board for extensive consideration of its merits, only to have Charles E. Wilson, a self-proclaimed big business man, attempt to reverse the decision without regard to its merits." *New York Times*, March 26, 1952.

[22] WSB industry members charged that the recommendations were a "conscious and admitted" effort to satisfy the union, later urged that the Board be abolished. The House Rules Committee voted an investigation of the WSB by the House Education and Labor Committee, which became the first of many committees to join the fray.

indignation reinforced prudence. The President was incensed at the steel industry for holding the union contract "hostage" until a price settlement was achieved.

On March 28 Wilson, Putnam, and Arnall met with the President. While conceding that Wilson was instructed to do the best he could, the President denied emphatically ever having given Wilson *carte blanche* authority to settle the steel dispute by yielding the whole of the price stabilization program to the industry. The President, in short, was outraged by Wilson's action for the very reason that Wilson had been outraged by that of Chairman Feinsinger. In both instances a vague mandate to proceed had been given and the results had been disappointing. Poor communication generated charges of bad faith! To Wilson the President's "repudiation" of him became betrayal; he promptly resigned, charging the President with having "changed the plan we agreed upon" and stating, "I can't accept public responsibility for national stabilization actions which I cannot control."[23] Wilson's resignation and the resulting uproar blocked any renewal of bargaining, either between the union and industry on wages or the industry and government on prices.[24] The strike deadline of April 8 loomed close ahead.

John R. Steelman, Assistant to the President, replaced Wilson as Mobilization Director and promptly tackled the steel dispute. His first task was to get the union and the industry to the bargaining table, his next to work out a compromise on prices. Steelman re-adopted the earlier strategy of seeking a wage settlement prior to making any commitment on prices.

Wage bargaining began in New York, with Chairman Feinsinger participating as a special mediator. Thursday, April 3, nearly four months after "bargaining" had begun, the steel industry made its *first* offer: 14.4 cents an hour and various fringe benefits. However attractive the offer might have looked earlier, the steelworkers now found it unacceptable.

As the strike deadline approached, the White House weighed alternatives. Taft-Hartley seemed manifestly inappropriate. The emergency provisions, if applied, would paralyze the bargaining

[23] For a blow-by-blow account of the Wilson story, see Dan Seligman, "The Last Days of Charlie Wilson," *Fortune*, 45 (June 1952), pp. 85-88.

[24] Negotiations scheduled to begin Monday, March 31, were canceled. With Wilson's departure went the agreement or commitment (if any) on price that had been worked out with the steel industry in the New York meeting.

and destroy any chance of settlement. They offered an eighty-day delay and the WSB procedure had already provided ample delay. Price seemed a paramount issue and the act was surely not designed for disputes between business and governments. Rejecting Taft-Hartley left but one alternative, the weapon of seizure. The argument for seizure was familiar. It maintained production, preserved the status quo, and enabled the government to pressure both parties to settle. Reluctantly, the White House ordered the Justice Department to "prepare the necessary papers" to accomplish seizure.[25] The order was both bluff and precaution. News of the "planned seizure" was leaked to the press. To the last the underlying hope was that the steel dispute would, somehow, be settled.

Even as the steel furnaces were being banked and Justice was preparing for seizure, Feinsinger reported "progress." However, on the week end of April 5-6 the administration passed a point of no return. Thereafter the Taft-Hartley Act might be used to stop a strike; it could no longer be used to prevent one. Barring a last-minute settlement, seizure was inevitable. In the late afternoon of April 8, just before the midnight strike deadline, Feinsinger reported failure to the White House; within hours a draft of a speech was put in final form. The President's bluff had been called.

SEIZURE—A PANDORA'S BOX

In a nationwide broadcast on April 8 the President announced seizure of the steel mills. He supported the steelworkers, and was sharply critical of the steel industry for its refusal to abide by the "rules of the game."[26] He pointed out that seizure was adopted with

[25] Section 18, Selective Service and Training Act, empowers plant seizures upon failure to fill mandatory orders placed through defense agencies. This route to seizure was carefully examined and rejected; the defense agencies argued that the technical problems were insufferable and Justice doubted the legality of seizure under Section 18. This left only the seizure based on "inherent powers," as in the early seizures of World War II.

[26] Said the President, "It is perfectly clear that the emergency provisions of the Taft-Hartley Act do not meet the needs of the present situation. . . . The fact of the matter is that the settlement proposed by the Board is fair to both sides and to the public interest. And what is more I think the steel companies know it. . . . The plain fact of the matter is that the steel companies are recklessly forcing a shutdown of the steel mills." The President urged that the wage dispute be settled, and the steel companies then file petition for any price increases to which they were entitled—thus observing the "rules of the game." *New York Times*, April 9, 1952.

great reluctance as the only way short of abandoning the stabilization program to assure weapons for our troops.

Reactions were prompt. The strike was called off; the steel companies moved into court to defeat what Randall of Inland Steel in a nationwide radio and TV broadcast called an "evil deed without precedent in American history, the discharge of a political debt to the CIO." The steel controversy was submerged by political furore and rousing debates on the constitutional issue of the powers of the President.[27]

Meanwhile, efforts to revive collective bargaining proved abortive. Preoccupied with fighting seizure in the courts, the steel companies were in no mood for bargaining. The first of many sessions in the White House failed; after seven days of fruitless effort the negotiations were recessed indefinitely.

Unable to bargain with the industry, the steelworkers turned their attention hopefully to their "employer," Secretary of Commerce Sawyer, hoping for a contract or at least for part of the wage adjustment recommended by the WSB. They met frustrations exceeding their worst expectations. On April 14 Sawyer promised that he would deal "promptly but not precipitately" with the wage matter.

[27] The administration argued that seizure was within the aggregate of the constitutional powers of the President. No claim of unlimited executive power was made—exactly the contrary was implied. On the morning of April 9 the President sent a message to the Congress pointing out the alternatives to seizure and indicating that if the Congress deemed some other course wiser, it had the power to undo his seizure action. The President posed three alternatives: (1) change in the stabilization rules or abandonment of the program, (2) a shutdown, or (3) specific seizure legislation tailored to the steel dispute. *New York Times,* April 10, 1952.

As Chief Justice Vinson noted later, the President's seizure gave Congress time to act. The President at no time denied the right of the Congress to countermand his action. Congress was highly critical of the President but rejected his invitation to act. Later, when the Congress considered action which would have forced an end to seizure, the President again tried without success to implicate the Congress. On April 21 he wrote the Congress, "I do not believe the Congress can meet its responsibilities simply by following a course of negation. The Congress cannot perform its constitutional functions simply by paralyzing the operations of government in an emergency." As for Taft-Hartley, the President noted that "nothing in the situation suggests that further fact-finding and further delay would bring about a settlement. . . . A Taft-Hartley injunction . . . would be most unfair since its effect would simply be to force the workers to continue at work for another 80 days at their old wages." *Congressional Record,* 82d Cong., 2d sess., 98:3 (April 21, 1952), p. 4192.

A week later, after unsuccessful meetings with the union and the industry, he asked ESA Administrator Putnam to draft an order raising the wages of steelworkers. The order was never issued. District Judge David Pine, hearing the companies' plea for an injunction, sought a commitment from the Justice Department that the government would not change wages (or prices) while the case was before him. The government would give no such promise; but neither did it act. Thereupon, Judge Pine acted—some thought—both promptly *and* precipitately. On April 29 he ruled the seizure illegal, charging that a strike "with all its awful results" would be "less injurious to the public than the injury which would flow from a timorous judicial recognition that there is some basis for a claim to unlimited and unrestrained executive power."[28]

Within minutes after Pine's decision steelworkers were walking off their jobs; the strike which so many had labored so hard to avoid began. Hurried talks in the White House yielded a decision to seek a "stay" of Pine's order, pending an appeal to the Supreme Court, and at the same time get the men back to work. The Circuit Court of Appeals acted promptly to grant the stay, refusing to attach a freeze on wages as requested by the steel companies.[29] This maintained seizure while the case was carried to the Supreme Court, and made possible a successful appeal by President Truman to the steelworkers to return to work. Almost as quickly as the strike began, it was called off.

The battle shifted to the Supreme Court. The companies asked the Supreme Court for an interim order to freeze the status quo; the Justice Department answered that "any change in the nature of

[28] *Youngstown Sheet & Tube Co. v. Sawyer,* 103 F. Supp. 569 (DC, D. of C. 1952). The issues were hopelessly blurred for the public after Pine's ruling. The Justice Department counsel shocked the court, the country, and most emphatically the White House with an assertion that the power of the President to meet emergencies—unlike that of court or Congress—was unlimited. Efforts at retraction never erased the impression that the President lay claim to unlimited power. Cf. letter to a Mr. Jones released by the White House and used as a vehicle to "set the record straight." *New York Times,* April 28, 1952.

[29] Solicitor Philip Perlman walked a tightrope. He had to avoid a freeze order at all costs, since it would make it difficult if not impossible to get the men back to work. Yet he had to reassure the court that the government would not put such a wage increase into effect in the interim. Perlman did this by telling the court his "best information" was that no immediate increase was contemplated.

the stay now in effect would probably result in a new crisis, with danger of still another interruption." From the sidelines, the steelworkers' brief noted mournfully:

If the stay order is granted, the union can bargain with the government. If as the companies request, it is denied completely, the employees can bargain with the steel companies. But if the order is granted but modified as the companies request, the union will have no employer with which it can bargain.[30]

Even as the Supreme Court took jurisdiction, the White House made a last-ditch effort at settlement. Calling Murray and six steel presidents to the White House for bargaining sessions at 10 A.M. Saturday, May 3, the President told the negotiators that the government would be prepared on Monday morning to order changes in terms and conditions of employment to be put into effect. "If we must take action it will be something that is not satisfactory to either side."

The words struck home. Bargaining got under way in an atmosphere of restrained optimism. Some progress was made. However, just as Fairless and Murray were settling to serious bargaining, the Supreme Court late Saturday afternoon issued an interim order forbidding the government to change terms and conditions of employment (except by mutual consent) pending the Court's ruling. This effectively destroyed the bargaining pressures. The Sunday discussions were fruitless and by late afternoon the negotiations broke off amid angry charges.

On May 12 and 13 oral argument was heard before the Supreme Court.[31] Quite obscured in the rich debate on the constitutional

[30] Brief for United Steelworkers of America, *Youngstown Sheet & Tube Co. v. Sawyer,* 343 U. S. 579 (1952).

[31] The government argued that the deep underlying fact of a national emergency "threatening the very existence of the whole nation" justified the extraordinary and extralegal action of the President. As for executive usurpation, Solicitor Perlman pointed out that at any time Congress could have acted to undo the President's seizure, or could have legislated a different solution. Moreover, the Taft-Hartley procedure was discretionary, not mandatory. The Congress had impliedly accepted an alternative route for handling emergency labor disputes when it enacted Title V of the DPA and later specifically refused to take away the disputes authority assigned to the WSB. Finally, the companies had an adequate remedy at law in the payment of just compensation.

powers of the President was the union's plea for prompt action. Seizure, said the steelworkers, has brought a "drastic alteration . . . of the balance of power in the collective bargaining relationship. . . . Without the possibility of strike, the bargaining power of labor shrinks."[32] This was an accurate prediction. Wage bargaining was at a complete standstill for the month it took the Court to decide the case. Nor was any progress made toward solving the price issue.

During this period the White House weighed various alternatives. No clear solutions were advanced. Plainly the President had a bear by the tail. If seizure were sustained, presumably a partial wage increase could be imposed. However, the price issue still had to be met.[33] The problem of steel prices was inseparable from that of the Defense Production Act and its extension for another year. If the Court did not block seizure, the Congress certainly would. An appropriation rider, effective June 30, could block use of any federal funds to pay any officers involved in the steel seizure, thus ending seizure. Defeat in the Supreme Court or in the Congress would recreate the strike *and* the price impasse.

John W. Davis, industry counsel, rejected these arguments entirely. As for the "delay" and the resulting stoppage which would have occurred if Taft-Hartley had been invoked at the eleventh hour, Davis reminded the Court of the longshore case where an injunction was obtained in four days. "Neither the military nor the economic structure of the country would have fallen in that time," said Davis. He argued that the very existence of the Taft-Hartley Act militated against the President's right to use the alternative of seizure. While admitting there had been nonstatutory seizures before, Davis asserted there were no instances of seizure where an existing statute provided an alternative approach to the problem.

[32] The union brief also noted that if after a union voluntarily submitted to the WSB the President used Taft-Hartley, "no union conscious of its responsibilities to its membership would thereafter consent to voluntary submission to the WSB."

[33] One idea which gained currency in the White House and enlisted the support of some members of the Mobilization Advisory Board was to put the spotlight of pitiless publicity on steel prices. A public hearing was suggested so that the steel companies would state their case publicly—much as the union had presented its wage petition to the WSB—so that price pleas might be measured against the industry-earnings standard. The idea was never specifically rejected; it just never was followed up, largely because of lack of enthusiasm on the part of OPS.

THE STEEL STRIKE AND THE SEARCH FOR RESPONSIBILITY

On June 2 the Supreme Court announced its decision: the President lacked authority to seize the steel mills.[34] The Court decided a landmark case; it also precipitated a strike which, in its last days, lived up to its advance billing: "intolerable." At the same time that the Court denied presidential power it also affirmed the power of the Congress to act. The one common thread running through the majority and concurring opinions was that the nation's security was not dependent upon executive prerogative as long as the Congress retained the lawmaking power and the capacity to act.[35] The Court's suggestion that the Congress might act struck no fire. Though deeply disturbed that a steel strike should occur, the Congress was unwilling to take responsibility, much preferring its role of presidential critic.

Once again the President called the parties to the White House in a renewed effort to break the stalemate, meanwhile preparing a message to the Congress in the event of failure. For a brief time the prospect of a settlement glowed brightly, then faded. Intensive bargaining June 6-9 resulted in substantial progress.[36] A tentative

[34] *Youngstown Sheet & Tube Co. v. Sawyer*, 343 U. S. 579 (1952). The function of the Court is to decide cases in controversy, not to aid the executive in the settlement of labor disputes. However, it is doubtful under all the circumstances whether the Court's decision was called for by the necessities of the case. As Paul Freund has pointed out, "the consequences of the abrupt order of retransfer could hardly have been worse and might have been avoided." He suggests that the Court order "might have required a retransfer of the properties unless within a designated short period further executive or legislative action were taken, meanwhile forbidding a change in working conditions save by agreement." Such a brief waiting period, he suggests, "might have sharpened the sense of responsibility of the government authorities." Paul Freund, "The Year of the Steel Case," *Harvard Law Review*, 66 (November 1952), p. 89.

[35] For conflicting reactions compare E. S. Corwin, "The Steel Case: A Judicial Brick Without Straw," *Columbia Law Review*, 53 (January 1953), pp. 53-67; John Roche, "Executive Power and Domestic Emergency: The Quest for Prerogative," *Western Political Quarterly*, V (December 1952), pp. 592-619; and Lucius Wilmerding, "The President and the Law," *Political Science Quarterly*, LXVII (September 1952), pp. 321-334.

[36] On Monday, June 9, the President, in order to forestall Senate action that might be disruptive, wrote to Vice-President Barkley, stating that there was a reasonable hope of settlement and that any action by the Senate might "cause a breakdown of the negotiations." A phone call on Friday from Steelman to Majority Leader MacFarland had forestalled the Senate from voting on proposals to "recommend" that the President use Taft-Hartley.

understanding on wage rates and most fringe items was reached. The union-shop and Sunday-overtime issues were discussed at length and counterproposals on the union shop were made. However, on June 9 the monotonous lines were played again. The parties were reported as "completely deadlocked," perhaps because the bargainers were more preoccupied with what the government would do next than with solving their own problems. (A mutual pledge was made to cooperate with the government in reopening facilities to meet urgent military requirements, but despite many conferences the pledge was never honored.)

Eight days after the Supreme Court's decision, President Truman took the steel dispute to the Congress. Telling his staff of his decision to address the Congress personally, the President said, "Let's put the cat right on their back." Tuesday, June 11, the President pointedly reminded a joint session of the Congress that at any time it could have provided a different solution of the steel dispute but that "the Congress took no action." According to the President, two main possibilities existed: government operation of the mills or use of a labor injunction of the type authorized by Taft-Hartley. The President then sought to put responsibility for action squarely upon the Congress. "The Congress," he said, "can choose either of these alternatives. I cannot. I could only use the Taft-Hartley approach . . . by far the worse of the two approaches." The President then argued that the only way of achieving the threefold objective of assuring steel production, treating both parties fairly, and encouraging collective bargaining was a seizure law providing "fair and just compensation" to both owners and employees.[37] Logically the President's position may have been unassailable; politically it was unattainable. It was true that the Congress could authorize an immediate suit by the government for an injunction, whereas the President would have to go through the formality of appointing a board of inquiry and awaiting a report before he could act.

The arguments were lost on the Congress. The President's alternatives were ignored. Before day's end, the Senate passed (49-30) the Byrd amendment "recommending" that the President use the Taft-Hartley Act. Next day the Senate rejected (54-26) the Morse proposal, which permitted presidential seizure but required congressional concurrence for the continuance of seizure.

[37] *New York Times,* June 11, 1952.

The strike that couldn't be allowed was now in full swing. Negotiations were stalled as the union, the industry, and government each waited for someone to make the next move. Congress had specifically and unmistakably denied any responsibility for taking the initiative. As for the White House, it had no plans. After nine days of intensive maneuvering, each of the participants laid the blame elsewhere. The President and Congress, reflecting the antagonisms of the union and the industry, were in deadlock, each convinced of the other's moral delinquency. Democracy's capacity for compromise was, for the moment, submerged in self-justifying antagonisms.[38]

The country behaved with astonishing calm. Doomsday had not arrived. The strike had few immediately visible effects; the world moved on, and the shooting war in Korea with it. The war of words died down even as the strike deepened, as day piled on day, week on week, and the earlier predictions of catastrophe finally began to have meaning. Of this, the general public seemed unaware. From the exaggerated fear that even a day's stoppage spelled disaster the nation swung to the far more dangerous exaggeration that the prolonged strike really didn't hurt much. Seasonal lassitude and the fascinations of the upcoming political conventions added to the general lack of urgency.

What were the barriers to settlement? On the surface the price impasse loomed as forbidding as ever; OPS Director Arnall still insisted that the government would not buy peace at the cost of abandoning its stabilization program. But his words carried less conviction. The price issue had for all practical purposes melted away. No written commitment and no public announcement had been made, but the steel industry knew it could expect a $5.20 a ton price increase whenever the labor contract was signed. The price barrier was gone: the "steel case" was once again simply a labor

---

[38] "The Steelworkers," said Murray, "will never surrender. . . . No group is big enough to whip this union." The union chief began touring the steel mills in an effort to keep the pressure on. Though he made some settlements with smaller companies, Murray was never able to split the industry. The companies also moved to the offensive. The propaganda batteries, stilled for a while, began again. Full-page ads blossomed throughout the land, crying the evils of monopoly union shop. The steel industry would "never surrender" its workers to the union shop.

dispute. It was, however, one in which the participants had been rubbed raw by events. Since the strike began, the parties had never been far apart, certainly on wages. Even on the thorny issue of the union shop real progress had been made during the June 5-9 sessions at the White House. Attitudes, not issues, kept the parties from a settlement. As Abe Raskin noted,

The process of what is politely called collective bargaining can be endless especially when emotional, political and economic factors are so intertwined. . . . The chief stumbling block is . . . the bitterness that has developed in the six months of struggle over the steel contract. Cordial labor-management relations are being eaten away by the weary weeks of bickering and frustration.[39]

A labor dispute had become a pawn in the struggles within and between the executive, the courts, and the Congress. At every stage of the interminable affair, government intervention aggravated rather than eased the conflict—and did to the bitter end.

SETTLEMENT EFFORTS RENEWED

Not until June 20 were efforts at settlement renewed. Union negotiators met with Bethlehem, one of the Big Six, and reached tentative agreement on a modified version of the union shop.[40] On Friday the agreement was rejected by the Big Six, who were able to hold Bethlehem Steel in line. Try as he would, Murray was unable to split the steel industry.[41]

The strike dragged on; neither side seemed in a hurry to settle. The union refused to take less than the Bethlehem formula. The companies, meeting in secret session on July 3, decided against further concessions. The union-shop issue was alleged by the industry to be the principal barrier to settlement. But surely there were other

[39] *New York Times,* June 15, 1952.

[40] The Bethlehem formula provided no change for old employees; new employees could withdraw from the union within thirty days after hire. Upon employment they must apply for membership in the union and authorize dues deductions, but this could be revoked by registered letter to both union and company within twenty days.

[41] The union charged conspiracy and requested the NLRB and the Justice Department to investigate. Settlements were reached with Pittsburgh Steel (fourteenth largest) but all other settlements were with small producers and left the balance of power undisturbed.

factors as well. The political conventions loomed close on the horizon. The steel strike was an albatross around the President's neck. Moreover, the strike was cutting consumer goods inventories and insuring high demand once settlement was reached.[42] Public sentiment was building up against the President for his stubborn refusal to use Taft-Hartley and against the union for its adamant insistence on the union shop.

On July 10, exactly one month from the President's futile plea to Congress, the parties renewed bargaining, this time in secret sessions in Pittsburgh. Again optimism mounted. A settlement looked near. As the wage bargaining got under way, U.S. Steel executives met with Steelman on the price issue. A clear understanding was reached, though no signatures were affixed to the document. The steel industry was promised $5.20 a ton ($4.50 plus 70 cents for a recent ICC freight rate increase). However, on Saturday, July 14, the weary labor negotiators announced failure. The industry proposals, involving several minor changes in the Bethlehem formula, were unacceptable to the union.

It was not a failure the White House could tolerate. With increasing force, the steel strike was beginning to strangle the mobilization program. Pressure by the military for the White House to "do something" grew ever more determined. Steelman forced a resumption of the talks, threatening to lock the negotiators in a room until they settled.[43] On July 20 the talks were resumed, again with no success; the proposed escape clause, providing workers fifteen days at the start of the contract in which to withdraw, remained at issue.

Short of a settlement by the tiniest of margins, the parties seemed helpless to come to terms. Secretary of Defense Lovett indirectly provided the final push. On July 23 he called a press conference. In anger and anguish, the Secretary pointed out that the steel strike was worse than any enemy bombing raid. No raid could have knocked out our entire capacity for nearly two months, and all self-inflicted! The mobilization program, said the Secretary, was grind-

---

[42] Joseph Loftus reported the belief that "large supplies of some types of steel is a major influence in the companies' decisions and that when these inventories are reduced a price increase will be more meaningful and bargaining will be conducted on a more realistic basis." *New York Times*, June 25, 1952.

[43] Strong intervention was essential. The union was about to call the 170-man wage committee together formally to reject the last offer—a fresh declaration of war.

ing to a halt. These strong words were not lost on the White House or the parties. Plainly the strike could not be tolerated much longer. And it would not be enough for the White House to say that Congress should act.

Determined somehow to break the deadlock, the President called the parties to the White House on Saturday morning, July 24. He met only with Murray and Fairless. The President's comments were brief and to the point. He told them they could settle the dispute *that day;* no one else could settle it for them. The stoppage had to be ended. They knew it as well as he did. He would now leave them alone. If they wanted help, John Steelman would come in. It was up to them.[44] Within hours Fairless and Murray reached an agreement which paved the way for a general settlement. After fifty-three days the strike that "couldn't happen" was finally over, on terms close to those proposed early in the strike. A union-shop provision similar to the Bethlehem proposal was accepted. The agreement specified that a new employee must apply for union membership to take effect within thirty days unless revoked by the applicant in the last fifteen days of the thirty-day period following employment. All union members were given the right to drop membership during the last fifteen days of the contract. It was an odd ending to the great union-shop controversy. For all practical purposes the steelworkers won the union shop. (The union now has virtually complete membership in the plants.) Yet the companies could claim a limited victory. They had sacrificed no principle; the right of each employee to decide for himself whether he wished to join the union and remain in it was fully protected.

By any standard the cost of the stoppage was heavy. The impact on the civilian economy is detailed elsewhere.[45] The real significance

[44] The President had with him a staff paper suggesting that the parties submit the remaining issues to arbitration, the arbitrator to be selected by the President in the event of failure to agree. It appears that the President never referred to the proposal.

[45] See Irving Berstein's account on pages 38-42 of this volume. Chamberlain and Schilling place the stoppage third among seventeen emergency strikes between 1941 and 1952 in terms of "hardship to the public." Neil W. Chamberlain and Jane Metzger Schilling, *The Impact of Strikes* (New York: Harper, 1954), p. 241. Their elaborate formula for measuring "impact" is a worthwhile effort to substitute economic measurement for guesswork. However, to exclude "defense considerations" is to ignore what in most instances must be the heart of the analysis. For example, dare we ignore the ramifying effects of atomic energy?

of the stoppage, however, was in the damage to the defense program. The ramifying effect of the strike on mobilization schedules was incalculable. Plainly, the result was to delay production of military end items which would have been badly needed in the event of all-out war. The steel strike coincided with (and contributed to) a slackening of the mobilization effort and a general feeling that the risks of total war were fading. It is no answer to say that the country survived. No one can measure the vulnerability to enemy attack or count the cost had we been plunged into war. In the latter event the President's seizure action might have appeared wholly justified, the attitude of Court and Congress wildest folly.

SUMMARY AND CONCLUSIONS

This tale of the 1952 steel dispute brings us full-circle to the thesis outlined at the beginning.

Presidential intervention in *emergency* disputes is inevitable. Against the backdrop of Korea and the Chinese Communists' invasion, no President conscious of his responsibilities could have heard the warnings of the Secretary of Defense and the Mobilization Director and failed to act. If the parties to big disputes will not work out their own salvation, the government must intervene. Government is the only agency by which the community at large can act. Government intervention may be clumsy, inept, and wrong-headed, but such intervention cannot be banished without solving the situation which brings it about.

Responsible political leadership will always seek to *prevent* emergencies from developing. This is, after all, one of the objects for which governments are established. There was no economic Univac enabling President Truman to determine the exact moment when the steel stoppage would shift from "serious" to "critical" and then to "intolerable." His action was premised on the advice and information before him. In retrospect, government intervention may look premature. But governments do not act in retrospect; they act amid the compulsions of the present. In 1952 a nationwide steel strike posed a clear and present danger to the mobilization program of the nation and to the foreign policy the President sought to execute.

The intervention of government is likely to complicate and prolong an emergency dispute. The steel dispute was especially complicated because it was entangled with wage and price stabilization issues. The parties maneuvered interminably through government: a *terra incognita* of administrative agencies, courts, and committees of Congress. Familiar rights, duties, and expectations were obscured, and both the union and the industry felt themselves victims of unfairly imposed obligations. The point is not that "collective bargaining failed," but that the entire process of group negotiation and diplomacy, of which collective bargaining was only a part, faltered and failed.

Emergency disputes are intimately bound to the larger political environment. The steel dispute was shaped at every turn by considerations relating to the Taft-Hartley Act, the Defense Production Act, and the upcoming 1952 elections. As the struggle deepened, political antagonisms were aroused. Common points of view came to be regarded as sinister conspiracies. Both the union and the industry sought to mobilize countervailing power where they could: the union in the executive branch, the industry in Congress and the courts.

Presidential intervention must command the support of the political community. The physical and legal power of government in emergency disputes is slight. In our society government is one of many competitors for power and influence, and the executive branch is hemmed in by the Congress and the courts. The power of the President is directly dependent on his power to mobilize a favorable public opinion. In the 1952 steel dispute the driving sense of urgency in the White House and the mobilization agencies was never successfully communicated to the parties, the Congress, the Supreme Court, or the public at large. The impact of a steel strike, exaggerated at the outset, was dangerously minimized in its final stages. At the root of the struggles was a wide split on the *extent* of the national danger and its implications for presidential power. Steel was caught up in cross currents of public opinion. Our words revealed the national indecision: *police action, partial mobilization.* The whole apparatus of stabilization was jerry-built, reflecting the deep uncertainties of the policy makers and the people. In these circumstances, it is not surprising that the President failed to win the battle for public opinion.

The 1952 record in steel suggests a final warning. Both labor and management have enormous power, which impels the use of countervailing power by government. Like it or not, government will intervene in emergency disputes, creating new risks as well as new avenues of maneuver. Problems not solved by those directly responsible will be solved by outsiders, perhaps in blundering fashion. As for government, each branch has the power to immobilize the other. Power, whether of groups or of government, must be used sparingly if we are to survive in a hostile world.

No one can save us from ourselves. Vast as are the powers and sanctions of the President, he cannot force agreement when powerful groups contend mightily for advantage. Neither the emergency provisions of Taft-Hartley, the disputes machinery of the Wage Stabilization Board and its like, nor any other law, mechanism, procedure, or gadget can substitute for basic social responsibility.

· IV ·

THE BUGABOO OF SOVEREIGNTY

AND NATIONAL EMERGENCY DISPUTES*

BY BENJAMIN AARON

University of California, Los Angeles

The term "national emergency dispute" seems to stimulate lurid
fantasies in the minds of otherwise sober and conservative citizens.
Cartoons suggested by those ominous words typically reveal John L.
Lewis bestriding a prostrate economy like a colossus and breathing
defiance at a fearful Uncle Sam, or show a group of smug-faced
business tycoons thumbing their noses at the same timorous Uncle,
while the wheels of industry grind to a halt.

What is the basis for such highly colored notions? Are some disputes "national emergencies" precisely because one or more of the
parties involved have challenged the power of government to intervene? Let us consider briefly one of the most frequently cited
instances of resistance to governmental processes by a private group
and see what light it throws upon these speculations.

In October 1946 the federal government was in possession of the
major portion of the country's bituminous coal mines, having seized
them the previous May pursuant to an executive order. Disagreement over the interpretation of an agreement entered into in May
of that year between John L. Lewis and Secretary of Interior Krug,
as Coal Mines Administrator, led to notice of termination of the
agreement by the union. The government promptly sued the union
and Lewis in federal district court under the Declaratory Judgment

---

* The writer wishes to acknowledge the assistance of Mr. Elliot Stanford in
the preparation of this chapter.

Act, seeking judgment to the effect that the defendants had no power unilaterally to terminate the Krug-Lewis agreement, and also injunctive relief against the threatened stoppage resulting from the miners' "no contract-no work" policy. The federal district court immediately, and without notice to the defendants, issued a temporary restraining order against (1) continuation of the notice of termination, (2) encouragement of the miners to strike or cease work, and (3) interfering with the court's jurisdiction and its determination of the case.

Despite the issuance of the restraining order, the miners left the pits. In a subsequent proceeding against the defendants for contempt they argued that the court had no jurisdiction in the premises and that the Norris-LaGuardia Act prohibited the granting of the temporary restraining order at the instance of the United States.

The legal points raised by the defendants were overruled and they were tried and found guilty of both civil and criminal contempt. The court fined the union $3,500,000 and Lewis $10,000. It also issued a preliminary injunction, in terms similar to those of the restraining order, to be effective until the final determination of the case. On appeal to the United States Supreme Court, the action of the trial court was affirmed, by majority vote, in all respects save the fine assessed against the union, which was reduced.[1]

A dispassionate examination of the foregoing facts hardly supports the theory that the mine workers' union or its irascible leader engaged in rebellion against the United States or challenged its sovereignty. The dispute arose over an interpretation of legal rights, and the conduct of the defendants was no more resistant to authority than that of a corporation which opposes by all means at its disposal an indictment under the antitrust laws. Certainly, there was nothing trivial about the legal issues raised by the union, as a reading of the Supreme Court opinions will demonstrate.[2] While the actions of the miners may have been ill-advised, they were certainly not rebellious in a political sense.

The thesis of this chapter is that national emergency disputes, whatever else they may import, do not involve a challenge to the

[1] *United States v. United Mine Workers of America*, 330 U. S. 258 (1947).

[2] Five opinions were written, and seven of the nine justices expressed their views. The Court's opinion, delivered by the Chief Justice, was concurred in without qualification by only two other justices.

legal authority of the government to act. This is not to deny that companies and unions must be viewed as political as well as economic institutions, but merely to assert that historical political developments in this country have established the sovereignty of government so securely that it cannot be challenged by any private group. Stated in another way, the proposition advanced here is that no private group any longer challenges the exclusive legal authority of government—that is, its sovereignty—to prescribe rules regulating the conduct of parties involved in major disputes. Employers or unions may, it is true, criticize the rules prescribed or other action taken by government; they may urge one or more branches of government to act, or to refrain from acting, in a way most favorable to their own interests. Viewed in even the most unfavorable light, however, those activities cannot be regarded as anything more than placing selfish economic interests above the welfare of the American people; they can by no stretch of the imagination be transformed into an explicit or implied challenge to the sovereignty of the state.

The following discussion, therefore, is largely negative in character. Its purpose is to clarify, without specifically dealing with, the basic problem of what the government ought to do about national emergency disputes by removing from the area of debate the spurious issue of sovereignty.

PROPERTY AND SOVEREIGNTY

In his perceptive essay, "Property and Sovereignty,"[3] Morris R. Cohen observed that "as a legal term 'property' denotes not material things but certain rights," of which the most basic is the right to exclude others. This is true despite the fact that the "character of property as sovereign power compelling service and obedience may be obscured for us in a commercial economy by the fiction of the so-called labour contract as a free bargain and by the frequency with which service is rendered indirectly through a money payment." Men must work to obtain money for purchasing necessities for subsistence; thus, "dominion over things is also *imperium* over our fellow human beings."[4]

Writing in 1927, Cohen could discern on the American scene no

[3] *Cornell Law Quarterly,* 13 (December 1927), pp. 8 ff.
[4] *Ibid.,* p. 13.

change in the traditional theory of rights, molded by the struggle in the seventeenth and eighteenth centuries against restrictions on individual enterprise, which he described as follows:

These restrictions in the interest of special privilege were fortified by the divine (and therefore absolute) right of kings. As is natural in all revolts, absolute claims on one side were met with absolute denials on the other. Hence the theory of the natural rights of the individual took not only an absolute but a negative form; men have *in*alienable rights, the state must never interfere with private property, etc.[5]

There was, of course, ample evidence at the time to support Cohen's conclusion that the sovereign power of property had successfully resisted government control, particularly in the area of employment relationships. Despite the increasing tendency of publicists and writers on constitutional and administrative law to consider the limitations of private property necessary for public safety, peace, health, and morals, the law continued to be construed by judges whose opinions mirrored the traditional concept of the sovereignty of private property. Thus, to cite but a few illustrations, the United States Supreme Court had ruled that a state was prohibited by the Fourteenth Amendment from limiting the number of hours worked in bakeries to not more than ten per day or sixty per week ("we think that a law like the one before us involves neither the safety, the morals nor the welfare of the public, and that the interest of the public is not in the slightest degree affected by such an act");[6] that the federal government was barred by the Fifth Amendment from making it a crime for an interstate carrier to discriminate against an employee because of his membership in a labor organization ("In all such particulars the employer and the employé have equality of right, and any legislation that disturbs that equality is an arbitrary interference with the liberty of contract which no government can legally justify in a free land");[7] and that an employer's "yellow-dog" contracts with his employees constituted a property right, which the courts would protect by injunction from interference by a union ("Unionizing the miners is but a step in the process of unionizing the mine. . . . Plaintiff is

[5] *Ibid.*, p. 21.
[6] *Lochner v. New York*, 198 U. S. 45, 57 (1905).
[7] *Adair v. United States*, 208 U. S. 161, 175 (1908).

as much entitled to prevent the first step as the second . . . and to be protected against irreparable injury resulting from either").[8]

The Great Depression and the social revolution brought about by the New Deal changed all that; so much so, in fact, that many property owners, particularly employers, began to wonder if any of the traditional rights of property remained. The tidal wave of legislation in the thirties—especially the Norris-LaGuardia Act, the amended Railway Labor Act, the Wagner Act, and the Fair Labor Standards Act—swept away much of the old law, depriving employers of rights they had previously enjoyed on the basis of their property ownership, and imposing on them duties toward their employees and the labor unions representing them that went far beyond any former reach of government.

More recent developments have indicated an intensification, rather than a diminution, of this trend. The enactment of the Taft-Hartley Act in 1947 marked the high point of governmental interference in the affairs of management. Though remedying some of the alleged evils in the Wagner Act, of which employers had bitterly complained, the new law relieved businessmen of none of the basic duties imposed by the earlier statute; moreover, it prescribed additional rules concerning the substantive provisions of collective agreements. Despite current talk of less governmental interference in private affairs, the concept of the sovereignty of private property in the area of employment relations has scarcely more applicability today than the doctrine of the divine right of kings has in modern political affairs.

Of particular significance for this discussion is the fact that "national emergency disputes" are a post-World War II phenomenon. The term came into common usage during the strike wave of 1946, and although foreshadowed by the language of Section 10 of the Railway Labor Act (which established procedures for dealing with a dispute threatening "substantially to interrupt interstate commerce to a degree such as to deprive any section of the country of essential transportation service"), it was not given general application in any statute prior to the Taft-Hartley Act. The reason for the relatively recent development of the concept is clear enough: prior to World War II there were virtually no controversies of such

[8] *Hitchman Coal & Coke Co. v. Mitchell*, 245 U. S. 229, 248 (1917).

magnitude as to create a national emergency. Some disputes, such as the Pullman strike of 1894, the Coeur d'Alene disturbance of 1899, the anthracite strike of 1902, and the steel strike of 1919, attracted national attention; but this was because of the importance of the issues involved or the occurrence of violence, rather than the existence of any threat to the national health or safety. The mass-production industries, which are the potential breeding grounds of most national emergency disputes, were not organized to any substantial extent until the thirties, and it was not until the forties that union strength in those industries was sufficiently great to precipitate disputes affecting the national health or safety.

By the forties, however, as we have seen, the principle of governmental regulation of labor-management relations had been firmly established, and the notion that the sovereignty of private property was inviolable had by that time been abandoned by all but a few unreconstructed individualists in the business community. Hence, while the wisdom of governmental intervention in labor disputes has been frequently questioned and often bitterly denounced by employers, they have seldom challenged the legal power of the government to intervene. In the steel case of 1952 the seizure of steel properties by order of the President was contested and was ultimately declared unconstitutional by the Supreme Court;[9] but even in that case only the presidential power of seizure in the absence of specific statutory authority was challenged, not governmental intervention as such. Indeed, during World War II many properties had been seized under authority of the Selective Service Act, the First War Powers Act, the War Labor Disputes Act, and other statutes. Railroad properties had been seized as recently as 1950. In short, the most that can be said about the 1952 steel case in this respect is that it involved a challenge of the *manner* of intervention by one branch of government, the executive, rather than a denial of the *right* of government to restrain the use of private property.

So ingrained has the idea of governmental intervention in major disputes become in the thinking of management that there is considerable agitation in the ranks of industry for greater freedom on the part of state authorities to intervene under circumstances in

[9] *Youngstown Sheet & Tube Co. v. Sawyer,* 343 U. S. 579 (1952).

which the federal government declines to act. Of course, like the labor unions, employers have learned to evaluate in advance the probable consequences of governmental interference and to act accordingly: Taft-Hartley injunctions are usually welcome, while appointments of nonstatutory boards of inquiry are apt to be viewed with the greatest suspicion, particularly when those boards are given power to make recommendations.

THE SOVEREIGNTY OF UNIONS

The concept of sovereignty has been a dominant force in shaping the structure of American unions. In brief, the concept of union sovereignty assumes ownership by a given union of specific work. "Title" to this property (or jurisdiction) is symbolized by the union's charter, which it receives from the parent federation. Ownership of a job territory is no different than possession of any other property right; its essential feature is, as previously noted, the right to exclude others. George E. Barnett declared this concept to be "comparable in rigidity with the theory of sovereignty of the State,"[10] and, more recently, it has been observed that the "central role which the concept of jurisdiction [sovereignty] has played in the American labor movement" can be attributed in part to the same individualism and the same high valuation of property rights that have characterized the American community generally.[11]

Despite the importance of this concept to the labor movement, its effects upon the formal relationships between unions and employers have been negligible. The latter, as a group, have never conceded union claims of sovereignty over job territories as a matter of right, although they have frequently been compelled to recognize such sovereignty as a matter of fact. Employers who have found themselves involved in union jurisdictional warfare have turned increasingly to the courts and to federal and state legislatures for relief; many have refused to abide by decisions of union or union-management tribunals on jurisdictional matters.

[10] "The Causes of Jurisdictional Disputes in American Trade Unions," *Harvard Business Review*, 9 (July 1931), p. 401.

[11] John T. Dunlop, "Jurisdictional Disputes," *Proceedings of New York University Second Annual Conference on Labor* (Albany: Matthew Bender, 1949), p. 482.

Similarly, the concept of union sovereignty has had virtually no effect on the formal relationships between unions and the government. Indeed, the National Labor Relations Act established a basic policy—the right of workers to organize and to bargain collectively through representatives *of their own choosing*—that struck at the very heart of the theory that jurisdiction is a property right.[12]

Only in the area loosely described as "internal union affairs" has the sovereignty of unions been accorded some recognition. For many years the courts displayed considerable reluctance to take jurisdiction of quarrels between unions and their members, on the theory that unions, being unincorporated, nonprofit associations, should be treated no differently than church groups, clubs, and fraternal organizations.[13] More recently, however, and particularly since the end of World War II, courts have shown an increasing willingness to intervene in disputes between unions and their members, and some governmental control over that relationship has been established by state and federal legislation.[14]

While unions have frequently opposed the manner of governmental regulation of their dealings with management or with their own members, they have, like employers, seldom challenged the legal right of the government to intervene. Indeed, it was governmental regulation on a massive scale in the thirties that enabled unions to build up sufficient economic strength to precipitate major strikes in the succeeding years.

These facts help to explain the completely inconsistent attitudes of unions toward governmental intervention in major disputes. Frequently, unions have welcomed active governmental interference, as in the case of the famous argument over "examining the books" in the General Motors-United Auto Workers dispute of 1945-1946, or in the appointment of a nonstatutory board of inquiry in the steel dispute of 1949. On the other hand, governmental intervention has been resisted by unions in those cases, such as the

[12] See Benjamin Aaron, "Union Procedures for Settling Jurisdictional Disputes," *Labor Law Journal*, 5 (April 1954), pp. 258 ff.

[13] Zechariah Chafee, "The Internal Affairs of Associations Not for Profit," *Harvard Law Review*, 43 (May 1930), pp. 993 ff.

[14] Benjamin Aaron and Michael I. Komaroff, "Statutory Regulation of Internal Union Affairs," *Illinois Law Review*, 44 (September-October 1949), pp. 425 ff.

1952 strike against Douglas Aircraft by the United Auto Workers, in which it was felt that private economic pressure would produce a more favorable settlement than public adjudication. Likewise, governmental interference is generally opposed by unions when it takes the form of an injunction and enforced "cooling-off" period.

In short, a review of the position taken by unions involved in all the disputes which might conceivably be characterized as national emergencies indicates clearly that they accept the virtual inevitability of governmental intervention and that they frequently promote such intervention as an aid in securing their objectives.

SOVEREIGNTY AND PUBLIC OPINION

The concept of sovereignty, in so far as it holds any meaning for the American people, is generally thought of in terms of relationships between formal political entities. The term has no precise definition in common usage, but as applied to our dealings with other countries, it is used by the man in the street to signify freedom of action, the right to do whatever we deem advisable in our own interest, without regard to the wishes of other nations. This notion underlies the attacks by proponents of the Bricker Amendment on the President's constitutional treaty-making powers and also explains why some of our citizens oppose continued American participation in the United Nations.

In domestic affairs, also, the concept of sovereignty has a limited scope, being applied almost exclusively to the relationships between the federal government and the several states. In this context, however, the term "sovereignty," while still loosely used, implies not only freedom of action but legal authority; for both the states and the federal government are subject to the Constitution, which is the supreme law of the land. Conflicting claims of sovereignty between the federal government and the states are likely to arise in a number of situations. Sometimes a federal statute or a judicial decision by the United States Supreme Court outlaws a state law or policy, as in the recent instance of educational segregation, despite the claims of the affected states that this action unlawfully encroaches upon their sovereignty. In other situations one or more states may seek to enforce laws or policies in an area already covered, to a greater or lesser degree, by federal statute. The extent of a state's freedom to legislate in the field of labor-management relations, particularly in those areas not specifically dealt with in the Taft-Hartley Act, is one such problem that remains largely unsettled.[15]

In contrast to the relationships described above, those between private voluntary associations and the federal or state governments are seldom considered or discussed in terms of sovereignty. This fact can be explained largely in terms of our history. Modern European governments emerged slowly, after centuries of conflict between rulers and private groups, such as churches and the nobility. In these struggles for power, doctrines of sovereignty, such as that of the divine right of kings, were of prime importance, since they provided both the legal and the moral foundations for the claims of the rival groups. In the United States, however, the legal authority of government has never been challenged by groups other than those of religious zealots who profess allegiance to no temporal power. Even in our one great internal upheaval, the Civil War, the basic issue was not so much a struggle for power between government and private groups as a showdown between the federal government and the seceding states over the preservation of the union.

The United States thus holds a unique position among the great countries of the world in that, from the very outset of our national history, our Constitution has proved sufficiently flexible to permit a workable balance between the authority of government and the rights of individuals and private groups. The fact, for example, that the constitutionality of executive orders and legislative enactments may be challenged in the courts, and judicial authority or discretion may be curbed by statute, or even influenced by the President, through his appointive power, helps to explain why voluntary associations in this country have seldom felt the need to challenge the supremacy of government, taken as a whole, over their private domains.

It thus becomes clear why the pluralistic theory of the state explored so intensively by Laski, as well as the application of the concept of sovereignty to relationships between government and

[15] See Archibald Cox, "Federalism in the Law of Labor Relations," *Harvard Law Review*, 67 (June 1954), pp. 1297 ff.

private associations, has never had much acceptance in this country. For Laski, the "true meaning of sovereignty" was to be found "not in the coercive power possessed by its instrument, but in the fused good-will for which it stands." He conceived of the "will of the State . . . competing with other wills, and, Darwin-wise, surviving only by its ability to cope with its environment." When the state ignores competing wills, it "finds its sovereignty by consent transformed into impotence by disagreement."[16] This theory fails, however, to take into account the checks and balances within our own government. The executive will may be thwarted by Congress or the judiciary; the legislative will, by the judiciary or the executive; and the judicial will, by Congress or by the President. In the United States there is, in fact, no single "will of the State," as Laski used the term; the three branches of government function, to a degree, independently of each other, and as previously noted, their independent actions may represent a clash, rather than a unity, of wills. It is seldom indeed that private associations refuse to recognize the sovereignty of government thus defined.

Moreover, Americans seem to have accepted, without thinking much about it, the distinction, in Sir Frederick Pollock's phrase, between "legal sovereignty—the formal authority to make rules not formally controllable by any other defined power—[and] political supremacy—the power of directing the action of legal sovereignty by lawful means: of which the first is a matter of law, the second a matter of fact."[17] To illustrate, the bitter opposition of the building trades unions to the union-security provisions of the Taft-Hartley Act involved no challenge of the government's legal sovereignty, that is, the authority of Congress to enact labor legislation; but the large number of "bootleg" closed-shop agreements in the construction industry indicates some diminution in the government's political supremacy, that is, the power of the executive to enforce the Act "by lawful means" through the National Labor Relations Board and the courts.

Americans, as is well known, are not greatly given to philo-

[16] Harold J. Laski, *Studies in the Problem of Sovereignty* (New Haven: Yale University Press, 1917), pp. 12-14.

[17] Mark DeWolfe Howe, ed., *Holmes-Pollock Letters* (Cambridge: Harvard University Press, 1944), II, p. 26.

sophical speculation about the nature of their government; on the other hand, they take a lively interest in the practical effects of its operation. Though the legal sovereignty of government is accepted as a matter of course by private associations, the manner in which that sovereignty is exercised arouses the utmost concern. Reverting to Pollock's terminology, the principal problem in the relationship between government and private associations in this country, as is apparent from the previous discussion of employer and union attitudes toward governmental intervention, concerns the political supremacy, rather than the legal sovereignty, of government.

In any test of the government's political supremacy, public opinion usually plays a decisive role. Lack of public support spelled the doom of the "great experiment" of prohibition, just as public opposition or apathy has effectively nullified countless state and municipal laws and ordinances. National emergency disputes, however, appear to be an exception to the general rule. It seems clear that governmental intervention in those situations can almost never be frustrated by popular indignation or indifference. (One possible exception would be a law requiring the immediate drafting of all strikers, which might be frustrated by lack of cooperation by local draft boards.) While the entire economy may be affected indirectly by the controversy, only the disputants feel the immediate impact of governmental action, and usually they are the only ones who must alter their conduct as a consequence. As a practical matter, it is almost impossible to incite the general public to such a degree that the government will be forced to give ground. The principal reason for this fact is that any action taken by the government, however unpopular it may be in some quarters, is designed to insure the continuation or resumption of production or distribution, which is the prime concern of the public at large. Even the widespread indignation aroused by the President's seizure of the steel mills in 1952 had no effect on the outcome of that particular dispute; it took a decision of the United States Supreme Court to stay the administration's hand. There is no evidence that in the past public opinion has compelled the reversal of action by Congress or by the President in any national emergency dispute, and the prospect of such a thing is highly unlikely.

Another reason why resistance by private groups to governmental intervention in national emergency disputes is almost certain to be futile is that these controversies tend to occur more frequently in wartime or in periods of heightened international tension. During such crises there is generally a greater unity of purpose among the several branches of government, a unity that frequently is evidenced in legislation vesting the President with broad powers. Through the medium of executive orders, the full power of the government is thus brought to bear upon the disputants. In subsequent, quieter times the government's action in a specific case may conceivably be held to have been unconstitutional, although, more often, the issues become moot by the time court review is possible; but in any case, effective resistance against the government at the time the dispute occurs is virtually impossible.

CONCLUSION

If the foregoing observations are correct, and the relationship between the concept of sovereignty and the problem of national emergency disputes is as tenuous as has been represented, we must ask why the subject merits discussion at all.

The answer is to be found in the attitudes and public statements of those interested or directly involved in such disputes. Whenever the government is forced to act, it usually does so in a manner more acceptable to one side than to the other; and the party which stands to gain most from governmental intervention almost invariably seeks to create the impression that any resistance to, or even criticism of, the government's actions by the other party is tantamount to a challenge to the sovereignty of the state. Thus, in the 1949 steel dispute, the refusal of the steel companies to accept the recommendations of a presidential fact-finding board before entering into further negotiations with the union prompted Philip Murray to denounce Benjamin Fairless, as representative of the steel companies, for "adamantly flaunting the union, the government, the people," and for maintaining with "an air of arrogance" a "public be damned" attitude.[18] However unrestrained such language may seem, it is but a simulacrum of that which has been applied to John L. Lewis during the coal strikes of recent years.

It must also be remembered that strikes are news and that big

[18] Bureau of National Affairs, *Daily Labor Report*, September 15, 1949, p. AA-2.

strikes are big news. Public taste and the nature of news reporting in this country, which stresses speed rather than analysis or even accuracy, result in the reporting of big strikes in dramatic and oversimplified terms. Consequently, it is not surprising that Fairless' unwillingness to accede to a set of recommendations by a fact-finding board, or Lewis' expressions of dislike for an injunction against his union, are magnified and distorted by some segments of the press until they take on the appearance of subversive acts against the government.

In this writer's opinion, however, the public statements by parties to major disputes and the highly colored press accounts of those controversies are deserving of no more serious consideration than the extravagant accusations and dire predictions voiced by rival candidates and reported in newspapers during a political campaign. Certainly, they provide no basis for the conclusion that either party is challenging the sovereignty of government.

It remains true, nevertheless, that public attitudes on *how* and *when* the government ought to intervene in future national emergency disputes can and should be influential in shaping legislation dealing with that subject. In the last analysis, the relationship of government and private groups in national emergency disputes may be most meaningfully explored from the point of view taken by Dicey:

The problem to be solved, either as a matter of theory or as a matter of practical necessity, is at bottom always and everywhere the same. How can the right of combined action be curtailed without depriving individual liberty of half its value; how can it be left unrestricted without destroying either the liberty of individual citizens, or the power of Government?[19]

These are questions of policy, not of authority, and are basic to both an understanding and a solution of the problem. Discussion of the issues can only be beclouded, however, by considerations of sovereignty, whether of the government or of private groups; for, as we have seen, the problems of conflicting sovereignty, to the extent that they ever existed, were settled long ago.

[19] A. V. Dicey, *Law and Public Opinion in England* (2nd ed.; London: Macmillan, 1948), pp. 467-468.

PART II

WHAT IS THE TAFT-HARTLEY EXPERIENCE?

The Taft-Hartley Act is the "great experiment" in detailed public regulation of labor-management relations. Probably no part of the statute has excited so much interest and controversy as the emergency provisions. How adequate is our machinery for handling emergency disputes? Chapter V traces the legislative history of the emergency provisions and reminds us of the historical circumstances and the climate of public opinion from which they arose. On the great issues posed by emergency disputes, identifiable and contrary viewpoints emerge. Chapters VI and VII are opposite sides of the same coin, the first setting forth the views of "labor" and the second of "management." Chapter VIII is an evaluation which tests the emergency provisions against the experience and goals of a free but ordered society. The factual record of the cases that have arisen under Taft-Hartley appears in Appendix A. The text of the statute is in Appendix B.

· V ·

A LEGISLATIVE HISTORY

OF THE NATIONAL EMERGENCY PROVISIONS

BY FRANK M. KLEILER

National Labor Relations Board

The emergency section of the Taft-Hartley Act grew out of troubled industrial relations in the years immediately preceding 1947. A combination of events produced the most vigorous peacetime effort in the history of the federal government to deal with strikes affecting the public interest. The same events created a flood of state laws dealing with disputes involving public utilities.[1]

Two days after the surrender of Japan, President Truman issued a statement signalizing the liquidation of the War Labor Board and announcing his intention of calling an industry-labor conference for the purpose of working out methods of minimizing the interruption of production by labor disputes in the reconversion period. The War Labor Disputes Act[2] was still on the books, but its early expiration was anticipated. The WLB officially ceased func-

[1] Ten states passed laws in 1947 providing, among other things, for the use of injunctions against public utility strikes. Irving Bernstein, "Recent Legislative Developments Affecting Mediation and Arbitration," *Industrial and Labor Relations Review*, 1 (April 1948), pp. 406-420.

[2] 57 Stat. 163 (1943), 50 U.S.C. § 1501-1511. This Act put the powers and duties of the WLB upon a statutory basis, and it required the National Labor Relations Board to conduct a "last offer" vote thirty days after a dispute notice was filed. It also empowered the President to take immediate possession of any plant, mine, or facility in the event of an interruption of production as the result of a strike or other labor disturbance which would impede the war effort.

tioning on December 31, 1945. A somewhat limited wage stabilization responsibility was assigned to a new board which would not handle disputes.

The President's Industry-Labor Conference failed to agree upon any program for dealing with disputes not settled by collective bargaining and conciliation. Most congressmen had little or no faith that representatives of management and labor could work out their differences in such a way that the public interest would be protected.

The year 1946 broke records in strike statistics. There were more and larger work stoppages than ever before.[3]

At the start of 1946 the automobile industry was still engaged in tremendous strikes, notably affecting General Motors, which had begun late in 1945. Not having had new cars for several war years, people were paying fantastic black-market prices. As the automobile stoppage ended, a nationwide steel strike began in January 1946, following rejection by industry spokesmen of the recommendations of a presidential fact-finding board. A steel strike threatening a shortage of materials for other industries in the transition from wartime production was hard to take.

A bituminous coal mine strike began on April 2. On May 4 President Truman, through the office of War Mobilization and Reconversion, issued a report terming this strike a "national disaster." The government seized the coal mines on May 22, but production was not resumed until after an agreement was signed on May 29 by the Secretary of the Interior and the United Mine Workers of America to cover the indefinite period of government operation.

In the railroad industry the Railway Labor Act—which had long been proclaimed as a model procedure for dealing with disputes in basic industries—appeared to break down. The government seized the carriers in May after the engineers and trainmen rejected the recommendations of a presidential emergency board. A strike occurred despite seizure, and on May 25 the President appeared

[3] The Bureau of Labor Statistics reports 4,985 stoppages in 1946, involving 4,600,000 workers and 116,000,000 man-days idle. These figures are higher than comparable figures available for any prior year. When measured by per cent of total employed, however, 1946 did not break the record set in another great postwar strike year, 1919. Workers involved in stoppages in 1919 constituted 20.8 per cent of the labor force, compared with 14.5 per cent in 1946.

before a joint session of Congress seeking emergency legislation that would give him the power to prevent future strikes having widespread effects on the public and the nation's economy.

Great Lakes shipping was tied up by a stoppage in August. In September a strike of unlicensed maritime personnel paralyzed all shipping on the Atlantic, Pacific, and Gulf coasts for over two weeks. Eight days after that strike was settled, a nationwide stoppage of licensed personnel virtually tied up all deep-sea shipping in American ports.

On November 21 the bituminous coal industry, still held by the government, was struck for the second time in the year in the face of a temporary restraining order issued by Justice T. Alan Goldsborough of the United States District Court for the District of Columbia. On December 3 the court found the union and its president, John L. Lewis, guilty of contempt and ordered the union and Lewis to pay heavy fines.[4] The district court action promptly was appealed to higher courts.

There were many other large, costly strikes. If in those days there were any labor relations experts entertaining the view that "national emergency" disputes were few and far between, they were notably inarticulate; but opinions on what to do with labor disputes were a dime a dozen. A new and large crop of labor experts had emerged from the recently deceased tripartite national and regional war labor boards. Management and labor representatives exhibited more vigor than usual in pressing for partisan advantages. Labor spokesmen, however, were on the defensive. Management advocated legislation intended mainly to control and restrict unions in the "public interest."

While the strikes were proceeding with unabated fury, Congress was trying to legislate on labor problems. The House had already passed the Case bill (H.R. 4908)[5] when the President addressed the joint session of Congress on May 25 in connection with the railroad strike. Following the President's address the Senate passed the Case bill, declining to give the President the kind of legislation

[4] *United States v. United Mine Workers of America*, Civil No. 37764 (DC, D. of C., Nov. 18, 1946), 11 CCH Labor Cases ¶ 63,438.

[5] *Congressional Record*, 79th Cong., 2d sess., 92:1 (February 7, 1946), pp. 1067-1070.

which he requested. The vote in the Senate was 49 to 29; that in the House was 230 to 116. The bill went to the White House on May 29.

When introduced by Representative Mary Norton, H.R. 4908 simply provided for the appointment of boards to make recommendations in labor disputes seriously affecting the public interest and for strike delay during fact finding and for five days thereafter. The bill was amended on the floor of the House by substituting the language of H.R. 5262, introduced by Representative Case of South Dakota. Case's bill covered a wide range of matters in addition to emergency disputes. Thereafter H.R. 4908 acquired many other amendments. The emergency section of the bill as it passed the Senate empowered the President to appoint a commission to make recommendations for settlement and provided for the so-called prestrike cooling-off period which had become familiar under the Railway Labor Act. It went much further than the Railway Labor Act, however. That statute provided no penalties for strikes called without observance of the procedures laid down, but the Case bill would have penalized strikers by depriving them of their rights under the National Labor Relations Act.

President Truman vetoed the Case bill on June 11, characterizing it as a "collection of separate unrelated measures which are likely to increase rather than decrease industrial strife." In his veto message he reiterated his request for temporary legislation to stop strikes against the government during the reconversion period.[6] Efforts to override the veto failed, but the event deepened the conflict between President Truman and the Congress. In part the story of the Taft-Hartley Act is a story of this deepening conflict.

The temporary legislation which President Truman had requested on May 25, in so far as emergency disputes were concerned, was more drastic than the Case bill which he vetoed. Designed primarily to outlaw strikes in government-seized properties, the President's bill, among other things, provided that employees striking a plant seized by the government would be deprived of seniority rights, would lose their rights under the Wagner Act or the Railway Labor Act, and would be subject to induction into the armed forces of the United States. The House passed the temporary legislation which

[6] *Congressional Record*, 79th Cong., 2d sess., 92:5 (June 12, 1946), p. 6074.

the President requested, but the bill died in the Senate. Labor leaders denounced it as a move designed to bring about a return to "slave labor," a term which they thus warmed up for their later characterization of the Taft-Hartley Act. In the Senate the bill was branded as "dictatorial" and "unconstitutional" by opponents of the bill in the Democratic party as well as in the Republican party.

With the fires of criticism and complaint stoked by the 1946 strike wave, the President's veto of the Case bill, and the President's request for emergency legislation, labor was an important issue in the elections that fall. More particularly, the administration's handling of labor problems was an issue, and the Republicans assumed after November that their victory gave them a mandate from the people to revise the national labor policy. The term "mandate" may be too strong in interpreting the 1946 election returns, but nobody can dispute a conclusion that the elections strengthened what was already a majority sentiment in Congress that government policies had gone too far in favoring unions.[7]

A wide assortment of ideas was available, and the trends were clear. Organized labor was going to be regulated. Union spokesmen offered no proposals of their own. Their role was one of resisting legislation.

As 1946 ended, President Truman declared the termination of the period of hostilities of World War II. His declaration automatically ended the government's plant-seizure powers on December 31 and started tolling the six-month time limit for other sections of the War Labor Disputes Act, notably those providing for thirty days' strike notice.

Federal labor policy was high on the agenda of the Eightieth Congress when it assembled in January 1947. The Democrats were in the White House, but the Republicans had majorities in both branches of Congress. Senator Robert A. Taft of Ohio was chairman of the Senate Committee on Labor and Public Welfare. Repre-

[7] Hartley, in his book on the Taft-Hartley Act, reported significantly: "One hundred and twenty-eight House members voted against the Case bill and sought reelection. Of this number, 45 lost at the polls. Two hundred and forty-five House members voted for the Case bill and sought reelection. Of this number, 223 were reelected; only 22 were defeated." Fred A. Hartley, Jr., *Our New National Labor Policy* (New York: Funk & Wagnalls Company in association with *Modern Industry Magazine,* 1948), p. 2.

sentative Fred A. Hartley, Jr., of New Jersey was chairman of the House Committee on Education and Labor.[8] They were confident that they could put through Congress a comprehensive labor relations statute, but they had to reckon with the probability of a presidential veto. That much seemed clear from the experience with the Case bill, but they were so confident of the temper of the Congress that the prospect of a veto did not dismay them.

The new committee chairmen set about their work vigorously, and early began to lay out an ambitious legislative program. Provision for handling national emergency strikes was only one of many items. The closed shop, jurisdictional disputes, featherbedding, secondary boycotts, reorganization of the National Labor Relations Board, pension plans and welfare funds, communism in the labor movement, and political contributions by labor organizations were up for consideration along with many other problems.

In his January message to Congress President Truman urged early enactment of legislation to prevent certain "unjustifiable" union practices such as jurisdictional strikes, certain kinds of secondary boycotts, and a few other measures; but he proposed nothing in connection with emergency disputes except the creation of a study commission consisting of twelve congressmen and senators and eight representatives of labor, management, and the public to be appointed by the President. He suggested that the first business of the commission should be to investigate and make recommendations on how to handle the "special and unique problem" of nationwide strikes in vital industries without endangering our general democratic freedoms.

Only by the use of extraordinary war powers, the President said, have we been able to avert the paralyzing effects of such strikes, and the war powers will soon be gone. In their place there must be created "an adequate system and effective machinery in these vital fields." Calling for careful study and a bold approach consistent

---

[8] This was a new committee. Under the congressional reorganization law which went into effect at that time, the Committee on Labor and the Committee on Education were merged. The Labor Committee, incidentally, was hit hard by the 1946 elections. Six Democrats who served on that committee during the Seventy-ninth Congress were defeated at the polls. With a few exceptions most of the old Labor Committee members who survived to serve on the new committee in the Eightieth Congress had supported the Case bill.

with the preservation of rights, he concluded that "the need is pressing."

Congress agreed with the President that the need was pressing, but the legislators had no interest in creating any study commissions. Having authored several abortive bills to amend the Wagner Act and to deal with strikes during his years of service in the Senate, Senator Taft had fairly definite ideas of what he wanted for legislation. He regarded proposals for a study commission as delaying action. He promptly obtained the services of two experienced lawyers in the labor relations field, Gerard D. Reilly and Thomas E. Shroyer, to advise him on the technicalities, and he set them to work drafting his bill. Reilly had been solicitor for the Department of Labor from 1937 to 1941 and a member of the National Labor Relations Board from 1941 to 1946. After leaving the NLRB, he practiced law in Washington for only a few months before becoming special counsel to the Senate Committee on Labor and Public Welfare in 1947. Once the Taft-Hartley Act was passed, he resumed his law practice. Shroyer was a regional attorney for the NLRB when he went to Washington in 1947 as counsel to the Senate Labor Committee. He served the Committee until 1952 and then entered law practice in Washington, representing employers in labor matters.

On the House side the chief draftsman for Chairman Hartley was Gerald D. Morgan, a Washington attorney who had worked from 1935 to 1945 in the office of the legislative counsel of the House of Representatives. He was not a labor specialist. In testifying before a congressional committee later, he indicated that in drafting the Hartley bill he frequently consulted Reilly and Theodore Iserman, who represented Chrysler Corporation and several other large companies in labor matters.[9]

The Senate committee opened hearings on January 23, the House committee on February 5. The leading bill in the Senate at first was the Ball-Taft-Smith bill (S. 55), which was characterized as the "new Case bill" because of its similarity to the one vetoed by

[9] *National Labor Relations Act of 1949*, Hearings on H.R. 2032 before a special subcommittee of the House Committee on Education and Labor, 81st Cong., 1st sess. (March 7-21, 1949), p. 1162.

the President and because it was equally comprehensive. There was a wide assortment of bills in the House.

The hearings were significant chiefly for the disagreements which they revealed between administration and congressional leaders, between labor and industry spokesmen, and among the neutral experts on labor relations. This was true with respect to proposals for handling national emergency disputes as well as with respect to the other legislation under consideration. So many witnesses had so much to say about so many different subjects, however, that the hearings themselves supply little or nothing to the legislative history of the emergency provisions of the Taft-Hartley Act. The Senate group concluded its hearings on March 8 and the House on March 15. Each committee promptly went into executive session.

Meanwhile, the United Mine Workers' appeal from Judge Goldsborough's decision was argued in the Supreme Court, and early in March that high tribunal issued an opinion of major significance in connection with the shaping of legislation on emergency disputes.[10] By a five to four vote the Supreme Court ruled that the Norris-LaGuardia Act does not apply where the government has seized actual possession of the mines or other facilities and is operating them and the relationship between the government and the workers is that of employer and employee. The opinion included dicta to the effect that, absent seizure, the government would have no status to appear in the courts and seek to enjoin strikes. "We agree," said the majority opinion, "that . . . Congress, in passing the Norris-LaGuardia Act, did not intend to permit the United States to continue to intervene by injunction in purely private labor disputes."

To the law students this court opinion meant many things, but to the legislators it meant simply this: Either they would have to pass legislation specifically authorizing seizure so that the government could seize strike-bound or strike-threatened property and then get the strike enjoined, or they would have to pass legislation specifically amending the Norris-LaGuardia Act to provide for injunctions under some conditions. It was an injunction-minded Congress, and the only real problem was how best to authorize injunc-

[10] *United States v. United Mine Workers of America*, 330 U. S. 258 (1947).

tions. Although bills were offered which would authorize seizure, the congressional leadership preferred the more direct route.

On April 3 the House Committee reported out H.R. 2861, which, among other things, provided district courts with jurisdiction to issue injunctions upon application of the government in connection with labor disputes when the cessation or substantial curtailment of commerce existed and the public health, safety, or interest was imperiled or threatened thereby.[11] No action was taken on this bill, because exactly one week later Representative Hartley introduced his comprehensive bill (H.R. 3020) containing approximately the same provisions but also covering virtually the entire range of matters which subsequently became the scope of the Taft-Hartley Act. It was reported favorably the next day.[12]

For emergency disputes the Hartley bill provided that "whenever the President finds that a labor dispute has resulted in, or imminently threatens to result in, the cessation or substantial curtailment of interstate or foreign commerce in transportation, public utility, or communication services essential to the public health, safety, or interest,"[13] the President shall direct the Attorney General to petition a district court for an injunction. After other provisions for guidance of the court, for specific amendment of the Norris-LaGuardia Act, for review by higher courts of any district court injunction, and for thirty days of settlement efforts by conciliation, the bill set forth distinctive procedures for secret ballots on settlement offers and, finally, for establishment of fact-finding boards under auspices of the Court of Appeals for the District of Columbia.

The provisions for the secret ballots differed from the provisions ultimately written into the Taft-Hartley Act. The Hartley bill provided for votes at two different stages. The first one would come at the end of the thirty-day period following the injunction. The ballot was to ascertain (1) whether the employees desired to accept their employer's offer of settlement then current, and (2) if, so, what person or persons they wanted to designate as their representative to embody their acceptance in a contract with their employer.

[11] House Report No. 235, 80th Cong., 1st sess. (1947).
[12] House Report No. 245, 80th Cong., 1st sess. (1947).
[13] Note that by this language the emergency provisions covered more than national emergencies and could be applied to most large public utilities.

The bill provided that if the dispute were not settled by means of such a secret ballot, the Director of Conciliation was obligated to notify the chief justice of the United States Court of Appeals for the District of Columbia, who then would create a special advisory board of himself as chairman and two other members, one designated by the union and the other designated by the employer or employers. Such an advisory board would investigate the dispute and within thirty days "render and make public its opinion as to the proper settlement of the dispute." The board was to "reach its conclusions and render its opinion solely on the basis of the facts of the case, and shall not be bound by any demands or offers of settlement of either party, or by the existing terms of employment, or by any opinion of any other board created under this section for any other dispute."

Then there was provision for another secret ballot to be conducted by the government on whether the employees wanted to accept and be bound by the terms of the special board's opinion and, if so, whom they wanted as their representative to make a contract.

On April 15 the House adopted a rule to allow only six hours' debate on the Hartley bill. Debate commenced the next day and was concluded on April 17. A nationwide telephone strike was then in its second week, and some of labor's critics were complaining that the Hartley bill was too moderate because it failed to *prohibit* absolutely strikes of that character. On the other side, Representative Javits of New York unsuccessfully offered an amendment which would have substituted for the injunction provisions a procedure for national seizure.[14] The bill, without any amendments to the emergency dispute provisions, passed the House by a vote of 308 to 107.

On the same day that the House approved the Hartley bill, Senator Taft introduced his bill (S. 1126), which was immediately reported favorably by the labor committee of which he was chairman. So far as can be discerned from the bills, there was no collaboration between Senator Taft and Representative Hartley or between the House and Senate labor committees. There were important differences throughout the bills, though they were generally

[14] *Congressional Record*, 80th Cong., 1st sess., 93:3 (April 17, 1947), p. 3637.

parallel in scope. The differences were substantial in the emergency provisions.

The Taft bill provided that whenever in the opinion of the Attorney General a threatened or actual strike or lockout affecting substantially an entire industry imperiled the national health or safety, he could appoint a board of inquiry to investigate the issues involved in the dispute and to make a written report to him. The report could not contain any recommendations. Upon receipt of the report the Attorney General could petition a federal district court for an injunction, with the Norris-LaGuardia Act specifically made inapplicable. While the strike was enjoined, the parties would be required to make an effort to settle their differences with the assistance of the Federal Mediation and Conciliation Service. At the end of a sixty-day period (unless the dispute had been settled by that time), the board of inquiry would report to the Attorney General the current position of the parties to the dispute and the efforts which had been made for settlement. The bill provided for the Attorney General to make the report public and for the National Labor Relations Board, fifteen days later, to conduct a vote among employees to determine whether they wished to accept the employer's last offer. Upon receipt of the certification of results five days later, the Attorney General would have to move the court to dissolve the injunction. The court would be required to grant such a motion, and thereupon the Attorney General would submit to the President a full and comprehensive report of the proceedings. The President would transmit the report to the Congress for consideration and appropriate action.

In explaining the rationale underlying these provisions, the majority report of the Senate Committee on Labor and Public Welfare emphasized the John L. Lewis case. It said:

While the committee is of the opinion that in most labor disputes the role of the Federal Government should be limited to mediation, we recognize that the repercussions from stoppages in certain industries are occasionally so grave that the national health and safety is imperiled. An example is the recent coal strike in which defiance of the President by the United Mine Workers Union compelled the Attorney General to resort to injunctive relief in the courts. The committee believes that only in national emergencies of this character should the Federal Government be armed with such power. But it also feels that this power should be available if the need arises. It should be remembered that the Supreme Court decision in *U.S. v. United Mine Workers* (decided March 6, 1947), did not hold in broad terms that the Government was exempted from the Norris-LaGuardia Act. The majority of the court relied in part upon the fact that the Government had previously seized the mines under the War Labor Disputes Act and that the calling of the strike by the officers of the United Mine Workers was undoubtedly a breach of the criminal provisions contained in that statute. This act, however, is only temporary legislation and expires June 30, 1947.

We concluded, therefore, that the permanent code of laws of the United States should make it clear that the Attorney General should have the power to intervene and secure judicial relief when a threatened strike or lock-out is conducted on a scale imperiling the national health or safety.[15]

Although they were no more effective, the senators opposing the Taft emergency provisions were more articulate than Hartley's opponents in the House. The minority report of the Senate Labor Committee set forth a comprehensive criticism of the emergency provisions, and with variations the same points were used repeatedly in the Senate debate which opened on April 23 and continued through May 13. Foremost in the minority report was the following complaint that the Taft bill diffused responsibility:

Under these sections of the act the Attorney General, boards of inquiry, Federal district courts, Federal Mediation Service, the President, and the Congress would all be participating in the handling of a single labor dispute. We believe that the handling of labor disputes should be concentrated in one agency. Diffusion of responsibility would confuse the handling of these important matters. The public would be unable to fix responsibility when one of these critical labor disputes is mishandled.[16]

The opponents of the Taft bill suggested little in the way of specific legislation for dealing with emergency disputes. They fell back upon President Truman's plea for a joint study commission. Only by such a study, said the minority report, could a solution to this problem be found. To the argument that the majority's remedy for dealing with the problem was better than none, the minority

[15] Senate Report No. 105 on S. 1126, 80th Cong., 1st sess. (1947), pp. 14-15.
[16] Senate Report No. 105 on S. 1126, pt. 2, "Minority Views," 80th Cong., 1st sess. (1947), pp. 15-16.

replied that "this remedy may be worse than the disease." Until a solution was found, said the minority, "let us not be stampeded into action that can lead only to more strikes and industrial chaos."

The committee minority, nevertheless, made about eight specific criticisms of the emergency provisions of the Taft bill, which, in simplified form, are summarized below:

1. The fact-finding functions provided in the Taft bill should be vested in the Secretary of Labor.

2. The injunction provisions would make the coercive effect of government action entirely one-sided.

3. The standards for identifying cases that might affect the national health or safety were inadequate.

4. The bill contained no statutory standards to determine at what stage of the negotiations a strike might be threatened.

5. Because no injunction petition could be filed until after receipt of a board of inquiry report, there would be a tendency to appoint such boards at early stages in the negotiations and thereby frustrate free collective bargaining.

6. The broad scope of the phrases "threatened or actual strike or lock-out" and "imperil the national health or safety" would lead to heated debate as to their meaning and would tend to aggravate rather than settle labor disputes in key industries.

7. Reports of boards of inquiry without recommendations might be useless. Whoever appointed a board of inquiry should have discretion as to whether recommendations should be made or not.

8. Experience under the War Labor Disputes Act demonstrated that strike votes such as those provided in the Taft bill were futile.

In one way or another most of these criticisms were answered or at least considered in the course of Senate debate. With the emergency provisions constituting only one segment of a comprehensive bill for the regulation of labor-management relations, however, it is apparent from the legislative history that each of the features of the bill and the criticisms of it did not get the sort of searching analysis that might have been given them if a bill dealing with emergency disputes had been considered separately. Nevertheless, it cannot be said that the emergency provisions were submerged in the welter of debate on other features of the Taft bill. At times their importance was identified with remarkable clarity.

One proposal which the Senate rejected had particular significance in relation to emergency disputes, but the proposal was not considered exactly in the context of the emergency provisions. It was the proposal to ban industry-wide bargaining. As the Hartley bill was passed by the House it contained a provision (Section 12) making "monopolistic strikes" unlawful. In effect, this provision would forbid a strike by a union against more than one employer if the strike action could be identified as resulting from any conspiracy, collusion, or concerted plan of action between employees of competing employers unless the employees had a common bargaining agent. Another provision of the bill, Section 9(f)(1), would permit employees of competing employers to have a common bargaining agent only if (1) the bargaining agent represented less than one hundred employees of each employer and (2) the plants of the competing employers were less than fifty miles apart.

What these provisions were intended to do, said the House committee in its majority report, "is to put a stop to strikes that paralyze the economy of our country and imperil the health and safety of our people." Referring to laws forbidding competing employers to conspire together to close their plants, fix their prices, and otherwise to restrain trade, the committee majority said, "There is no justification for permitting employees of competing employers to enter into conspiracies that have the same effect."

The Taft bill contained a provision which would prevent the NLRB from treating industry-wide associations of employers as a single employer, but it rejected the House idea of outlawing industry-wide or area-wide bargaining. Senator Ball and others offered an amendment to the Taft bill which was generally consistent with the House approach although differing in method. The Ball amendment would have limited the geographic scope of collective bargaining units and would have prevented any labor organization from exercising authority over a subordinate local in the determination of wages, hours, and working conditions. The Ball amendment was bitterly debated on the Senate floor. On May 7 it was defeated by one vote, 44 to 43.

The Taft bill was amended in several important respects during the course of consideration by the Senate, but the amendments did not change the emergency dispute provisions. When debate ended on May 13, the Senate substituted the language of the Taft bill for that of the Hartley bill. As thus amended, H. R. 3020 passed the Senate by a vote of 68 to 24, the majority line-up basically a Republican and Southern Democrat coalition.

The Senate and House conferees worked from May 15 to 29 in reconciling and compromising the differences between the two Houses of Congress. Mr. Hartley's later comments on the conference are interesting:

We had to retain as much of the House measure as we could without jeopardizing the final two-thirds majority in the Senate.

As the situation developed the conference became a battle of nerves and, more than that, a battle of public relations.

We had to create the general impression that most of the original Hartley bill had been discarded by the conferees in favor of the so-called milder provisions of Taft's bill. . . .

Too many weeks and months of effort by too many people had gone into its creation for the personal feelings of any of us to be considered.

The recorded vote in the Senate against industry-wide bargaining prohibitions certainly dictated my course in this respect. Similarly, the Senate had shown clearly that it wanted no part in restoring the right of private injunction in labor disputes. It was obvious to me that two-thirds of the Senate had no intention of approving a measure containing those particular provisions, for this would have required many Senators to reverse announced positions. Such reversals are not easy.

Consequently, even before the conference opened I announced that the House would not insist on the provisions banning industry-wide bargaining, nor the right of private injunctions against labor abuse.[17]

The conference committee report rejected the Hartley bill's provisions with respect to emergency disputes in favor of the Taft bill. The only important modification of the emergency provisions of the Taft bill adopted in conference was the substitution of the President for the Attorney General as the official responsible for invoking the emergency provisions and creating a board of inquiry in any particular dispute.

The House agreed to the conference report on June 4 and the

[17] Hartley, *op. cit.*, pp. 75-77.

Senate on June 6. Two weeks later President Truman vetoed the legislation, which by then had come to be called the Taft-Hartley Act. Among his criticisms of various sections, the President said the bill would establish "an ineffective and discriminatory procedure for dealing with major strikes affecting the public health or safety." The President specifically objected to the use of injunctions without providing sanctions against employers, to the prohibition against recommendations from the boards of inquiry, to the possibility that a strike or lockout might occur before a board of inquiry could make a report, to the last-offer ballots, and to the requirement that after the elaborate procedure was exhausted it was mandatory for the President to transfer the whole problem to the Congress even though that body might not be in session at the time. Thus, the President pointed out, major disputes over contract terms might ultimately be thrown into the political arena for disposition. "One could scarcely devise a less effective method for discouraging critical strikes," he added.[18]

The House by a score of 331 to 83 voted to override the veto the same day it was received. After two days of debate the Senate on June 23 overrode the veto by a vote of 68 to 25.

As a legislative history, the foregoing narrative is of course oversimplified. To the extent that legislation can sometimes be better understood by looking to see what was rejected, it may be well to recall what Congress discarded in the process of adopting the Taft-Hartley Act. It specifically voted down the scheme for outlawing industry-wide bargaining. Without voting on other proposals, Congress also rejected various plans for fact-finding boards with power to recommend settlements, for compulsory arbitration, and for seizure. Except for the Hartley bill's provisions, however, none of these other proposals was reported out of committee during the first session of the Eightieth Congress. Accordingly, they are relatively unimportant in any general account of the Taft-Hartley Act.

The important fact about the legislative history is that the emergency provisions survived the Senate Committee and the Senate-House conference in almost the exact form that Senator Taft wanted. In his own committee and in the conference he made

[18] *Congressional Record,* 80th Cong., 1st sess., 93:6 (June 20, 1947), pp. 7485-7488.

numerous compromises in other parts of the bill to gain support, but the emergency section of the law is almost pure Taft. To the extent that it provided for injunctions against strikes, this part of the bill was popular with an overwhelming majority in Congress; but the Taft concept of how to handle emergency disputes was far more sophisticated than that of the average injunction-minded legislator.

Senator Taft recognized that the injunctive process does not deal with the main causes of labor trouble. He regarded injunctions only as a device for enforced delay to give mediation, fact-finding, and energized public opinion an opportunity to produce a settlement. He wanted no recommendations from the fact-finding board simply because he believed that government boards with power to recommend settlements come dangerously close to compulsory arbitration. He opposed compulsory arbitration as vigorously as he opposed seizure. If compulsory arbitration were available as a routine remedy, Taft contended, there would always be pressure to resort to it by whichever party thought it would receive better treatment through such a process than it would receive in collective bargaining. If a national emergency dispute could not be settled during the delay process, Taft believed, then no authority lower than the Congress should deal with it. He felt strongly that if the safety and health of the people were finally threatened, an emergency law should be designed to deal with the particular emergency. In the debate on his bill he told the Senate:

I have had in mind drafting such a bill, giving power to seize the plants, and other necessary facilities, to seize the unions, their money, and their treasury, and requisition trucks and other equipment; in fact, to do everything that the British did in their general strike of 1926. But while such a bill might be prepared, I should be unwilling to place such a law on the books until we actually face such an emergency, and Congress applies the remedy for the particular emergency only.[19]

Compared with other provisions of the Taft-Hartley Act, the emergency section is relatively simple. Because it was largely the Taft bill all the way through, the legislative history of the emergency section likewise is simple. The historical events that created

[19] *Congressional Record*, 80th Cong., 1st sess., 93:3 (April 23, 1947), p. 3836.

the environment in which the law was passed, however, were not simple, and those events explain the whys and wherefores of the emergency provisions more vividly than the whys and wherefores are explained by the bills, reports, and debates which constitute the technical legislative history.

The record-breaking wave of large strikes created the need. The imminent expiration of wartime legislation made the need more imperative. The antilabor sentiment found in the 1946 election returns fixed the attitude. The distrust in Congress of the President eliminated any possibility of increasing the chief executive's authority to handle labor disputes.

Uniquely designed to emphasize the paramountcy of Congress over the President in emergencies while simultaneously providing a method for prompt government action to delay strikes, the virtues of the Taft bill were readily apparent. Not even the supporters of the Hartley bill were much dismayed when the House conferees went along with the Senate on the emergency provisions. As a product of its times, Senator Taft's proposal for handling the troublesome strike problem looked good enough to Congress, and Congress did not want to take the time to shop for anything better.

VI

LABOR LOOKS AT

THE NATIONAL EMERGENCY PROVISIONS

BY ARTHUR J. GOLDBERG AND JACK BARBASH

Congress of Industrial Organizations

Something more, probably, needs to be said about the perspectives that we bring to this problem of emergency disputes than is suggested in the "Labor Looks at" part of the title assigned to this chapter. Indeed, the sketching of this perspective is one of the most important contributions we can make, at this point. The congressional hearings and the periodicals are bulging with pro and con viewpoints on the Taft-Hartley law and on its national emergency disputes provisions in particular. It is doubtful that another pro or con analysis alone will be significant, the point of diminishing returns possibly having been reached a long time ago.

Any law reflects a system of values and the application of these values to the techniques required to deal with the problem at hand. Invariably the techniques are more apparent to the naked eye than are the values.

Particularly is this true of labor relations law. For one thing, in this branch of law and legislation, we have not had the advantage of a slowly evolving system. The full momentum of the problem has come upon us so precipitately that our legal institutions have adapted on a makeshift basis, and we have been forced to apply categories operative in other areas to this strange new field of labor-management relations.

The Taft-Hartley law and its national emergency provisions well demonstrate this. Like the whole law these provisions reflect two sorts of responses to labor-management relations. On the one hand we see a clear-cut power play at work, the object being to cut down the influence of unions in the United States, rather than really to deal with emergency disputes. But there is also reflected, we are sure, a genuine concern for the public interest on the part of some, but a concern lacking in insight into unions or collective bargaining as going enterprises.

It is conceivable, with boundless faith in the educability of human beings, that if we are able to agree on the underlying values, we can make some headway in dealing with this perplexing problem of national emergency disputes.

Let us, then, try to set down what in our minds, at least, is the common ground that we occupy in labor-management relations with special reference to emergency disputes. In brief compass, we think these values can be stated as follows:

1. Collective bargaining, backed up by the union's right to strike and by the employer's right to say "no" to union demands, is an indispensable ingredient of a free society.

2. With respect to the regulation of strikes in certain situations, the essence of the national emergency problem—the threat to the national health, safety, welfare—whatever we call it—must be imminent and critical to justify regulation.

3. Finally, when the government does move in, it should operate as a community guardian and not as an ally of either side.

When these common values are blended into the experience which we have accumulated about labor-management relations in the United States, we come out with a set of social skills—techniques. At this point a caveat is in order. Techniques applied to complicated human problems are rarely equal to the total solution of these problems. When we talk about techniques we mean ways of dealing with a problem, with the fair chance only that some of the techniques will work in the way we expect they will. There is no neat solution and in certain situations the techniques simply won't work. And then at the critical point we will just have to improvise.

This insight is relevant to the handling of emergency labor disputes. We have been so obsessed with the search for a total solution that we have resorted to gadgetry. If, as experience tells us so emphatically, we perceive that there are no final answers, we will then take steps which, to be sure, may be short of theoretical perfection but are also likely to avoid the frustrations which come either from an impotence to do anything or from an impotence to do everything.

If there were no values to plague us, the emergency dispute problem would be simple. We could say, "Let's outlaw strikes" or "Let's outlaw them in certain industries"—period. This is an elementary enough technique and it doesn't require much social intelligence to apply it.

But it isn't enough to say of a set of techniques, "They stopped the strike—what more do you want?" The question of at what cost the strikes were stopped is of compelling relevance—at what cost to our ways of doing business, to our way of life, and at what cost to our liberties.

FAIRNESS

A major consideration in establishing ways of dealing with emergency disputes is fairness. As we have said, government cannot function as an ally of either side in a dispute. The Taft-Hartley provisions on national emergencies violate the standard of fairness at several points. The most flagrant is the use of the injunction to prohibit a strike for an eighty-day period. This injunction by its very nature automatically resolves every issue in the dispute against the union by restraining the strike. The underlying merits become irrelevant because whatever they are the union may not call a strike.

At the same time the injunction has relieved the employer of union pressure for at least eighty days, as well as providing him with a cost reduction inducement to hold back agreement for the period during which the injunction runs.

The ballot which polls the employees on whether they will accept the last offer of the employer is of course a conspicuous attempt to divide the union from its constituents, quite aside from the question of whether it works, which it doesn't. In the interests of equity if not efficacy, it would be just as reasonable to poll the stockholders or the public.

In effect, then, the injunction and the last-offer ballot seek to put the power of government inevitably behind the employer in every case.

RELEVANCE

The procedures should have some relevance to the posture of the dispute. There ought to be no rigid schedule of procedures such as Taft-Hartley dictates which must be applied no matter what. As is well known, the Taft-Hartley law prescribes a relentless march of government intercessions—board of inquiry, eighty-day strike injunction, mediation, last-offer ballot, dissolution of injunction, presidential report to Congress.

However, many disputes do not lend themselves to this rigorous sequence and in some instances this leads to absurd results. In the meat-packing dispute of 1948, the board took three weeks to report.[1] Meanwhile the strike was on. The board was prohibited by law from making recommendations so that there was no effective way of settling, or no basis for mediating, the dispute. In two of the coal disputes the issue between the parties was the pension fund, and it was clear from the outset that it was *this* issue that had to be disposed of. The first coal dispute (March 1948) was settled when a third party to the administration of the pension fund was agreed to by the union and the employers. In the second coal dispute (June 1948) a settlement was reached when Federal Judge Goldsborough handed down a decision on the pension fund dispute. Both of these developments were quite unrelated to the Taft-Hartley machinery.

Some of the absurd consequences are illuminated by the last-

[1] For the basic facts on the cases involving utilization of emergency disputes procedures under the Taft-Hartley law, we have relied on U.S. Bureau of Labor Statistics, *Work Stoppages, "National Emergency" Disputes Under the Labor-Management Relations (Taft-Hartley) Act*, 1947-June 30, 1952, Series 5, No. 2 (undated). With respect to subsequent disputes in 1953 and 1954 we have used the Bureau of National Affairs, *Daily Labor Report*; longshore, 1953, No. 237 (December 7, 1953), p. A-3; atomic energy, 1954, No. 156 (August 12, 1954), p. A-4. The first-named author of this chapter was involved in the American Locomotive case as general counsel to the United Steelworkers of America.

offer ballot requirement. In the Pacific Coast Maritime dispute (1948) last-offer ballots were mailed to sailors all over the world on August 30 and 31, but two days later the NMU had reached an agreement with the employers. It is very likely that the overwhelming majority of the sailors aboard the ships received their ballots days and weeks after the settlement had already been reached. In the American Locomotive case (1953) the employer could not clearly formulate his "last offer." In the 1953-1954 longshore case it was not apparent who the bargaining agency was; hence there was no union authorized to receive a last offer if the employer had made one (which he didn't).

The attraction that procedures for their own sake have for some people is difficult to diagnose. Acting in accord with what he presumed to be the intent of the administration, Senator Smith (N.J.) in 1954 introduced amendments to the Taft-Hartley emergency disputes provisions[2] which, if slotted into the procedures already required, would have resulted in the following mandatory sequence of steps:

1. The union serves a sixty-day notice on the company, as required by Section 8(d)(1). This is in addition to any notice the union has already served under the terms of the collective bargaining agreement.

2. The union serves a thirty-day notice on the Federal Mediation and Conciliation Service as required by Section 8(d)(3).

3. The union serves a thirty-day notice on the state mediation agency, as required by Section 8(d)(3).

4. Under Section 203 of Taft-Hartley, the Federal Mediation and Conciliation Service will use its best efforts to mediate the dispute.

5. The President finds, under Section 206, that the strike will imperil the national health or safety and appoints a board of inquiry.

6. The board of inquiry makes a report, which cannot include recommendations.

7. The Attorney General, under Section 208, petitions a federal district court to enjoin the strike for eighty days, and the district court issues the injunction.

8. At the end of sixty days (changed to forty days by the Smith

[2] S. 2650, 83d Cong., 2d sess. (1954).

bill) the President reconvenes the board of inquiry, which reports the current position of the parties and the company's last offer.

9. After sixty days (changed to forty days by the Smith bill) the NLRB conducts a secret ballot on whether the employees wish to accept the final offer of settlement made by their employer. The Board certifies the results of this ballot to the Attorney General. No consequences flow from this ballot whichever way it goes.

10. Under Section 209(c) of the Act as amended by the Smith bill, the President reconvenes his board of inquiry. This time it makes recommendations for the settlement of the dispute.

11. At the expiration of eighty days from its issuance, the injunction is dissolved.

12. The President, under Section 210, submits to the Congress a full report of the proceedings together with any recommendations he may have for appropriate action.

13. Employees are now free to strike.

14. They notify the NLRB of the commencement of the strike, as required by Section 8(f) of the Act as proposed by another section of the Smith bill.

15. The NLRB directs the taking of a secret ballot among the employees on the question of whether they wish to continue the strike.

All these steps would have been required by the Taft-Hartley Act, as amended by the Smith bill, in every national emergency dispute. If the strike took place before the President moved under the national emergency provisions, the NLRB's strike-vote ballot under the proposed Section 8(f) would take place at an earlier stage, but the total number of steps would be the same. This is a pertinent example of the obsession with gadgetry that we referred to earlier.

FLEXIBILITY AND UNCERTAINTY

Obviously there has to be a large measure of flexibility in government procedures in dealing with emergency disputes, which are almost by definition extraordinary and lacking in conformity to a pattern. Flexibility is essential for another reason and that is the need for some uncertainty on the part of the disputants if they are not to utilize the government as a calculated part of their strategy.

Unions and management would, on principle, prefer to settle their differences through collective bargaining, without extraordinary intervention by the government. But if either side is confronted with a ready-made situation where it can forecast with reasonable accuracy the timetable of government intervention, then such intervention inevitably becomes part of the strategy and the dispute is therefore less likely to be settled by private negotiations.

Just how this operates in a concrete situation is illuminated by the 1950 coal dispute.[3] John L. Lewis anticipated that the coal mine operators would not bargain while they were in a position to pressure for recourse to the Taft-Hartley emergency provisions. Lewis calculated that they counted on an injunction against the union which in turn they expected him to violate. As a result, though the union and the operators met for nine months, there was no bargaining and there were no demands.

As Lewis had counted on, there was a Taft-Hartley injunction, there was a government request for a show-cause order as to why Lewis and the union should not be held in contempt; but, as apparently nobody had expected, Federal District Judge Keech would not hold either Lewis or the union in contempt. President Truman then asked Congress for special legislation to seize the mines. Agreement was reached two days after the President asked for seizure authority and three days after the district court refused to find contempt.

The special insight which is applicable here is this: The imminence of shutdown and strike is normally a powerful inducement to agree on a basis somewhat less than the parties might have been willing to agree on when the pressure was less urgent. This normal pressure on the parties to agree on their own is seriously impaired by the inevitability of government intercession taking the parties off the spot.

The obverse side of the flexibility-uncertainty approach, perhaps, is the notion that collective bargaining between the parties ought not to be left in abeyance while the government is in the picture.

[3] *Wage Stabilization Program,* Hearings before the Subcommittee on Labor and Labor-Management Relations, Senate Committee on Labor and Public Welfare, 82d Cong., 1st sess. (1952), p. 187.

Now, to be sure, the parties are required to bargain during the effective period of the injunction, but as a practical matter this does not happen.

INJUNCTION VS. COLLECTIVE BARGAINING

An injunction was issued in nine of the twelve cases in which emergency disputes procedures were invoked. It is instructive to see what happened to collective bargaining against the backdrop of an injunction.[4]

1. Atomic energy dispute, 1948. Settlement after the injunction was discharged.

2. Bituminous coal, March 1948. Dispute was settled during the period of the injunction, but the settlement came as a result of a federal district court interpretation of the pension fund agreement rather than as a result of the injunction.

3. Maritime dispute, 1948. The dispute was settled on the Atlantic and Gulf coasts just before the expiration of the injunction. On the Pacific coast the dispute was not settled until eleven weeks after the injunction was vacated.

4. Atlantic coast longshore, 1948. Agreement two weeks after the injunction was dissolved.

5. Bituminous coal, 1950. Settlement took place during the injunction but after the federal district court refused to hold Lewis and the union in contempt when the miners refused to return to work after the issuance of injunction. It is likely that the threat of seizure here was what brought the parties to settlement.

6. Copper, 1951. Some of the disputes were settled before the injunction and some during the injunction.

7. American Locomotive, 1953. Final agreement was not reached until after the injunction had expired.

8. Atlantic coast longshore, 1953-1954. Settlement was not reached until long after expiration of the injunction.

9. Atomic energy, 1954. Agreement was reached after the injunction had expired.

Thus, injunctions were issued in nine cases. In five cases no agreement was reached until after the injunction had expired. In two of the cases agreements were reached before, during, and after the

[4] See footnote 1, p. 112.

injunction. In an additional two cases, both bituminous coal, agreement was reached during the life of the injunction, but it was a court decision unrelated to the Taft-Hartley procedures that provided the turning point in each of the disputes. This recital of the facts makes it rather plain that collective bargaining is either hobbled severely or just stops while the injunction is in force.

SELECTIVITY

Selectivity of use of the emergency procedures emerges as another operating criterion which ought to be applied. From one point of view it can be argued that the Taft-Hartley provisions have been invoked in only twelve cases in a period of seven years, seven of them in one year (1948). We cannot say for sure whether or not the use of Taft-Hartley procedures was justified by the existence of a genuine emergency in each case.

There are authorities who doubt whether we have had a real "emergency" strike. David Cole has said, "There has been no strike in the last dozen years which truly threatened the national welfare."[5] Edgar Warren, after detailed study, has concluded, "Vital services have never been completely curtailed because of strike activity."[6]

All of this is admittedly in the realm of judgment, and we do not wish to underestimate the tensions and pressures which a President is subjected to when there is clamor for something called "action." We suggest, however, the possibility that much of the clamor for action arises because of the availability of the procedures.

This much we can say: Judicial approval of the use of emergency procedures in the American Locomotive case[7] opens up the use of these procedures in situations which are far from being national emergencies in any critical sense. The federal court's interpretation of the reach of the national emergency disputes provisions in this case virtually makes their use available in any local plant producing something for national defense, although the statutory language

[5] David Cole, cited in W. P. Reuther and A. J. Goldberg, *CIO Case against Taft-Hartley* (Washington: 1953), p. 70.
[6] Edgar L. Warren, "Thirty-Six Years of 'National Emergency' Strikes," *Industrial and Labor Relations Review*, 5 (October 1951), p. 12.
[7] *United States v. United Steelworkers of America*, 202 F. 2d 132 (2d Cir. 1953).

talks about a "strike or lockout affecting an entire industry or substantial part thereof" (Sec. 206). The American Locomotive case involved a strike of 1,500 workers of whom 950 were working on products for the atomic energy program. This is a far cry from the national coal and transportation strikes which the legislative history shows the Taft-Hartley draftsmen had in mind when they wrote the national emergency dispute provisions.

ALTERNATIVES

What do we have to offer instead of the present national emergency provisions? We have discussed this in other places. Here we will simply say this much: The best way to cope with genuine national emergency disputes is to continue to place responsibility on the parties themselves to settle their disputes through collective bargaining, without blueprinting any general solution or a rigid timetable of procedures to be taken by the government in the event collective bargaining fails. This means that the executive branch, including the President, could resort to any or all voluntary techniques suitable to resolve the dispute, short of coercive sanction.

This does *not* mean, however, that the nation is left prostrate in the face of a crisis. If there is a crisis, Congress is or can be made available to act with a remedy designed to meet the peculiar circumstances of each emergency situation.

It is of some interest, we think, that a committee appointed by Governor Robert B. Meyner of New Jersey to recommend legislation relating to public utility labor disputes comes out with almost the same answer. New Jersey, of course, has one of the pioneering postwar statutes prohibiting strikes in public utilities and providing for compulsory arbitration. The governor's tripartite committee recommended repeal of the legislation, and all of the interests in the tripartite committee agreed (except one of the three employer members, who wrote what might be called a separate opinion).

There are many quotable sections of the report which support the position we take here, but we will let the issue rest by quoting a few sentences which we think have general application.

"It is a mistake simply to assume there must be a law, and that without some law New Jersey will be helpless. Other jurisdictions have gotten along satisfactorily without laws under which strikes may be forbidden, and we know that the present type of law has been unsatisfactory. The writing of another law may again give a false sense of security." The report then goes on to cite the existing general legal remedies which are available to the governor in case of a utility strike or any other emergency.

Short of an emergency "unlike any we have ever had, which approaches the proportions of disaster . . . it would be better to let the normal forces of economics, public duty, and public opinion expressed through the executive branch in the form of intensive mediation and persuasion, work out the difficulties."

If a disastrous shutdown does occur, the governor as the state's chief executive has ample constitutional power to meet the sudden emergency. The governor could "quickly bring the Legislature together in extraordinary session. The Legislature could work out a course of action designed to meet that particular problem, or it could ratify and approve the course which the Governor has already instituted for the protection of the public."[8]

For the purposes of our formulation, read "President" for "governor" and "Congress" for "legislature."

How does this approach meet the criteria of values and techniques which we have previously outlined?

1. Because we are utilizing an extraordinary remedy (congressional action) for an extraordinary situation it would be rarely used—therefore, selectivity.

2. Because the parties could not know for sure what the Congress might do, there would be uncertainty and maximum pressure on the parties to settle the dispute on their own power—therefore, unpredictability and major reliance on collective bargaining.

3. Because the President and the Congress would be acting on a specific dispute there would be a better chance of suitability and flexibility.

Now the objection can be raised to our approach that the intervention of the Congress at the final stage would create a climate of hysteria. This is a reasonable objection and it could happen. But we remind you that in all of the clamor and din raised in connection with the 1951-1952 steel dispute, the Congress let the dispute take

[8] The Governor's Committee on Legislation Relating to Public Utility Labor Disputes, *Report to Governor Robert B. Meyner* (1954), pp. 17-18.

its own course when the President confronted them with the problem of what to do after he had done what he could. Similarly, it was the Congress which rejected President Truman's proposal to draft the striking railroad workers in 1946.

Our approach is a calculated risk, to be sure, but we believe that it involves less of a risk to the civilized settlement of national emergency disputes than the prefabricated assembly line techniques of Taft-Hartley.

Those who argue that the threat of force of one kind or another must be routinely in the offing in any emergency disputes scheme are reminded that nonstatutory fact finding and kindred voluntary forms of intercession were utilized by the executive in sixteen major disputes between 1945 and 1951; and that in eleven of these cases the recommendations of the boards turned out to be the basis of settlement. This is not an argument for fact finding in every dispute but for the force of voluntary procedures generally in settling disputes.

VII

INDUSTRY LOOKS AT

THE NATIONAL EMERGENCY PROVISIONS

BY ALEXANDER R. HERON
Crown Zellerbach Corporation

No one should attempt to portray what industry sees when industry looks at the national emergency provisions. There is no such thing as an industry view on any question; there are tens of thousands of industry views on every question.

A collection of opinions on the emergency provisions could be obtained from a hundred or a thousand people responsible in the management of industry. These opinions would be largely reflections of the basic attitudes which the spokesmen would reveal on scores of other questions. Many would have their foundations in the political, economic, or social philosophies accepted by the spokesmen. A few would be based on relatively valid experience. Perhaps most of them would reflect the associations or reading habits of the speaker. On this, as on most questions, there is no authorized spokesman for industry.

Some national organizations have recorded definite opinions on the emergency provisions. For our purposes, we may disregard opinions on details and look at those which deal with the principles of the provisions.

One organization, in 1946, urged that where a labor dispute would constitute a national emergency, or where national health or safety is endangered, the President should be empowered to appoint a fact-finding panel to hear both sides and make public the facts, without recommendation; and that the parties be obligated to maintain the status quo until ten days after the publication of the facts.[1]

However, the same organization, four years later, labeled fact finding as of no help in labor disputes, but possibly valuable in acquainting the public with the facts. It declared that strikes affecting wartime production should be handled under the national emergency provisions of the Labor-Management Relations Act. It urged that every avenue of good-faith collective bargaining and the procedures of the Labor-Management Relations Act be exhausted before a War Labor Board be permitted to assume jurisdiction.[2] It also emphasized the opinion that no special agency was needed during war or mobilization for the purpose of handling labor disputes; furthermore, that the right to strike should be maintained, with no pledge of either labor or management against strikes or lockouts.[3]

Actual experience with the emergency provisions is rare among those who constitute the management group in industry. This is almost equally true of hearsay experience. Many of us will gladly comment on the ineffectiveness of the emergency provisions in the steel dispute of 1952. Then either our own memories or an alert listener will point out that this particular dispute ran its course completely without recourse to the emergency provisions.

Some industry spokesmen see the emergency provisions as another extension of government powers into a field from which government should be largely excluded. This attitude is seldom carried to its logical conclusion. There is always the qualification that government must step in at the proper time, in certain kinds of disputes, to protect the public interest. The location of this point of necessary government intervention will be different from man to man, from industry to industry, and from time to time. It is

[1] National Association of Manufacturers, *Public and Industrial Peace* (1946), p. 18.

[2] National Association of Manufacturers, *Industry Believes* (December 1951), pp. 26-27.

[3] National Association of Manufacturers, *Industry Believes* (February 1953), pp. 18-19.

probable that the location of this point is becoming more remote in the minds of most management thinkers.

There are still opinions close to the belief that every strike is against the public interest and should be unlawful. There is still a measurable group resentment of the statutory authorization or licensing of the strike; a feeling that what was once an unlawful conspiracy, and is still a conspiracy but a lawful one, should be again an unlawful conspiracy.

Against this is a growing acceptance by management of the thesis that a strike, a conspiracy to withhold the labor of an entire group of employees, is a necessary result of the evolution of our economy. Those who share this opinion are frequently unhappy over the immaturity shown by strike leaders and strike followers. At the same time, they pin their hopes on the attainment of reasonable maturity on the part of workers, union leaders, and management leaders. They believe this maturity can be obtained only through experience, and the cost of that experience is not too much to pay for the improved ability to act as responsible citizens of a democracy.

Assuming that this is the most frequent attitude in management, there is still a diversity of attitude toward the emergency provisions of this or any other statute. Almost no management spokesman will say that no emergency provisions are necessary, or that the general powers of government to maintain peace and order are sufficient to cover all industrial disputes. Almost no one will deny the possibility of a labor dispute which will, in fact, threaten the "national health and safety," even in peacetime. On the other side is the strong opinion that national emergencies have been carelessly defined.

This view is supported by Cyrus Ching, who has had a major responsibility for appraising the national emergency nature of labor disputes, in these comments:

A good case can be made for the statement that the nation has never really suffered seriously from a strike. . . . There have been few, if any, real national emergencies resulting from labor-management conflicts.

. . . many times since enactment of the Taft-Hartley law, in 1947, with its national emergency strike section, the Federal Government has dealt with a situation on the basis of a national emergency when, in looking back, it really was not that at all.

All of the people who are affected by the shutdown of an industry, including the retailers, wholesalers, stockholders and other groups, bring pressure to bear on Congress, the President, and the Government agencies, demanding action. . . . I can say, in looking back on my own experience, pressures of that kind led me to refer matters to the President and we in the Federal Mediation Service proceeded on the basis that it was a national emergency. I confess that in regard to some of the instances there now is serious doubt in my mind as to the correctness of the label.[4]

Many of the judgments or feelings about the need for emergency provisions rest upon emergencies which have been or would be purely local. We react indignantly against a strike which may completely cut off the supply of milk, or power, or transportation for a million people. It is rarely that such an emergency can reasonably be given national character. Obviously a local strike affecting construction, transportation, or power facilities for an atomic energy project can be so classified. But in peacetime the list is not much longer than that, in theory. In practice there are few instances in which definite moves have been made toward using the Taft-Hartley emergency provisions. Two have involved atomic energy, two were directly related to the Korean emergency. Three actions involving coal can be broadly considered as involving one continuous dispute; likewise four actions involving transportation.

Perhaps the steel dispute of 1952 is the outstanding challenge to our emphasis on the national hazards which constitute an emergency. The strike resulting from that dispute was substantially complete. It involved the largest essential product in the national defense program. It occurred at a time of national emergency just short of war. And yet there is no strong evidence today that the defense program, the effort in Korea, or any other vital phase of the national welfare was seriously injured by that strike.

A thoughtful student of the subject has pointed out that we have, in fact, survived every emergency dispute in our history, but that if we had become suddenly involved in war, the losses in our defense production would have been extremely severe. Perhaps the

[4] Cyrus S. Ching, *Review and Reflection* (New York: Forbes, 1953), pp. 103, 106, 109.

general reaction of industry would be that the condition of all-out war would justify emergency action far beyond that provided in the Taft-Hartley Act. It would be intolerable merely to postpone a strike in a vital war industry, and then give implicit approval to the strike at the end of the injunction period. It must be remembered that the Taft-Hartley provisions were written at a time when we were presumably entering upon an era of peace, without even the problems of a cold war, to say nothing of the limited war situation created in Korea. In other words, we must measure the attitudes toward the emergency provisions as they would function in times of peace.

When the seizure issue of the steel dispute moved through the judicial tests to the Supreme Court, counsel for the steel company repeatedly emphasized the fact that Congress had provided emergency machinery through the Labor-Management Relations Act. They argued that seizure was beyond the general powers of the President, and in any case it was invalid for the specific reason that he had not used the machinery provided by legislation. Implicit in this argument was the assumption that the emergency provisions of the Taft-Hartley Act were adequate to protect the public interest. But probably few will argue that these provisions, by themselves, would be adequate to cope with emergency disputes in time of all-out war.

The organization mentioned above, in 1954, after the experience in Korea, took a firm position against special boards for purposes of settling labor disputes and against any government agency being allowed to recommend or impose a settlement. It reiterated the belief that the emergency provisions (LMRA) should be the only authorized action in the event of a dispute that imperils the national health, safety, or security, but with one significant addition: "Any restraining order issued to maintain the status quo in national emergency strikes and lockouts—for the purpose of protecting the public —should be of such duration as is necessary."[5]

These are some of the reasons why it is difficult to cite an industry viewpoint on the emergency provisions; in fact, why it is unlikely that there is a definable industry viewpoint. However, some conclusions about the attitude of "industry" can be reached by even

[5] National Association of Manufacturers, *Industry Believes* (April 1954), p. 15.

casual observers. Impressions can be drawn from the testimony before congressional committees: testimony by some individual on his own behalf, by a loosely designated spokesman for "industry" or for some industry, or by a carefully credentialed representative of an association. Inferences can be drawn from public speeches, interviews, or pamphlets. Still more authentic may be the pleadings and arguments by counsel for companies or industries in court proceedings. Such declarations are always calculated to inform and influence public opinion, even when addressed directly to legislators or jurists.

One conclusion seems inevitable. Industry looks at the emergency provisions much more favorably than does labor. This conclusion may be extended to the viewpoint on emergency provisions in principle, in addition to those of the Taft-Hartley Act alone.

The hearings and debates leading to passage of the Taft-Hartley Act called forth an orderly and responsible presentation of experiences, opinions, and arguments. These were not free from prejudice, of course, but they were necessarily different from the oratorical and editorial declarations of the ten years from 1937 to 1947. They had to be sufficiently orderly and organized to be presented to committees of the Congress.

In these hearings, the advocates of emergency provisions were not the spokesmen for organized labor, although there were advocates on behalf of unorganized workers. They were frequently bona fide spokesmen for the public. But they were probably predominantly spokesmen for industry and business, whether volunteers or delegates.

A small library could be stocked with the publications and speeches on behalf of business, during Wagner Act days, pointing directly or indirectly to the need for some kind of emergency provisions. Throughout the collection one can find a recurring frustration over the difficulty of insuring that the government agency concerned would use such powers properly.

It is not only indicated by history that more favorable attitudes toward the emergency provisions are held by management than by labor; it is also logical that this should be the case. These emergency provisions, or almost any other emergency provisions, are more likely to provide direct restraints upon unions than upon the owners and managers of industry. Fundamentally, the emergency provisions are intended to prevent strikes. There has been no measurable concern over possible interruptions due to overt acts by management.

It is natural for management people to look upon the emergency provisions as machinery to prohibit unions from striking, rather than to prohibit management or industry from taking any conceivable action. It is also natural for them to reject the idea that any action by management in a labor dispute would need prohibition, in order to protect the public safety, health, and welfare. People in management have the responsibility for continued operation and success of the respective enterprises which they guide. They believe that any action by management that would endanger the public safety, health, and welfare would inevitably damage the enterprise and probably endanger the tenure of the management.

It is safe to say that management in industry looks at the emergency provisions as curbs on strikes that would create public emergencies.

Most members of management oppose government intervention and government controls in principle. Yet the emergency provisions are clearly a form of government intervention. This requires reasoning to distinguish this from other forms. First, as indicated above, it is presumed to be intervention to prohibit unions from striking. Second, this intervention is supposed to give the parties a fair chance to negotiate their own settlement. Government assistance in conciliation and mediation is not objectionable in this view. But there is no widespread desire by management for such assistance as fact finding, recommendations, or arbitration.

There is a belief on the part of most management people that settlements can be reached in most labor disputes if rash actions can be avoided or postponed. Of course, they mean rash actions by unions—not by management. Presumably the emergency provisions insure this postponement and exert pressures for settlement, where a national emergency is involved. Union spokesmen assert that an enforced delay is likely to weaken the solidarity of the employee group and undermine the tactical position of the union leadership. Management people will argue that a cause or an issue which justified the strike on one date will equally justify it eighty days later, if the issues have not been settled or compromised.

The emergency provisions assume a guarantee of maintenance of the status quo during the period of an injunction, if an injunction issues. Management people are not intolerant of the arguments of union leaders that this involves a possible injustice. At the same time, they do not concede that it constitutes slavery. They emphasize the destruction of the negotiating process if any government power could be used to force a change from the status quo during the life of an injunction.

A large and articulate body of management people believes sincerely in collective bargaining. These people find themselves completely allied with spokesmen for organized labor in bitter opposition to compulsory arbitration. But they have not yet been joined by labor in opposition to government fact finding and recommendations as half steps toward compulsory arbitration.

Management people bitterly oppose the device of seizure in labor disputes without specific statutory authority. They would oppose legislation for such authority if it implied or specified the power of a government agent to decide, settle, or compromise the issues in dispute.

These oppositions have some roots in fear, based on experiences of government concessions to the demands of labor. But they have deeper roots in another fear. Management sees any such dictation by government as a threat to the principles of collective bargaining. Labor fought to establish those principles against the opposition of a previous generation of management. The new generation in management has learned that collective bargaining, in principle, is democratic, is modern, and is constructive.

The basic attitude of this new generation in management, toward the emergency provisions, may be this:

1. Some emergency provisions are needed to prevent actions by unions which would seriously endanger the public safety, health, and welfare.

2. The use of emergency provisions should be avoided except in cases of extreme danger.

3. The emergency provisions should be both designed and interpreted to encourage collective bargaining, and to prevent its displacement by government dictation.

By these criteria, it is probable that most people in management look favorably on the present emergency provisions.

· VIII ·

AN EVALUATION OF

THE NATIONAL EMERGENCY PROVISIONS*

BY FRANK C. PIERSON
Swarthmore College

When the Taft-Hartley Act was first put on the books, most disinterested observers were critical of the law's provisions dealing
with national emergency disputes. It was felt that this section of
the law was at one and the same time unfairly weighted against
labor organizations and ill designed to maintain industrial peace.
Underlying this view was a conviction that labor disputes in our
kind of society, even those involving industries of great national
importance, can be settled only by agreement between the parties,
and that the procedures established under the Act represented an
important departure from the principle of voluntarism in labor
relations.

Today, while the predominant sentiment among disinterested
groups remains critical, there is less readiness to indulge in broad
attacks on this aspect of the law. Several reasons may be noted.
First, experience under the Act does not indicate that the government will invoke the emergency procedures frequently or under
a wide variety of circumstances. Despite forebodings to the contrary,
the present Republican administration seems less ready, if anything,
to use the national emergency machinery than its predecessor, this

* This chapter has benefited from suggestions made by David L. Cole and
Whitley P. McCoy; they would not, however, concur in some of the conclusions
reached.

part of the law having been applied in only twelve disputes to date, seven in 1948, one in 1949-1950, one in 1951, one in 1952-1953, and two in 1953-1954.[1] If international tensions subside, the prospect is that the machinery will be used even more sparingly in the future.

Second, in the cases in which the national emergency procedures have been applied, there is little evidence that the unions involved have been hamstrung in their dealings with employers or that they have been prevented from exercising powerful bargaining pressures to win contract improvements. In three of the twelve cases (the Pacific coast maritime and both Atlantic coast longshore disputes), strikes occurred after the eighty-day waiting period had ended.[2] In all twelve cases except the Atlantic longshore dispute of 1953-1954, important contract demands were at issue, and in every instance but one the unions secured substantial gains. The sole exception was the telephone dispute of 1948 in which no general wage increase was obtained, but this result can hardly be attributed to the national emergency disputes machinery.[3] Indeed it is hard to believe that any of the settlements eventually arrived at would have been materially different if this machinery had not been in existence.

[1] Strikes in defense and other nationally important industries were fewer in 1953 and 1954 than in most postwar years, but regarding those which occurred, notably the sixty-three-day strike at the General Electric jet aircraft engine plant in Evendale, Ohio, and the fifty-four-day stoppage at North American Aviation in Los Angeles, the Eisenhower administration showed little disposition to invoke the national emergency procedures.

[2] Not much weight should be placed on the second (1953-1954) Atlantic coast longshore dispute in evaluating the national emergency procedures since it involved rival representation claims of the "old" ILA and the "new" ILA-AFL unions, not a dispute between a union and employer. No strike occurred in this dispute immediately after the original injunction was dissolved on December 4, 1953, but a twenty-eight-day unauthorized strike occurred on the New York waterfront three months later. Ultimately, the "old" ILA won out in the representation dispute.

[3] In the telephone dispute, a strike was threatened and the President appointed a board of inquiry, but the strike did not materialize, no injunction was issued, and the parties eventually reached agreement without the necessity of the board's submitting a report to the President. The union suffered something of a defeat in the 1948 meat packing strike, since the final settlement was very close to the terms originally offered by the employers. However, the union received a nine cents per hour general increase; it should also be noted that no injunction was issued in this case.

Third, even from a procedural point of view, relations between the so-called big unions and employers do not appear to have been much altered by this section of the law. Bargaining between the "titans" has for a long time had its public or ceremonial, as opposed to its nonpublic or off-the-record, aspects. The obligations imposed on the parties by the national emergency provisions largely fall in the former area; while complicating and sometimes actually interfering with the processes of reaching settlements, the chief effect of the national emergency procedures has been to add certain formalities to bargaining relationships.[4] Thus, unions must now move their bargaining schedules ahead to allow for the possibility of an eighty-day waiting period; each of the parties must be prepared to appear before government investigators and to have its case aired in a public forum. Even John L. Lewis has to exercise a certain care in the way he approaches strike actions; a misstep in 1948 cost him $20,000 and cost his union $1,400,000! None of the procedural requirements of the law, however, touch on vital interests of the parties. They are carrying on their dealings with one another in about the same way as before.

Fourth, and perhaps most important, critics have been hard put to suggest a *clearly* better method for dealing with national emergency disputes that would be *substantially* different from the one now in effect. Broadly speaking, there appear to be just three policies, either singly or in combination, which the government can elect to follow: mediation with no compulsory features, compulsory postponement with some type of investigatory procedure, or compulsory settlement. Few impartial observers are prepared to argue that the first policy would be adequate for all situations, even if it is felt that chief reliance should be placed on mediatory tech-

[4] The example usually cited to indicate how the national emergency procedures have tended to promote industrial strife is the west coast longshore dispute of 1948. Harry Bridges told the board of inquiry in this case he would use the cooling-off period required by the law to build up strike psychology and lay plans for subsequent strike action. Whether matters in this case were made worse by reason of the national emergency procedures cannot be definitely determined—the fact remains that a strike lasting for nearly three months occurred when the eighty-day period expired. Board of Inquiry Created by Executive Order No. 9964, *Report to the President on Labor Disputes in the Maritime Industry* (1948), p. 10.

niques. The third has hardly any adherents although a few authorities, notably Gregory, McCabe, and Slichter, have recommended programs which encroach seriously on the traditional freedom of unions and employers.[5] This leaves the second approach as the one commanding most support, the approach embodied in the Taft-Hartley Act. Thus, with varying degrees of distaste, reluctance, and even surprise, most impartial observers come out, after all, rather close to the position adopted by the framers of the national emergency provisions.

If the foregoing strikes the reader as damning the law with faint praise, this is precisely the impression intended. The best case that can be made for the national emergency section of the Taft-Hartley Act is essentially a negative one; that is, viewing the record overall, the Act's effects do not appear to have been unduly harmful. If a more positive criterion is applied—if, for example, the question is asked whether the law has made a significant contribution to promoting industrial peace in nationally strategic industries—a different appraisal results. In only one case, the atomic energy dispute of 1948, are there clear grounds for believing that the emergency procedures proved helpful in heading off a threatened strike. In three other cases, the telephone and coal contract disputes of 1948 and the atomic energy dispute of 1954, no strikes occurred after the law was applied, but this was apparently due to circumstances unrelated to the national emergency procedures. In the eight remaining cases strikes occurred anyway, and the emergency machinery proved ineffective, if not actually harmful, in bringing about settlements.

Even on this more exacting level of appraisal, however, care has to be exercised in reaching an over-all evaluation of the law. Of the eight cases in which strikes occurred, injunctions were eventually issued in all but one, the meat packing case of 1948; in none of these cases, except the bituminous coal contract dispute of 1950,

---

[5] See Charles O. Gregory, *Labor and the Law* (rev. ed.; New York: W. W. Norton, 1949), pp. 478–490; Statement of David A. McCabe, *Labor Relations*, Hearings on S. 249, Senate Committee on Labor and Public Welfare, 81st Cong., 1st sess. (1949), pt. 3, pp. 1601–1602; and Sumner H. Slichter, "Revision of the Taft-Hartley Act," *Quarterly Journal of Economics*, LXVII (May 1953), p. 178.

was there a stoppage during the period the injunction was in effect.[6] This, however, is different from saying that the injunctions prevented these strikes, much less that the cooling-off device was of any material help in bringing about a final disposition of the disputed issues. Indeed, in only two of the cases in which injunctions figured, the bituminous coal pension case of 1948 and the American Locomotive case of 1952-1953, were the disputes settled during the statutory eighty-day period. Moreover, in three cases, as already noted, serious stoppages occurred after the eighty-day injunction had expired. While avoiding sweeping criticisms, most observers would doubtless still agree with Sumner Slichter's general appraisal that "this record . . . cannot be regarded as a good 'batting average' for the law."[7]

While the broad impact of the national emergency procedures is difficult to gauge, the effects of particular features of the law are easier to evaluate. A review of the twelve cases in which the machinery has been used reveals a number of points at which the law can be changed to advantage, either in the direction of simplifying or increasing the flexibility of its procedures, as well as a number of respects in which the law has met the test of experience reasonably well. No attempt is made to consider different approaches to the problem of national emergency disputes since these broader issues are dealt with by other contributors to this volume. However,

[6] In the 1950 coal case, John L. Lewis and the United Mine Workers were absolved of responsibility for the continuance of the stoppage in a trial for contempt of court. A settlement was finally agreed to by the parties soon after President Truman asked Congress for power to seize the mines. It should be noted that the board of inquiry played a helpful role in bringing the two parties together in this dispute.

[7] Slichter, op. cit., p. 171. General evaluations of the national emergency disputes provisions of the Taft-Hartley Act will be found in Donald E. Cullen, "The Taft-Hartley Act in National Emergency Disputes," Industrial and Labor Relations Review, VII (October 1953), pp. 15-30; Charles M. Rehmus, "The Operation of the National Emergency Provisions of the Labor Management Relations Act of 1947," Yale Law Journal, LXII (June 1953), pp. 1047-1063; George W. Taylor, "Is Compulsory Arbitration Inevitable?" Proceedings of the First Annual Meeting (Champaign: Industrial Relations Research Association, 1948), pp. 64-77; Edgar L. Warren, The Settlement of Labor-Management Disputes (Rio Piedras: University of Puerto Rico Press, 1951); and Edwin E. Witte, "Industrial Conflicts in Periods of National Emergency," in Arthur Kornhauser, Robert Dubin, and Arthur M. Ross, eds., Industrial Conflict (New York: McGraw-Hill, 1954), pp. 435-441.

if the changes proposed here were adopted, the law would operate in a different fashion from what it does at the present time.

COVERAGE AND APPLICATION OF THE LAW

The President is authorized to invoke the national emergency procedures when in his opinion a threatened or actual strike "affectting an entire industry or a substantial part thereof" will "imperil the national health or safety." The opinion has been expressed that a strike in a single firm or plant could conceivably imperil the nation's health or safety and that the above language may prove unduly restrictive. This fear was laid to rest when President Truman's action invoking the law in a case involving the Dunkirk, New York, plant of the American Locomotive Company was upheld by the courts. In ruling on the case the U. S. Court of Appeals, 2nd Circuit, concluded that the test of applicability was "not the extent of the strike within an industry but the extent of the effect of a strike upon an industry and the national health and safety."[8] In this instance, the plant manufactured pipe and other products needed at atomic energy installations.

Judging from experience, the language defining the coverage of the law is, if anything, too broad rather than too restrictive. Agreement as to the precise circumstances under which the procedures should apply, even among impartial observers, is not likely, but the danger of the government's intervening in too many disputes on the grounds they "imperil the national health or safety" is widely recognized. Nothing could destroy the machinery's effectiveness more quickly than to permit it to be used frequently, just to be "doing something" about important strikes.

Fortunately, as already noted, the Truman and Eisenhower administrations have resisted pressures working in this direction, the one exception being the meat-packing strike of 1948.[9] As matters

[8] *United States v. United Steelworkers of America,* 202 F. 2d 132 (2d Cir. 1953).

[9] The government in this strike stopped midway in applying the Act's procedures; after the board of inquiry submitted its initial report to the President, no injunction was requested by the President, and the parties were left to work out a settlement in spite of the fact that the strike continued for two and a half months.

stand now, barring a change in the military scene, it would appear that the procedures will probably be invoked only in major strikes in coal, steel, water transportation, communications, and a few critically important defense installations. As was the case in the steel dispute of 1949, the government may not even apply the law in these industries if other procedures seem more appropriate or if the effects of a strike would not prove too crippling. Nevertheless, as long as the present language is retained, the Act will constitute an open invitation for one party or the other to try to have the machinery applied on its behalf. If it were made clear that the law would be invoked only where there was a definite showing that an interruption to production would precipitate a crisis, actually endangering the physical welfare of the nation, there would be less clamor to have the procedures applied in every important strike and the parties would be less able to count on White House intervention as a way out of their difficulties.

At the same time, experience shows it would not be wise to specify, in advance, the industries in which the emergency procedures will be applied. Even if agreement could be secured on the matter, which is most doubtful, changing conditions would soon make any such listing out of date. A coal strike in 1948 is quite different from one in 1954. Who can say but what even the production of atomic energy will be much less "critical" a few months, or a few years, hence? Even within the very narrow range of industries in which national emergency strikes may conceivably occur, it is therefore wise to permit considerable flexibility in determining just where and when the law shall be invoked. By the same token, the discretion granted the President in this regard seems sound and should be retained.[10] Care would therefore have to be exercised in determining how far the present coverage of the law should be narrowed. It might be sufficient for the purpose at hand

[10] It can be argued that limiting the industries in which the procedures may be applied, as suggested above, would deprive the law of an important degree of flexibility. The issue becomes one of balancing the various considerations involved. In the writer's judgment, minimizing the element of government intervention in labor disputes is more important than maximizing the flexibility of the procedures to be followed. Once government intervention beyond the usual mediatory efforts becomes necessary, a high degree of flexibility should be provided.

simply to add the "clear and present danger" test to the definition of national emergency disputes now contained in the law.[11]

BOARDS OF INQUIRY

It is difficult to determine just what the framers of the emergency machinery intended in providing for boards of inquiry "to inquire into the issues" and report to the President on "the facts." Presumably, this feature of the law was designed to bring the impartial judgment of a group of eminent citizens to bear on the matters in controversy for the purpose of clarifying the issues and subjecting the parties to the pressures of an aroused public opinion. At the same time, the procedure under the law makes it well-nigh impossible for a board to make a thorough study of the dispute, since its initial (and most important) report must be issued before an injunction can be secured, and its findings must not include any recommendations as to how the dispute might be equitably resolved. Typically, this has meant that the boards have had about a week's time in which to dig into the facts, and the reports have been most perfunctory, merely repeating what is already known about the positions of the parties. Under these circumstances it is little wonder that the work of the boards of inquiry has received scant attention either by the parties or by the public at large. With the exception of the 1950 coal case, and to a lesser extent in the 1948 coal pension case, in which the boards performed certain "extrastatutory" mediation functions, there is no evidence that these bodies have contributed in any way to fulfilling the purposes for which they were established.

There is no reason why the initial inquiry reports have to be squeezed into the brief period between the time of a board's appointment and the President's request for an injunction. Even if it is felt that some type of certification procedure is necessary

[11] It is interesting to note that in connection with President Eisenhower's 1954 proposal to allow the states to deal with certain types of emergency disputes, the majority report of the Senate Labor Committee defined such emergencies as "labor disputes which, if permitted to occur or continue, will constitute a clear and present danger to the health or safety of the people of the State." *Labor Management Relations Act, 1947, as Amended,* Senate Committee on Education and Labor, 83d Cong., 2d sess., Rep. No. 1211 (April 15, 1954), p. 8. Senate bill S. 2650 to which this report refers embodied a number of administration proposals for changing the Labor-Management Relations Act, but they failed of enactment.

before an injunction is issued, the board's first report on the facts of the dispute need not be issued until later.[12] More controversial is the proposal that the boards of inquiry should make recommendations, although the late Senator Taft's change of mind on the issue is indicative of the trend in present thinking.[13] The drafters of the Taft-Hartley Act believed that if the boards were given this power, the parties (especially the employers) would be virtually forced to accept their recommendations, a form of compulsory arbitration which few would welcome.

While not completely groundless, this fear nonetheless seems exaggerated; much depends on the particular proposals made by the board in question, the language used, and the circumstances surrounding the case. The recommendations of the 1949 steel fact-finding board, for example, were presented in such a way as to occasion a considerable amount of bargaining before the dispute was settled.[14] Unless it is assumed that the boards established under the national emergency procedures are bound to be either

[12] In this connection, the Congressional Joint Committee on Labor-Management Relations recommended the following in 1948: "If the act were amended to permit the President to direct the Attorney General to seek an injunction when upon the advice of the Director of Mediation and Conciliation Service he is of the opinion that the threatened strike or lock-out will imperil the national health or safety, without the intervention of the emergency board, the Director's objection is met. The emergency board could then be called into existence upon the issuance of the injunction." *Labor Management Relations*, Joint Committee on Labor-Management Relations, 80th Cong., 2d sess., Rep. No. 986 (December 31, 1948), pt. 3, p. 21.

[13] Among the twenty-eight amendments to the Taft-Hartley Act submitted by Senator Taft was a proposal to allow the boards of inquiry to make recommendations. The Senate voted in favor of his amendments, but the House did not. S. 249, 81st Cong., 1st sess. (1949). In his labor message to Congress on January 11, 1954, President Eisenhower proposed that the boards of inquiry should be authorized to make recommendations at the final step of the procedure but not before. A majority of the Senate Labor Committee approved this proposal. See Senate Committee Rep. No. 1211, to accompany S. 2650, p. 13.

[14] The board in this case was set up by presidential executive order but not pursuant to the national emergency dispute procedures. The results of its work were mixed; in recommending that there should be no general wage increase and that provision be made for a company-financed pension and welfare program, the board made an important contribution to a narrowing of the issues; however, the employers refused to settle on the terms recommended by the board and a strike followed. The final settlement followed the board's recommendation, except that the welfare program was jointly financed. A somewhat similar pattern of events followed the Wage Stabilization Board's recommendations for ending the dispute in the steel industry in 1952.

grossly partial or glaringly inept, there is no reason why the same result could not be achieved under the national emergency procedures.

A more serious question is the deleterious effects which this procedure might have on the continuation of bargaining by the parties, since one or the other would be likely to feel that it has everything to gain and nothing to lose by waiting until the recommendations are announced. In the so-called national emergency strike situations that have occurred, however, the parties have typically reached a stalemate in their dealings anyway; under existing legislation no recommendations are permitted, but bargaining has certainly not on this account been maintained on a flourishing basis. What was needed, at least in many of these situations, was a new set of proposals, backed up by the prestige and influence of the President's office, in order to get the dispute-settling process under way again.

The foregoing suggests that the boards of inquiry should have considerable latitude in the way they discharge their functions. Under some circumstances, emphasis in the board's work should be put on mediation efforts; under others, on merely summarizing the facts; under still others, on formulating recommendations for a fair settlement. Uncertainty as to just how the boards will function should lessen somewhat the adverse effects on bargaining relations between the parties and should also give the boards of inquiry more opportunity to discharge their responsibilities successfully.

INJUNCTIONS AND COOLING-OFF PERIODS

Rather than emphasizing the role of the boards of inquiry, the framers of the emergency disputes machinery placed chief reliance on ordering both sides to maintain the status quo for eighty days and on encouraging the parties to reach voluntary settlements in the interval. Critics of the law, in and out of academic circles, are generally agreed that a cooling-off period, as such, is of little or no value in labor disputes, especially if resort is made at the outset to a court order compelling the employees to continue working against their will. The record tends to bear out this conclusion. In only two of the nine cases in which injunctions have been issued were settlements reached during the eighty-day period. In the first, the 1948 coal pension case, a settlement was reached after the parties had agreed upon Senator Styles Bridges as the third member of the pension fund's Board of Trustees. In the second, the American Locomotive dispute, a strike which had continued for three months ended when an injunction was secured, and a tentative basis for settlement was reached through mediation just before the "final offer" ballot was to be held.[15] In two other cases, the atomic energy disputes of 1948 and 1954, settlements were reached very soon after the expiration of the eighty-day period. In all these cases, as well as in the other five disputes in which injunctions were involved, one or two basic questions were at issue which had to be resolved before settlements could be reached. These key issues were so important to the parties that merely to postpone the strike deadline could not be expected to deflect either side from its ultimate objective or general strategy.

Compulsory postponement carries with it the heavy but inescapable cost of temporarily removing from the parties the pressure imposed by a strike, or strike threat, to continue active bargaining. In every one of the nine cases in which the eighty-day delay was involved, agreement was reached only after a strike action became imminent or actually occurred. While the postponement-investigation-balloting steps were being taken, the parties' efforts to reach settlements languished, but as the terminal step in the procedure drew near, bargaining quickened and the basis was usually laid for reaching agreement.

This points up again the need for keeping the procedures flexible. Even in national emergency disputes, the best interests of the public are not always served by attempting to compel the parties to postpone a strike action, especially if there is reason to believe that a short strike will be enough to induce a settlement or that the government's most vigorous efforts to secure a postponement will be flouted anyway. Under these circumstances, even if the strike continues, the inquiry board should be empowered to explore the pos-

---

[15] Charles M. Rehmus, *op. cit.*, p. 1051. Government officials close to this case report that the union devoted all its energies to coping with the injunction procedure and to carrying out strikes at the other plants of the American Locomotive Company, so that effective negotiations were quite impossible until close to the end of the injunction period.

sibility of a mediated settlement or to recommend terms on which the parties might be expected to agree.

In contrast to the foregoing, emphasis under the present law is placed on compelling the parties to postpone any strike action through the injunction procedure, this being the next step which the law authorizes the President to take after he receives the board of inquiry's initial report. The charge often made by union spokesmen that this procedure imposes an inequitable burden on labor organizations hardly seems justified on the basis of actual experience under the law. In none of the nine cases in which injunctions have figured have the unions suffered material harm. On the contrary, in each of these cases the union involved has won substantial gains. Moreover, in at least two instances in which court orders were not issued, the unions indicated they wished injunctions had been granted.[16]

At the same time, imposition of an injunction almost immediately after the government's formal entry into an emergency dispute is likely to introduce another controversial element into an already difficult situation, thus impeding rather than facilitating a final settlement. If it seems advisable to attempt to postpone a particular strike—a step, as indicated above, which should not be taken as a matter of course—the law might well simply grant the President authority to request the parties not to change the status quo for a limited period of time. This is the procedure followed in the railroad industry, and almost without exception such requests to postpone action have been honored by both parties in this field. Whether unions and employers in other industries in which national emergencies might occur would respond in similar fashion is open to question, but their reaction could hardly be less favorable than to injunctions. In this connection William Leiserson, who has had extensive labor relations experience in the railroad and other industries, has stated: "There is no need to resort to injunctions and court procedures to secure maintenance of the status quo pending a

[16] In the 1948 telephone dispute, the union hoped an injunction would be issued to prevent an "imminent" strike; the request was not granted, but the strike never materialized. The CIO packinghouse workers also desired an injunction in the meat packing strike of 1948, but no injunction was issued.

fact-finding investigation."[17] Generally speaking, the nine emergency dispute cases in which injunctions have been issued lend support to this view.[18]

This change in the procedure would not wholly preclude the use of injunctions. If a union or employer should prove completely obdurate and were to refuse to comply with the President's request, he could still ask for an injunction, going to Congress if it is decided he does not have the necessary power.[19] Alternatively, if Congress decides to retain the injunction as part of the national emergency machinery, the law could provide that it will be used only if one or other of the parties refuses to comply with the President's request to maintain conditions of employment unchanged during the eighty-day period. Under this alternative, the President should also probably be empowered to seize the property, if such a step seems necessary, so that the widest possible latitude of action is maintained.[20]

FINAL-OFFER BALLOT

There is now well-nigh universal agreement that the requirement to hold a vote among the employees on the employer's "last offer" in national emergency disputes should be dropped from the law as

[17] William M. Leiserson, "For a New Labor Law," *New York Times Magazine*, February 6, 1949, reprinted in *Labor Relations*, Hearings on S. 249, Senate Committee on Labor and Public Welfare, 81st Cong., 1st sess. (1949), p. 950.

[18] In this connection the United Mine Workers have to be treated separately from other unions. Whether the Pacific coast longshoremen would have responded to a request by the President to postpone their 1948 strike without an injunction cannot be answered with much assurance, but neither can the question whether the use of the injunction prolonged the west coast longshore strike which occurred after the eighty-day cooling-off period ended. See footnote 4.

[19] This conclusion is in line with the position taken by Senator Ives on national emergency procedures. See his amendment to S. 249, 81st Cong., 1st sess. (1949), presented to the Senate on June 16, 1949, *Congressional Record*, 81st Cong., 1st sess., 95:6 (June 16, 1949), p. 7800. The Ives proposal was later incorporated in S. 1075, 83d Cong., 1st sess. (1953) and will be found in *Taft-Hartley Act Revisions*, Hearings, Senate Committee on Labor and Public Welfare, 83d Cong., 1st sess. (1953), pt. 1, pp. 10-11.

[20] In 1949, Senator Taft proposed to give the President the power to seek an injunction or to request seizure; this proposal, one of his twenty-eight amendments, was approved by the Senate but defeated in the House. See footnote 13. The issue of seizure is a most complicated one, and since it is dealt with elsewhere in this volume, no attempt is made to discuss it here.

soon as possible. As the Act now stands, the NLRB is required to conduct such a poll in every unsettled dispute between the sixtieth and seventy-fifth day of the eighty-day injunction period. Almost all impartial observers, at the time the law was passed, were of the opinion this provision would prove completely useless. Events, if anything, have shown their criticisms were too mild.

If the vote requirement were merely an expensive formality, as indicated by the fact that the workers have overwhelmingly rejected the employer's "last offer" in each of the four elections that have been held to date, perhaps the amount of mischief caused would not be great. The record indicates, however, that the very attempt to define and vote on the employer's final offer tends to discourage active bargaining in the most crucial part of the eighty-day period. The task of stating precisely the employer's last offer, which of necessity is subject to frequent change until a final settlement is reached, is no small feat in itself.[21] Once it is on the ballot, the positions of the two parties tend to freeze for and against the terms of the offer, making further concessions which are needed to end the dispute that much more difficult to obtain.

Senator Taft recognized the undesirability of this feature of the law, and in 1949 recommended that it be eliminated. In discussing the issue on the Senate floor he stated:

The vote was not a success. It is a very difficult thing to arrange on a nation-wide basis. The unions did not like it. In one or two cases, I think, the men voted to strike anyway. In one case [west coast longshore dispute], they would not vote at all. In general, Mr. Ching's recommendation [as Director of the Federal Mediation and Conciliation Service] was that that was an impractical procedure, and should be eliminated.[22]

If Congress overhauls the national emergency disputes machinery there seems no doubt but what this provision will be dropped.[23]

[21] In the American Locomotive case, the employer revised downward a proposal which the board of inquiry had previously reported to the President as being the firm's "last offer." Amid the general confusion caused by these developments, the NLRB, at the suggestion of the Federal Mediation and Conciliation Service, postponed the ballot "indefinitely."

[22] *Congressional Record*, 81st Cong., 1st sess., 95:6 (June 16, 1949), p. 7802.

[23] See, for example, S. 1026 and S. 1075, 83d Cong., 1st sess. (1949), reprinted in *Taft-Hartley Act Revisions*, Hearings, Senate Committee on Labor and Public Welfare, 83d Cong., 1st sess. (1949), pt. 1, pp. 9-11. This change, however, was not included in President Eisenhower's labor message to Congress in January 1954.

FINAL STEP IN PROCEDURE

The upshot of the elaborate procedure for dealing with a national emergency dispute that remains unsettled at the end of the eighty-day waiting period is that the injunction is lifted, the workers are free to strike, and the President refers the case to Congress with any recommendations he sees fit to make. This somewhat anticlimactic terminal step has been widely condemned, but no alternative thus far suggested has won general support.

A review of the cases arising under the Act throws no direct light on the effectiveness of this feature of the law since no dispute has as yet been referred to Congress for action. Of the twelve cases in which the emergency machinery has been used, five remained unsettled after the eighty-day period was up. However, in three of these five cases (the atomic energy disputes of 1948 and 1954 and the Atlantic coast longshore dispute of 1948), active bargaining took place soon after the expiration of the waiting period, and settlements were reached on this basis. In the fourth, the Atlantic coast longshore case of 1953-1954, the representation issues between the "old" ILA and the "new" ILA-AFL were involved, and the fact that subsequently there was a wildcat strike and that the dispute dragged on for many months after the original injunction was dissolved on December 4, 1953, can hardly be attributed to any imperfections of the law.

In only one case, the west coast longshore dispute of 1948, was there no prospect of an immediate settlement through bargaining between the employers and union after the eighty-day period had ended. Even in this instance, however, President Truman did not take the last step in the emergency procedure. Meanwhile the strike continued, and finally, about two months after the injunction had been dissolved, a bargained settlement was achieved. One can only conjecture why the dispute was not referred to Congress in line with the terminal step procedure; presumably it was felt that the best hope was for the parties to reach an agreement on the same terms as those won earlier by other unions in other ports, the basis on which the strike was in fact finally settled.

There is little reason to believe that the prospect of congressional action served as an important catalytic agent, inducing the parties in these cases to arrive at settlements immediately before or after the expiration of the eighty-day period. What is more likely to have finally put the agreement-making process into high gear in these disputes was the prospect of a strike. The fact remains that the last step in the procedure left the disputants uncertain as to what to expect in the way of ultimate action, a prospect that was probably somewhat helpful in persuading them to work out their differences between themselves. This, however, carries the uncertainty thesis to indefensible lengths. In the highly charged atmosphere of a national emergency dispute, Congress can hardly be counted on to deal with the issues at stake in a calm and effective manner. A better approach would be to authorize the President to take whatever final action he deems appropriate, subject to such broad limitations or principles as Congress feels necessary to impose in advance.[24] This would avoid making the terminal step unduly rigid without at the same time forcing Congress to pass on the merits of individual cases.

While it would be unwise to put anything more specific in the law, careful thought should be given to what kind of action might be taken if, in a given case, all prior steps in the procedure were to prove unavailing. The variety of circumstances surrounding particular disputes, as well as the wide range of possible lines of action, makes generalizing about the matter most difficult. At one end of the spectrum is the type of case just on the border line between an emergency and a nonemergency dispute; at the other is the type which clearly threatens the nation's very existence. If the law's applicability were narrowed in the way indicated above, this range of difference would be greatly lessened but by no means eliminated. A strike in coal or steel, for example, might present the first kind of emergency and a strike in atomic energy production, the second. Accordingly, there might well be grounds for following a limited course of action in the former case, even to the point of permitting a strike, whereas in the latter, such an approach would be out of the question.

It would be a fatal blunder, however, to assume that some simple

[24] The only change in the terminal step which President Eisenhower proposed in his labor message to Congress in January 1954, was to give the President power to reconvene the boards of inquiry, and to have the latter make recommendations for resolving the disputes. See footnote 13.

formula can be devised (resort to a permanent injunction, seizure, compulsory arbitration, or what not) whereby strikes in this second category of industries could be prevented. If primary emphasis were placed on a flat prohibition of strikes in such situations, it is as certain as anything can be in this complex field that worker resentment would quickly mount and the program would soon be brought into disrepute. Rather, attention should be given to devising more positive, long-range measures for dealing with the particular problems facing workers and employers in such industries. This appears to be the approach being developed as a substitute for the strike weapon in atomic energy production, and it is one deserving serious consideration in other critically important industries.

CONCLUSIONS

While offering little basis for sweeping changes, this review of experience under the national emergency provisions of the Taft-Hartley Act points to a number of specific improvements which, if adopted, would considerably alter the way in which the law is now applied. The principal improvements recommended are the following:

1. Although no specific listing of industries would be advisable, the coverage of this section of the law should be narrowed to make sure that the national emergency procedures will be used only in disputes which present a clear and present danger to the national health and safety.

2. The boards of inquiry not only should be given the right to make recommendations but they should also be given considerable leeway in the manner in which they discharge their responsibilities.

3. The injunction should be dropped as a regular part of the procedure; if it is retained, it should be used only as a measure of last resort when one party or the other refuses to comply with the waiting period request by the President.

4. The final-offer ballot should be eliminated; presumably if this were done, the waiting period could be reduced from eighty to sixty days.

5. In place of the present terminal step, the President should be empowered to deal with unresolved disputes in the manner he

considers most appropriate, subject to whatever broad limitations Congress considers necessary.

These proposals are not so basic as to entail a major overhauling of this section of the Act. Chief reliance would still be placed on waiting periods and boards of inquiry to facilitate settlements, and after a certain time has elapsed the parties would normally be free to engage in a test of their economic strength. These changes would, however, entail a shift in emphasis away from reliance on certain formal prohibitions and rigid procedures to a more flexible and imaginative use of third-party techniques. In any event, whether or not these changes are made, the crux of the matter is the spirit in which the law will be administered. If the emergency procedures are applied in a manner which is in any way vindictive or arbitrary, it would be idle to consider whether particular features of the law should be altered. In the last analysis, success or failure of the emergency disputes procedures will depend largely on whether workers and employers feel that the law is being administered in a fair and constructive way.

PART III

WHAT ARE THE ELEMENTS
OF A NATIONAL POLICY?

The preceding essays in definition and experience have laid the foundation for a discussion of policy in emergency disputes. Chapter IX evaluates procedural flexibility within the framework of prevailing public opinion. An illustration of the industry-by-industry approach is examined for atomic energy in Chapter X. Various unconventional devices are assessed in Chapter XI: the statutory strike, compulsory arbitration, some state public utility laws, and industry panels. In Chapter XII the possibilities and limits of seizure are weighed. Finally, Chapter XIII suggests the location of authority for national dispute settlement in a government resting upon the separation of powers.

THE "CHOICE-OF-PROCEDURES" APPROACH

TO NATIONAL EMERGENCY DISPUTES

BY W. WILLARD WIRTZ

Stevenson, Wirtz, Blair, and Minow

One possible conclusion from the debate about whether "emergency labor disputes" should be handled by injunction, seizure, compulsory arbitration, fact finding, or mediation is that the answer to this riddle lies perhaps less in any one of these devices than it does in all of them. Increasing emphasis is being placed upon "flexibility" as the essential quality in any satisfactory governmental approach to national crisis resulting from a collective bargaining stalemate. The key feature of a number of recent proposals is that the executive agency charged with responsibility in this area should be authorized to invoke, in a particular case, not a single preordained procedure but rather any one of several procedures.

This line of thinking starts from the simple fact that the elements in labor disputes, their causes and consequences, are invariably different. "Emergency" and "dispute" and "public interest" are being recognized as imprecise words, and "emergency dispute" as a term which is meaningless because it can mean so many different things. Experience with the procedure established in Title II of the Taft-Hartley Act has revealed its basic defect as being the prescription of a single form of compulsion for all "emergency disputes," regardless of circumstance or broader equities. There is a growing sense that there has been committed here the old mistake of assuming that since the language offers a single phrase to label a set of troubles, there must be a single remedy available to cure them.

These proposals for flexible procedures depend, too, upon a more subtle and refined logic. If the function of government in the area of industrial dispute were simply to stop strikes when the public interest becomes sufficiently affected, there would appear neither need nor justification for consideration of a variety of procedures. The labor injunction does that job, usually with great dispatch. If, at the other extreme, government's function here were to fix the terms upon which arguments will be settled, then some form of compulsory arbitration would be the only thing worth talking about. The "choice of procedures" theory develops from the reasoning that the function of government in this area is neither just to stop a fight nor to settle an argument, but is rather to implement and possibly even to force the settlement of serious disputes *by the collective bargaining process*. It is realization of the protean nature of collective bargaining and of the desirability of making this process work even in crisis which gives the argument of governmental "flexibility" whatever strength it has.

Americans are fond of reiterating the oneness of labor and management interests, the interdependence of their prosperity. The truth expressed here is likely to obscure the equal truth that there are real differences as to how this oneness of interest is to be effectuated. A thousand pies are to be cut, with no scientific or unalterable way of cutting them. The identity of interests really creates only an area of latitude within which there is room for serious differences of opinion. These differences may be resolved in various ways. Russian labor and management are today denied independent status; all questions are resolved by government fiat. Germany experiments with codetermination. The British have been having a go at nationalization. We in the United States have settled, for the time being at least, on the theory that even with its defects, collective bargaining best fits our idea and ideal of free economic institutions.

The essential quality of collective bargaining theory is that the "right" answers are those which are produced by the pressure of grouped ("collective") economic forces upon each other, dollars grouped in the corporate employer on the one hand, employees grouped in the union on the other. The rightness of the answers is defined, at least tentatively, in terms of the process which is relied upon to produce them. And it is recognized that, for better or for worse, the components of economic force which press against each other will vary widely with the various industries in which the bargaining process is used. There are basic differences in the character, financial structure, business prospects, organization, immediacy of public dependency, and degree of regulation in the coal, steel, transportation, and atomic energy industries. The forces which will exert pressure toward settlement in collective bargaining conferences in one industry will be ineffective or even nonexistent in another. Coal can be easily stored, and the industry is plagued by overproduction. Yet in transportation the situation is different, for there the nation's economic lifeblood flows through these arteries every minute and hour of the year. So "collective bargaining" too emerges as a single phrase covering an infinite variety of relationships—and basically dependent for its acceptance upon full realization that it is a form of letting free enterprise pursue freedom's essentially unscheduled course.

The "emergency dispute" issue becomes, in one way of stating it, whether the government will, when crisis results from private collective bargaining, turn to a form of compulsion or decision making lying entirely outside the collective bargaining scheme, or will, in the alternative, seek by special devices to make the bargaining process work despite the difficulties which have arisen. The case for the choice-of-procedures approach rests on the propositions that collective bargaining can and should be made to work even in these crises, but that this can be accomplished only if whatever governmental participation becomes necessary is geared to the essentially variable quality in the collective bargaining process. The corollary of this is, as has been stated, that the proper function of government in these cases is not just to stop an argument, nor to fix the terms for resolving it, but to implement its settlement by the parties themselves through the collective bargaining process.

THE 1949-1950 COAL CASE

Whatever substance there may be in these generalizations will better emerge by consideration, necessarily brief, of a specific case. The 1949-1950 coal case commends itself for this purpose not only for its illustration of the deadening effect upon collective bargaining of the single-compulsion form of governmental interposition in the dispute, but also because attempts were made in that case to introduce a kind of administrative "flexibility."[1]

The 1949-1950 coal strike went on, in one form or another, for about a year. Before it was over, the coal supply situation had become sufficiently acute that the Interstate Commerce Commission ordered reductions in train service, "coal emergencies" were declared in several states and by a number of cities, and scattered schools and institutions closed for lack of heat. Private collective bargaining had operated with notable ineffectiveness. Months of glaring across various tables had yielded what the presidential board of inquiry was subsequently to describe as "only a 'fantastic' assortment of vague demands"; the real issues had seemingly been buried deeper and deeper, while "the parties stood alternately in ceremonious insistence upon what would invariably be described subsequently as 'conditions precedent.'" The miners had kept insisting that agreement upon a wage increase was the "condition precedent" to any discussion of nonwage issues. The operators had been equally adamantine in demanding settlement of union security and other nonwage issues before they would discuss wages.

Special significance attaches to what happened at a collective bargaining session between the northern operators and the United Mine Workers Union on February 2, 1950. There, after these long months of sparring, union representatives made the following motion:

The mine workers move that we proceed to negotiate a contract and that in the negotiations all matters before the conference are subjects

[1] The author of this chapter was a member of the presidential board of inquiry in this 1949-1950 coal case. Comments made about it here are restricted to those for which there is basis in the published reports of the proceedings of that board.

for consideration and negotiation and are not to be considered as conditions precedent to agreement.[2]

Upon the introduction of this resolution, the operators withdrew from the conference.

Relatively close attention to the development of the 1949-1950 coal controversy warrants the conclusion that the union resolution at the February 2 session reflected a serious intention and desire to proceed finally with bargaining, which had been all form and no substance for the preceding ten or twelve months. There is similar basis for the conclusion that the operators' withdrawal from this conference reflected a decision that their bargaining position would be stronger if they waited the additional few days which were bound to bring presidential intervention under the Taft-Hartley Act and a consequent injunction against the strike in effect at that time.

A casting of moral judgments would permit the conclusion that the "fault" basic to the crucial February 2 development was that the union had waited to make its move until it was sure of rejection, that the government should have invoked the Taft-Hartley Act earlier, or that the operators' withdrawal was wholly unwarranted. But no moral judgment is either warranted or intended here. The point is simply this: Just when the 1949-1950 coal negotiations had reached a promising stage, bargaining broke down because one party recognized that its own inaction would result in the issuance of an injunction against the other party. The result, at least in part a product of the statutory inflexibility, was that there was no further bargaining in the ordinary sense.

The presidential board of inquiry was set up four days later. It resorted, in connection with the discharge of its fact-finding function, to what could probably be considered a minor experiment in flexible execution of the statutory obligation. Dispensing with the usual routine public hearings of statements by the parties, the board directed them instead to sit down and bargain—with the board members as observers. This was done. The "observed bargaining" session went on for eight hours.

This administrative tactic was reasonably successful so far as

[2] *The Labor Dispute in the Bituminous Coal Industry*, Report to the President, submitted by the Board of Inquiry under Executive Order 10106 (February 11, 1950), pp. 4-5.

uncovering the basic issues (mainly money) and assessing responsibility (mutual) for the bargaining difficulties were concerned. This was at least partly, it may be guessed, because the parties couldn't quite make out what the board was up to, and accordingly cooperated fully because of a vague fear of the unknown price of any other course of action. But if there was expectation that this observed bargaining might also conceivably bring about a break in the negotiation stalemate, that hope was frustrated. No agreement was reached. The board filed its sterile report on February 11, and an injunction was issued against the strike immediately thereafter.

There can be no way of *proving* that the failure of collective bargaining efforts in the four weeks following the February 2 meeting in the 1950 coal case was a consequence of the statutory procedures. It is a subjective judgment that it was, although there is the obvious fact, too, that this stalemate did not set in with the institution of the statutory proceedings but had been going on for many months before. Throughout this crucial four-week period, the parties' attention was occupied by a whole series of legal developments which had nothing to do with the merits of the bargaining controversy: the issuance of a preliminary injunction, later of a more permanent order, the contempt hearing when the miners refused to go back to work, and then the court's ruling acquitting the union. There can be only conjecture as to whether these goings-on slowed up what would otherwise have been the pace of collective bargaining. To one thing, however, the record bears ample witness: Nothing done in the carrying out of the Taft-Hartley Act procedures hastened the settlement of the 1950 coal case by so much as an hour.

The circumstances of the final settlement of that case offer one additional element of possible relevance to the consideration of the efficacy of more flexible governmental procedures. Perhaps that settlement came as the result solely of economic forces or of the working out of the well-laid plans of shrewd bargainers, unaffected by anything the government did or didn't do. Yet it seems more than coincidence that the settlement which was reached finally on March 3 coincided almost to the hour with the President's transmission to Congress of a recommendation that the mines be seized. There had been leaks and rumors and some direct reports of the plans for such seizure for several days before. The parties to the dispute had obtained relatively clear pictures of what the terms of seizure would be. The chairman of the board of inquiry had been kept in close touch, as a specially designated White House representative, with the progress or lack of progress in the bargaining between the operators and the union. The general assumption was that the terms of the anticipated seizure would be geared in one way or another to the parties' bargaining positions. It seems a reasonable conclusion, although again a subjective one, that the prospect of governmental seizure was an important factor in affecting the timing and perhaps even something of the terms of the eventual 1950 coal dispute settlement.

This history has dual relevance to the present discussion. It illustrates the either neutral or negative effect of the Taft-Hartley Act emergency dispute provisions on the bargaining to which they are applied. It offers, beyond that, what is perhaps the closest approximation in federal government experience to the use of a choice-of-procedures approach. There was fact finding here, mediation, an injunction, and finally threatened seizure.

The possible significance of the record of governmental participation in the 1950 coal case lies in its suggestion that a procedure only slightly different from the one improvised by the board of inquiry and the President's office would have offered promise of substantial effectiveness. The difficulty was that from the time the board met, and even before, everyone knew exactly what the government representatives had to do and what they could not do—regardless of what the circumstances might seem to warrant. These predetermined procedures were in no way instruments for implementing or forcing collective bargaining. Because they were predetermined, they had lost their effectiveness.

It is reasonable to believe that if the 1950 board of inquiry had had, as it met with the parties, power to make a report recommending that any of a *variety* of dispute-settling procedures be followed, the union and the operators would have settled that case in early February (when the board met with them) instead of a month later. It may be seriously doubted whether, going back a step in the proceedings, the operators would have withdrawn from that February 2 bargaining conference if they had known that the consequent governmental intervention might take the form of *either* an injunction against the union *or* seizure of the properties. It seems a conservative judgment that the intransigence of both parties in that case could have been substantially broken by responsible mediatory approaches by governmental representatives clothed with the authority to recommend publicly the institution of whatever procedures—injunction, seizure, fact finding with recommendations, compulsory arbitration—would have been considered best fitted to the circumstances if the intransigence persisted. The likelihood is that no actual resort to any of those courses would have proved necessary. The area of agreement which the parties found in a brief, ninety-minute session on March 3 was equally existent a month earlier, and there is fair reason to believe it would have been found then if the alternative had been the risking of uncertain procedural consequences.

ALTERNATIVES TO THE TAFT-HARTLEY APPROACH

There is, aside from this record of improvisation in the 1949-1950 coal case, little basis in actual experience for evaluating the merits and weaknesses of the choice-of-procedures approach to national emergency labor disputes. Massachusetts adopted legislation in 1947 (amended in 1954) which empowers the governor to use, virtually at his discretion, the instruments of mediation, what is almost compulsory arbitration, seizure, or a combination of these. This statute is discussed in some detail in Chapter XI of this volume. But there has been virtually no occasion yet to test the Massachusetts law, and it stands almost alone on the nation's statute books. Consideration of this general type of approach is, as a consequence, necessarily restricted to an abstract kind of analysis of its various possible implications.

Judgment regarding any governmental disputes-settling procedure can be meaningful only in terms of alternatives. If the alternatives are (1) a statutory prescription that an injunction be obtained in all cases, or (2) a legislative authorization to the executive to use whichever of several procedures appears most appropriate in a particular case, the reasoning which supports the choice-of-procedures approach seems to find much firmer ground.

THE INJUNCTION

Support for the exclusive use of the injunction is based primarily (where something more is reflected than an uncomplicated feeling that unions are evil) on the feeling that the government's only appropriate function in an emergency of this kind is to stop its *immediate* cause (the strike) and that this is properly accomplished in the most direct manner available and without reference to fault, equity, or other consequence. It is questionable whether the injunction will in fact always work more quickly to restore production than would other procedures. But even if it did, there would remain the question of whether this gain of a few hours would warrant doing this much violence to the institution of collective bargaining and to the established traditions of freedom of enterprise from governmental interference. A cataloguing of the experience of democratic capitalism reveals that we have in the main accepted painful kicks in our economic shins as the price of letting private economic units settle their arguments in rough and tumble style, and further that where we have felt compelled to deny to one or another such unit the power to use its economic force, we have almost always set up an alternative procedure (as in the rate-setting procedures for utilities) for determining the issue which would otherwise have been determined by the use of that force.

Collective bargaining is the only process we recognize for settling industrial disputes. Where its functioning seems to break down, the appropriate government obligation would appear to be not just to order the argument stopped—on one party's terms—but rather to take whatever steps are available to make the parties themselves reach in timely fashion that solution to their dispute which experience shows has always been the eventual product of bargaining. And if the collective bargaining process is to be pliant, the government's hand must be free to act with discretion in aiding the parties to reach agreement.

FLEXIBILITY AND UNLIMITED EXECUTIVE POWER

Account must be taken of the protest that the choice-of-procedures type of law would create in the executive department that kind of discretion in the exercise of power which permits of its corruption. There can be no complete answer to this criticism. Yet it must be kept clear that the only practicable measure of the misuse of power is in terms of its effect upon the subjects of that use. When, under the present law, a strike is stopped by an injunction, the exercise of governmental power is no less real for its having been authorized by a statute passed years earlier by Congress. If that injunction is either unfair or ineffective as applied to the particular case, the evil of the exercise of centralized power is no less than if it resulted from either the inadvertent or malicious error of an executive or judicial officer armed with discretionary authority to apply the injunction. There is as much power exercised in the one case as in the other, and the automaticity regulating the form of its exercise in the one instance is as great a potential source of injustice as is the possible abuse of discretion in the other. It has not been shown, and is probably not true, that the exercise of executive discretion in these situations would result in greater unfairness than does automatic application of a single legislative prescription. It does not appeal to reason to argue that recourse in all household emergencies to a particular bottle of patent medicine avoids the possibility of human error which arises if the doctor is called in.

The danger of abuse of executive power under "flexible" procedures is nonetheless real, however, for having its parallels. There has accordingly been a good deal of attention to various devices for counteracting or at least limiting this danger. These involve, in general, proposals for distribution of various parts of the function among different offices of government and for conducting the various procedures as openly as possible, probably with the participation of "public" representatives.

COMPULSORY ARBITRATION AND SEIZURE

Another criticism of the choice-of-procedures proposals is that the choice includes not only the injunction, which defeats collective bargaining in one way, but the alternatives of compulsory arbitration and seizure, which would defeat it in another. Here again there can be, in the absence of actual experiment, no completely confident answer to this reaction. It is essential that it be recognized, however, that the theory behind these proposals is that the availability of a variety of stern governmental devices will reduce the likelihood of any of them, or at least the worst of them, actually being used. There is in a sense a parallel here to the history of recent thinking about that other field of force. The nation grew up on the theory that building armaments was playing with matches, yet is moving now into adulthood on the perhaps desperate premise that armed power offers the only assurance that the arms will not have to be used.

MEDIATION AND MEDIATION PLUS

Mediation is accepted by the choice-of-procedures proponents as the form of governmental activity most compatible with collective bargaining. Their argument is that mediation will be more effective where the much less palatable alternatives of injunction *or* seizure *or* compulsory arbitration loom in the background. It was not seizure, but the *threat* of seizure, which seemed to break the deadlock in the 1949-1950 coal case. There is a good deal of reasonableness in the argument that a mediator would be better equipped to persuade, and the parties more inclined to accept persuasion or to make their own peace on their own terms, if that persuasion were backed up by power to institute alternative procedures if it failed. And it takes a strangely strong feeling about such a measure as compulsory arbitration wholly to understand the objection to it where every conceivable opportunity for reaching agreement in a national emergency has failed.

Recognizing the emphasis in the choice-of-procedures proposals on the central importance of the mediation process requires taking account of the possibility that the "best" answer in this troubled area may be a law providing only for mediation itself. Some of the most thoughtful students of the emergency disputes problem who have also had the fullest actual experience with it urge that there should be no law in this area except one recognizing the government's responsibility to bring the parties together and to reason with them—with no provision for added trimmings which might conceivably be helpful to the mediator in certain cases but which might also complicate his problem seriously in others.

Those who take this position of reliance solely on mediation oppose as strongly as do the choice-of-procedures advocates such arrangements as that embodied in the present statutory requirement for automatic imposition in all cases of an injunction. They sub-

scribe equally to the idea that flexibility is a basically essential element in any governmental disputes-settling policy, and to the notion
that the government's function even in these emergency cases is
not just to stop a strike but to implement the settlement of the
dispute by the parties themselves. The line between the two points
of view is actually a thin one. This becomes clear in the light of
the suggestion by those who would like to see the law provide only
for mediation that if there is ever a "real" emergency which mediation cannot temper, the Congress will undoubtedly step in with
some special legislative order, and if it doesn't, the President will.
So in a sense the difference is only between two approaches both
primarily and basically dependent on mediation, both equally
insistent upon creating broad governmental discretion, but one of
which would provide in advance for certain last-resort procedures
while the other would leave this matter entirely open until an
emergency actually materializes.

In one important respect, however, the choice-of-procedures type
of proposal meets an element of need which the exclusive reliance
on mediation fails to recognize. There is a prevailing attitude on
the part of people generally today—a "public" view—that the law
should include some kind of firm insurance against work stoppages
in essential industries. The attraction of the injunction is that it
satisfies this general feeling, regardless of how unfair and ineffective it may actually prove in practice. And "mediation," especially
when its nature as a form only of persuasion—without compulsion
—is explained, falls far short of filling the prevailing public conception of the need which is involved here. It is part of the recommendation of the choice-of-procedures approach that it may both
satisfy the public idea of the kind of thing that is needed to meet
the emergency disputes problem and at the same time provide
what is essentially a mediation process.

THE ROLE OF PUBLIC OPINION

It seems worth insisting that the popular reactions to a matter
of this kind cannot properly be ignored, even though they may
conceivably be the products of what experts in the field consider
regrettable lack of complete understanding.

An illustrative and only suggestive listing of some public attitudes which may well be "wrong" but which, nevertheless, probably prevail very generally would include these: that we have had some serious national emergency labor disputes; that an emergency exists when the newspapers say it does; that the causes of emergencies which take the form of stoppages of production in essential industries are strikes rather than whatever causes strikes; that union demands are in general more likely to be unreasonable than management offers; that the monetary loss of a strike to the strikers will never be made up; that stopping a major interruption of the national economy is more important than the terms on which it is stopped; that even compulsory arbitration is better than permitting a "dangerous" strike to continue; that governmental interference with the operation of market-place forces is not nearly so bad where the subject of control is a labor union as where it is a corporation; that the function of law is to offer certainty of results.

The popular subscription to some of these attitudes is more general than it is to others, and so probably is the degree of rational justification for them. Some of them are undoubtedly reflections of the hypnotic influence upon people's minds of the respectability associated with the preservation of the status quo, with good manners, and with the avoidance of unpleasant showdowns. No argument falls on deafer ears than the wholly rational one that a strike represents simply a *mutual* decision by employer and employee that *neither* will, for the time being, accept the other's offer regarding the price for the sale and purchase of the employees' services.

The proper functioning of democracy neither requires nor permits that the nation's lawmaking should proceed from a 100 per cent acceptance of every 51 per cent public attitude regardless of its quality. Yet it would be equally unjustifiable to proceed to the working out of a national emergency dispute procedure in disregard of popular notions on the ground either that logic denies them or that labor and management groups agree in rejecting them. Account is properly taken of the possible error which may result from attaching more significance to the viewpoints—rational or irrational—of democratic capitalism's producers than to the viewpoints—rational or irrational—of its consumers. We in this country are much more highly organized and much more articulate in our capacity as producers than we are (except possibly through government) in our capacity as consumers. It is good sense, therefore, to question particularly our "producer" conclusions to see how they check against our "consumer" interests. Even the virtual unanimity of labor, management, and "labor expert" rejection in this country of the idea, for example, of "compulsory arbitration" may well be tested against (1) the probable fact that the overwhelming public sentiment would prefer such a procedure to a costly strike, (2) the fact that the history of democratic capitalism's maturation has been marked by the substitution of other arbitraments for that of force, even economic force, and (3) the fact that a number of the other democracies have accepted systems embodying some form of compulsory arbitration. It is possible to be persuaded in one's own mind that compulsory arbitration is wrong, and yet to feel at the same time real doubt as to the roots of the conclusion.

It has become a kind of badge of sophistication in trade or learned discussion of emergency labor disputes to remark that "of course, we have never actually had an emergency labor dispute anyway." This is part of the labor leader's argument against the Taft-Hartley Title II injunction, and becomes the management spokesman's gambit when the talk shifts around to seizure or compulsory arbitration. The more neutral (whatever that means) advocate of no law or of a law establishing only mediation procedures constructs a completely convincing argument that there is really no right to strike in this country which would carry beyond the period of adequate supply of the commodity involved, because the country would rise up in unholy wrath if it were actually deprived of anything it has to have. Figures and facts are assembled to show that emergency labor disputes are created not by the bullheadedness of labor or management units but by legislatures which pass laws setting up special procedures for handling emergency disputes. "Show me," the argument goes, "when this country's economy has ever *really* been hurt by a strike."

Again it needs to be suggested that the expert's proof that we have never had a real emergency strike is probably less important than the fact that the public thinks we have. There is reminder here of the limerick:

> There was a faith healer from Diehl
> Who said, "I know pain isn't real

But when I puncture my skin
With the point of a pin,
I dislike what I fancy I feel."

Not only is the public (a group reaction as real in its effect as it is elusive in its definition) completely persuaded that there have been some nasty emergency labor disputes; it is also irrevocably committed to the view, whether naive or not, that it wants something definite done to see to it that there are no more of them.

Although most individual members of this "public" would articulate their objection to nationwide strikes in terms of economic consequences, it may conceivably be that the bridge across the gap between expert analysis and lay reaction is a realization of some of the noneconomic implications and effects of such strikes. If it be conceded that the 1949-1950 experience in the coal industry, to return to that example, did not actually hurt the nation economically, there remains the question of what it did to the country's psychology. There would be no way of proving the proposition that that experience and others like it have done quite a lot to set back the eventual and inevitable fitting of labor unions into their appointed places as accepted democratic institutions. Yet it seems relatively clear that unfounded antagonisms, not just toward particular unions but toward unionism generally, are fed by every major crisis of this kind. It seems very likely that these few cases, more distorted than reported in 90 per cent of the nation's press, create the attitudes in people's minds which are then communicated by democracy's sensitive processes to their legislative representatives and which control the thinking, or at least the voting, of those representatives when the subject of amending the labor laws next arises. It is not wholly fancy that prompts conjecture as to whether, if there had been no nationwide labor disputes in the past ten years, there would have been a Taft-Hartley Act, a seven-year stalemate on its amendment, or the present aberrational rash of "right-to-work" laws.

Account may well be taken of whether there are not, in these occasional crises, even contributions to a class consciousness sort of reaction which every responsible citizen of a democracy deplores. One wonders, too, what unmeasurable weakening of democracy's essential sinews results from what seem to be exposures of its government's inability to deal effectively with the exercise of private group power.

These are *not* arguments for the coal miners or for any other group of employees not pressing to the limit for whatever improvements in their terms and conditions of employment seem to them proper. It is absolutely essential that they be free to do so. The question is only as to the realism of the suggestion that we need no emergency dispute legislation because there has never yet been a really lethal emergency dispute. This realism seems incomplete, or at least no sufficient argument for not seeing to it that the cases which do arise, whatever they may be called, are dealt with in a manner best designed to take account of *all* their implications.

PROBLEMS OF FLEXIBILITY

It is by no means clear that the choice-of-procedures kind of proposal offers the ultimate promise in this connection. To take account of the special importance of public reactions in this field is to realize that these proposals, too, present real problems in this connection. The laws they call for would necessarily provide for what will appear to be complex procedures, not easily described or understood. This makes them susceptible to editorial or political attack in which a single feature, lifted from its context, can be used effectively to discredit the whole proposal. The adoption and retention of the automatic injunction procedure in the present law attests the fact that as the economy and society become more complex, and as the right answers become increasingly complicated, the wrong but simple answers enjoy a growing advantage in the political arena. There is, similarly, enough substance to the point about the danger of abuse of the discretionary authority contemplated by these plans to increase their vulnerability to political opposition. When the Democratic candidate for the Presidency outlined a kind of choice-of-procedures emergency dispute plan during the 1952 campaign, it was condemned in the newspaper editorial columns as a grasping for an absolute kind of executive power. This was too rich fare for a political campaign, for there was no opportunity to go into details which would have been necessary to answer the broadside of criticism. Although legislative councils would permit of fuller exploration of such details, there would remain a considerable degree of danger on this score.

Such a statute would not, furthermore, wholly satisfy people's expectations for certainty from the law. If the answer to the question "What happens if there is a nationwide strike?" must start out "Well, that depends," a good many minds will not even entertain the rest of the explanation. People think of the law too much as something that ought to offer definite answers, recognizing it too little as an instrument for living with some problems to which there can be no clear or certain answers. Here again the nation's acceptance of the Taft-Hartley injunction formula illustrates the prospect that even a law offering bad answers will be accepted, if those answers are specific, in preference to a law which simply lays out an approach to seeking the right answers in the particular facts of a situation when it arises.

CONCLUSION

There is no justification here, however, for the cynicism of a conclusion that there just isn't any good answer to this problem. Recognition of the political difficulties which must be anticipated in seeking the adoption of a better type of legislation does not mean that any of them are insuperable. The Massachusetts law offers promise of constructive experience. The increasing acceptance throughout the American body politic not only of the fact of powerful trade unions but also of their infinite potential for good is laying the basis for more objective consideration of what to do about such matters as "emergency disputes."

If the question is whether Congress is likely to adopt, this year or the next or the year following, a definitive, sound, and popular law for the handling of labor disputes, the answer must be that there is no likelihood of this. If the question is whether there is one of these choice-of-procedures formulas which offers a pat solution to this problem, the answer must be that there is no such formula. But if the question is where it seems most worth looking for guiding stars behind the clouds that fill this particular sky, it seems a fair conclusion that there is special promise in some of these proposals for establishing a pattern for flexible approach to emergency when it arises, instead of trying to fix in advance a single invariable set of compulsions to be applied regardless of what the facts and circumstances may be.

· X ·

THE EMERGENCY IS NORMAL—

ATOMIC ENERGY*

BY J. KEITH MANN
Stanford University

This is 1955. Already a decade has passed since Hiroshima. The great bomb, as it seemed such a short while ago, jolted us into having to care and to think about the perplexing problems of atomic and nuclear energy. One of those problems is the adjustment of the employment relationship for those engaged in the atomic energy program. Here, too, the awesome nature of the product has had its influence. Distinctive procedures were developed for handling conflicts between labor and management in the program. These procedures and other approaches to disputes settlement are common to the point of comparison, different to that of significance. Therefore it is proposed to describe the special disputes machinery devised for the atomic energy field and to examine its present relation to generalized national labor policy.

While to our atomic beginnings we may stand so close as to be far, we have a mind's eye view of emergency disputes in such industries as coal, steel, and railroads. These disputes are apt to have a drama and ritual of their own. The mine and mill and shop where they occur are part of the American scene. The powerful councils of the principals are familiar. By contrast, conflicts be-

* The writer wishes to acknowledge the helpful assistance of Stewart Macaulay, LL.B. Stanford, 1955, in the preparation of this chapter.

tween labor and management—or perhaps one should say, among labor, management, and the government—in atomic energy have rarely come to the center of the stage. Only the initiated can chart the course of collective bargaining in this program which came from nowhere, which operates in an aura of mystery, and which may develop in directions that now can be only dimly perceived. As would be anticipated in our crisis democracy, debates over national labor policy in this area have been carried on to date in a relatively low key.

Thus, no more than a preliminary appraisal can be ventured at this time, and especially by anyone far removed from the center of gravity of disputes settlement in the atomic energy program. This is doubly the case because of the emphasis on informality of procedures to be discussed. Moreover, a baptism in Washington or in the field makes one view with caution inferences drawn from the formalized record of official reports. Many nuances are thereby missed.

Although the great strikes and debates have occurred elsewhere, there is an authentic conjunction between the theme of this volume and the problem of handling conflicts between labor and management in the atomic energy program. As in industry generally, there is the acute problem of defining the scope of the emergency dispute. There is, in addition, the problem as to the method by which stoppages within the acknowledged area of emergency are to be controlled.

Where one comes out on questions of this nature is likely to be guided, if not determined, by where one goes in. If unions are selected and recognized as the representatives of employees, we are accustomed to thinking of disputes which may arise between labor and management as being settled through the collective bargaining process. Today that process approaches a felt tradition. It is believed that our conventional analysis is sound: a possible resort to strike or lockout is inherent in the working out of mutually acceptable terms and conditions of employment; and this for the elementary reason that the necessary incentive toward compromise is missing if there is no possibility of withholding services or denying demands. This is a freedom equally essential to labor and to management. It is a cost paid for the basic value of the collective bargaining institution—self-determination of the terms and conditions of employment which are to prevail.

The assumption of collective bargaining as a "norm" does not mean that it may not fail. But even if that occurs, the study of criteria for defining a "true" emergency dispute and of techniques for resolving it premises an attitude toward the public interest in preserving collective bargaining. That attitude negates the thought that all or, indeed, even a small precentage of disputes which may arise are to be classified as emergency in nature or that specialized procedures shall be available for their settlement. An emergency is by definition abnormal.

What happens, then, when collective bargaining is placed in an environment in which the temptation is to call every dispute an emergency and in which the risk of the occasional excesses of private negotiation is thought to be exceedingly high?

THE BACKGROUND OF BARGAINING IN ATOMIC ENERGY

The formative years during which a policy on the labor relations phase of the atomic energy program was being shaped have been described and analyzed effectively elsewhere. The excellent study by Donald B. Straus, *The Development of a Policy for Industrial Peace in Atomic Energy*,[1] is a solid foundation upon which others may aspire to build.[2] The Straus monograph is concerned with the

---

[1] *Planning Pamphlet No. 71* (Washington: National Planning Association, July, 1950). In the preface to his recent one-volume work on Lincoln, Carl Sandburg quotes James G. Randall as having stated that "footnotes should be held guilty unless proved innocent." While sharing the aversion to the iceberg approach, much is put under water here because this chapter is a call for study of certain questions believed important at this time. It is hoped that the practice ultimately will be deemed more a help than an affectation.

[2] Only a few studies dealing in detail with labor-management relations in atomic energy were found. Such studies include Dale G. Fallon, "A Study of Public Policy in the Field of Labor Management Relations Under the Atomic Energy Act of 1946," (Ph.D. thesis, Notre Dame University, 1952); James R. Newman, "The Atomic Energy Industry: An Experiment in Hybridization," *Yale Law Journal*, LX (December, 1951), pp. 1263, 1364-1388; William H. Davis, "Labor-Management Relations in Atomic Energy Affairs," in *Atomic Energy Industrial and Legal Problems* (Ann Arbor: University of Michigan, 1952), pp. 97-105; see also Robert A. Dahl and Ralph S. Brown, Jr., *Domestic Control of Atomic Energy* (New York: Social Science Research Council, 1951), p. 67. Studies examining collective bargaining and community impact of particular AEC installations, with special emphasis on the construction phase, are:

period ending June 1, 1950.[2a] As detailed in this and in the other sources cited, before Hiroshima no trade unions were permitted in operating facilities in the program. Conferences carried on between the highest officials of the federal government and the leaders of the CIO and AFL resulted in an understanding that for security reasons there would be no organizing activity attempted on research and operations facilities of the so-called Manhattan Engineering District. Traditional closed-shop understandings and recruitment through union channels marked the construction phase.[3] In March 1946, the Secretary of War informed the National Labor Relations Board that union organization and Board certification of bargaining units at Oak Ridge were possible, but the wartime ban was con-

---

Bureau of Labor Statistics, *Labor and The Savannah River AEC Project*, Bull. No. 1100 (1952) (this study was made by M. Mead Smith and also appears in the June, July, August, and September 1952, issues of the *Monthly Labor Review*); L. Reed Tripp, J. Keith Mann, and Frederick T. Downs, *Labor-Management Relations in the Paducah Area of Western Kentucky* (Lexington: University of Kentucky, 1954). A private organization, the Atomic Industrial Forum, Inc., supplies much material on current developments in a monthly memorandum restricted in circulation to its members. The principal government sources relating directly to this matter are: The Semiannual Reports of the AEC, 1-17 (1947-1955), which include as appendices when appropriate the periodic "Report to the President by the Atomic Energy Labor Relations Panel"; Federal Mediation and Conciliation Service, *Sixth Annual Report* (1954); *First Annual Report to the President by the Atomic Energy Labor-Management Relations Panel*, July 1, 1953, to June 30, 1954 (published 1955); *Labor Policy in Atomic Energy Plants*, Hearings, Joint Committee on Atomic Energy, 80th Cong., 2d sess. (1948), pt. 1; *Recommendations on Labor Relations Policy in Atomic Energy Installations*, Hearings, Subcommittee of the Joint Committee on Atomic Energy, 81st Cong., 1st sess. (1949); Atomic Energy Commission, *Report of the President's Commission on Labor Relations in the Atomic Energy Installations* (April 1949); *Collective Bargaining Representation at Atomic Energy Installations* (mimeo., 1949); *Employment Practices at Savannah River Project*, Report pursuant to H.R. 73, Special Subcommittee on Labor Relations to the Committee on Education and Labor, 82d Cong., 2d sess. (1952). A rich source of current material on activities of the Atomic Energy Labor-Management Relations Panel, collective bargaining activity at AEC installations, NLRB proceedings, etc., is made available in a Newsletter prepared by the Organization and Personnel Division of the AEC.

[2a] Since this chapter was written a penetrating analysis by a member of the AEC staff of the program to date has become available. David B. Johnson, "Labor-Management Relations in the Atomic Energy Program" (Ph.D. thesis, University of Wisconsin, 1955).

[3] Straus, *op. cit.*, pp. 8-10; *Ninth Semiannual Report of AEC* (1951), pp. 75-76.

tinued as to other installations.[4] Both AFL and CIO unions won representation rights at Oak Ridge. This introduction of collective bargaining into the atomic energy program occurred only shortly before the passage of the Atomic Energy Act of 1946 and the resultant transfer of the facilities to the civilian control of the Commission. It became incumbent upon the Atomic Energy Commission to develop a labor relations policy.

The problems confronting the Commission were great. As a starting point, there was the premise of continuity of operations. It had to be accepted on faith from the Commission and the Joint Committee on Atomic Energy that at this time even a momentary work stoppage on basic construction, operations, and laboratory facilities was against the national interest.[5] From the beginning the concept of the emergency dispute in atomic energy was that it included all; and this without regard to whether a dispute arose over a grievance or new agreement, of whatever issue, scope, or duration. Nevertheless, it was assumed that there was "a place for, and a need for, organized labor in the atomic energy program."[6] The great responsibilities of the Atomic Energy Commission led it to propose policy objectives containing an apparent contradiction of collective bargaining without the threat of work stoppages. Because of the framework of the Atomic Energy Act of 1946 and for efficiency of operation, it wished to have industrial participation in its program rather than direct government operation. Industry

[4] The letter is contained in *Labor Policy in Atomic Energy Plants,* pp. 132-133.

[5] It is not possible in this chapter to discuss individual disputes. It may be noted, however, that the introduction of collective bargaining at Oak Ridge proved difficult and led to hearings before the Joint Committee early in 1948. See footnote 16. The Commission made a "Report on Labor Problems Relating to Continuity of Production in the Atomic Energy Commission Program." Chairman Lilienthal stated his belief that "solutions can be found which are in keeping with the traditions of American labor-management relations." The report suggested that continuing study be given to the question of whether "special legal sanctions or other special means of enforcement should be provided for an Atomic Energy Commission labor policy. . . ." *Labor Policy in Atomic Energy Plants,* p. 117. A typical statement of the Joint Committee's point of departure was that of the then chairman, Senator Hickenlooper: "The Committee has already determined that . . . the continuity of operation of . . . facilities is vital in the public interest. That question has already been decided. . . ." *Ibid.,* p. 109.

[6] Letter of then chairman Lilienthal to Charles E. Wilson, President, General Electric Company, *Ibid.,* p. 134.

opposed compulsory arbitration.[7] The Commission wanted to achieve the least possible interference with management and labor. At the same time it felt a responsibility to assure that those having negotiating and disciplinary authority were loyal, that unit and jurisdiction questions did not breach security, and that there were no work stoppages.[8]

There was another facet to the problem of continuity of operations: what part of American industry was to be embraced by the policy? As indicated by the Commission in its 1948 Report to the Joint Committee, the same issue of national safety is present when disputes arise which shut off from a critical AEC installation supplies which have not been or cannot be adequately stockpiled.[9] Electric power and some chemicals were cited as examples. "Continuous operation of AEC installations depends upon a flow of materials from numerous suppliers in very diverse fields, who are widely scattered throughout the country. Machinery in addition to what now exists for avoiding labor dispute stoppages of AEC suppliers, therefore, would need to be adaptable to almost any field of industry in the event of an emergency."[10] It has been observed that the inference of such a policy might require measures assuring continuity of production in mining operations connected with furnishing raw materials to suppliers, in plants manufacturing equipment, and in transportation industries delivering supplies.[11] While the scope given in actual practice to specialized procedures applicable to the atomic energy program is more significant than such speculation, regard for a flow of critical material does remind of the potential dimensions of the problem of labor policy.

There were a number of factors in addition to the necessity to assure continuity of operations which complicated the problem of devising a workable procedure.[12] The peculiar structure of bargaining was one of these. The Commission has utilized the contractor

[7] Ibid., pp. 90-91, 125; see Davis in Recommendations on Labor Relations Policy in Atomic Energy Installations, pp. 6-8.
[8] Labor Policy in Atomic Energy Plants, p. 117.
[9] Ibid., p. 123.
[10] Ibid.
[11] Fallon, op. cit., pp. 35, 55.
[12] See Straus, op. cit., passim.

system to a large degree.[13] The AEC reimburses the contractor for costs. It therefore has a responsibility to maintain cost control. The contractor with non-AEC operations has an incentive to keep costs down, beyond pride in efficiency, if union organization or other factors point toward a pattern settlement. On the other hand—and this aspect proved to be particularly acute in construction—statutory and agreement provisions often stipulate payment of local rates. If a "project agreement" had not been signed, this sometimes resulted in local negotiation of "double-barreled" features which the contractor was willing to follow, if only Commission approval were forthcoming. In any event, the ritual of collective bargaining and the often delicate series of related compromises which lead to agreement were much affected by the "brooding omnipresence" of the Commission at the bargaining table. Although there were many persuasive reasons supporting the contractor system, there is more than a little logic in the proposition that a bargaining agent must be more than a conduit. The empty chair for the agency paying the bills obviously complicated collective bargaining.

There was also the problem of secrecy. The nature of the atomic energy program in an environment of international tension, coupled with the stringencies of the Atomic Energy Act, required the AEC to adopt a settled policy that the program be operated in a manner to assure that those participating in the program were loyal to the United States. This policy was an impediment to the collective bargaining process at several levels: negotiations, contract administration, and representation proceedings. An adjustment with the National Labor Relations Board was worked out with respect to the last, and certain mediators of the Federal Mediation and Conciliation Service received security clearance and were assigned to cases at atomic energy installations. Probably the secrecy factor would not in itself make collective bargaining impossible, but it was an aggravation for the parties accustomed to more normal conditions. For instance, labor officials sometimes charged that management raised the issue of security when it was not really

[13] The policy has been the subject of debate. See, for example, Newman, *op. cit., p.* 1332; Dahl and Brown, *op. cit.,* p. 80; Richard A. Tybout, "The Contractor System," *in* "The Impact of Atomic Energy," *The Annals,* CCXC (November 1953), p. 82.

relevant, in order to avoid full discussion and collective bargaining.[14]

Finally, the atomic energy program having only recently emerged, the pattern of union organization and the identity of the contractors were fluid and chaotic. While a period of experiment for the parties would not be unique to the atomic energy program, it added to the difficulties in the light of the paramount objective of uninterrupted production. Moreover, some of the work, in construction particularly, was rushed by a sense of peril related to national security. As a result, the advance planning of the work, survey of community housing and recreational facilities, and recruitment techniques and training of proper supervisory personnel were inadequate. These unusual conditions of work not only caused grievances but also raised questions concerning the efficiency of the work force which produced strains in relationships.[15]

THE PRESIDENT'S COMMISSION: INDEFINITE PROCEDURES
FOR DEFINITE RESULTS

In September 1948, President Truman appointed a Commission on Labor Relations in Atomic Energy Installations.[16] The Commis-

[14] See, for example, *Ninth Semiannual Report of AEC*, p. 82; see also footnote 47.

[15] See Tripp, Mann, and Downs, *op. cit.*, p. 20.

[16] The members of the Commission were William H. Davis (chairman), Aaron Horvitz, and Edwin E. Witte. John T. Dunlop served as consultant, and Donald B. Straus as executive secretary. The appointment of the Commission grew out of a strike threat at Oak Ridge in 1948 which prompted the government to resort to the injunctive procedures of the LMRA.

Earlier when the question had arisen as to the Atomic Energy Commission's responsibility in relation to the initial agreements negotiated at Oak Ridge, the Commission had employed David A. Morse, George W. Taylor, and Lloyd K. Garrison to analyze the proposed agreements. These experts, submitting their report on January 4, 1947, were of the opinion that "The situation at Oak Ridge raises a question whether the Commission, in view of its statutory responsibilities, can provide collective bargaining of the traditional sort as a basis for labor relations in the Oak Ridge area. . . ." Relationships there were, and still are, much complicated by competition and division in the labor movement. These consultants felt that the Commission had a responsibility to pass upon three major portions of the agreements: wages, provisions relating to continuity of work, and security.

In its report to the Joint Committee in January, 1948, the Commission noted that its staff also had held extensive conferences with representatives of both management and labor. Oscar S. Smith has carried the major load for the Commission in this area and is presently its Director of Organization and Personnel.

sion's task was to formulate a broad code of conduct to be observed by labor and management in the program. It was to include in its study the question of whether special legislation was needed to protect the national interest.[17] The Commission not only devoted its time and experience to the problem, but, in a sense, carried on national collective bargaining with top government officials, union and employer representatives, and workers.

The President's Commission reported in April 1949. It recommended against the enactment of special legislation and stressed the importance of preserving to the greatest possible extent under the admitted difficulties the normal incidents of collective bargaining. The Commission suggested special panel machinery and "status quo" procedures which would, if the promise fulfilled the hope, serve as an effective substitute for strikes and lockouts. The jurisdiction of the panel was to include any dispute unresolved by collective bargaining and mediation "which threatens to interfere with an essential part of the atomic energy program."[18] An unqualified no-strike—no-lockout sanction or pledge was not provided. But unions and contractors at government-owned, privately operated atomic energy installations were to agree not to interrupt production before the panel was given an opportunity to take jurisdiction. After the panel took jurisdiction the status quo was to continue until settlement or, if the panel issued recommendations, for thirty days thereafter.[19] An escape clause was provided in that a party could terminate its anticipated agreement not to interrupt production[20] by notifying the panel. Economic action could then be taken after twenty days if the case had not been settled. However, if the panel issued recommendations, the usual thirty-day "status quo" obligation was to apply. In short, this was special machinery tailored to the contemporary necessities of the atomic energy program. It was to come into play only after the parties and the Federal Mediation and Conciliation Service had exhausted avenues of agreement.

[17] Report of the President's Commission on Labor Relations in the Atomic Energy Installations, p. 1.
[18] Ibid., p. 9.
[19] Ibid.
[20] Agreements from contractors and unions not to interrupt production without giving the panel an opportunity to settle the dispute were later obtained by the AEC. Straus, op. cit., pp. 72-73.

The President and the Atomic Energy Commission adopted the recommendations of the report, and in April 1949, the Atomic Energy Labor Relations Panel, sometimes referred to as the Davis panel, was appointed.[21] The panel became the "strike" step in the collective bargaining process. Under circumstances in which the temptations to resort to some compulsory formula were so great, it was apparent that those who had worked out these arrangements were devoted to democratic institutions.

In consideration of emergency disputes and national policy, the procedures of the panel hold much interest. Unlike the national emergency provisions of the Labor Management Relations Act, the panel has no statutory base. In form, at least, voluntarism was preserved. Moreover, fact finding is only one of the techniques at the disposal of the panel. However broadly the panel's powers were defined, the crux of the idea was that resort to its services should not be easily available lest collective bargaining become a farce. The parties would be uncertain whether jurisdiction would be asserted over a specific case. Once jurisdiction was asserted, they also would be uncertain what approach the panel would take to the case. The choice was to be pragmatic and might include any one or any combination of the techniques which may be utilized for the obtaining of agreement.[22]

There is nothing novel in the techniques themselves. There is much comparable experience with methods utilized in state and federal mediation, voluntary arbitration, the National Mediation Board under the Railway Labor Act, the wartime labor boards, state compulsory arbitration adventures, and the national emergency provisions of the Labor Management Relations Act. It is the combination and concentration of techniques in one body which represents the departure. The Atomic Energy Labor Relations Panel is one of the very few "agencies" that come to mind, and perhaps the only body operating in at least a sense under governmental aegis, which would supply a body of empirical data for examination of the "choice-of-procedures approach" discussed by Professor Wirtz in the preceding chapter.

[21] The members of the Commission were appointed to the panel (see footnote 16). Davis was also named to be chairman of the panel.

[22] Davis, "Labor-Management Relations in Atomic Energy Affairs," p. 103.

The Davis panel: 1949-1952

The Davis panel was active from April 1949 to December 1, 1952. In three and one-half years the panel took official jurisdiction of fifty-nine cases.[23] Total case load figures, however, are likely to be deceptive in attempting to define the panel's role in the disputes-settling process. Naturally these disputes were of varying complexity. The flexibility of the panel's procedures is shown by its retention of jurisdiction over labor relations at Paducah in 1952 beyond any particular dispute which had arisen. There it developed machinery with the parties designed to produce more harmonious relations.[24] The panel helped to resolve many disputes in which it did not take official action and frequently counseled the AEC, contractors, and unions on their problems.[25]

It is not possible here to detail the background and resolution of particular disputes. It may be noted, however, that the panel was conscious of its objective of maintaining collective bargaining and expressed concern when its case load began to grow.[26] In conformance with the goal of preserving private negotiations, primary effort was toward mediation. Of the twenty disputes handled during the first eighteen months of the panel's existence, formal recommendations were required in only six. However, it became increasingly necessary to issue recommendations.[27] Classification is hazardous, but a rough breakdown offered by the panel indicates that of fifty-five cases, recommendations were issued in nineteen;

[23] See *Thirteenth Semiannual Report of AEC* (1953), p. 179.

[24] A prominent feature was monthly meetings to be held by international representatives of the crafts to discuss accumulated grievances and interunion problems, to be followed by joint meetings with the company. *Ibid.*, pp. 182-185.

[25] *Ibid.*, p. 179.

[26] In the first six months of its existence the panel handled four formal "cases," six in the second six-month period, and ten in the third. *Ninth Semiannual Report of AEC*, p. 129.

[27] Mediation by the panel presumably followed similar efforts by the Federal Mediation and Conciliation Service. The panel issued no recommendations in the first six-month period of its operation, two in the second, and four in the third. *Ibid.*, pp. 80, 129. The increase may, of course, be attributable to many external factors, as well as the possibility that the existence of the panel in itself was a contributing cause.

twenty-two disputes were referred to the parties or to another agency;[28] a settlement was mediated in thirteen disputes; and jurisdiction was not taken in one case.[29] Doubtless the methods overlapped a great deal. For example, often extended mediation would precede resort to recommendations.

The Ching panel: 1953 to date

The resignations of the members of the Davis panel, submitted with the change in administrations, were accepted by the White House in March 1953. In that spring a new Atomic Energy Labor-Management Relations Panel, here referred to as the Ching panel, was established within the Federal Mediation and Conciliation Service.[30] President Eisenhower directed that the new panel exercise substantially the same jurisdiction as that of the prior panel. Its procedures were worked out jointly by the panel, the Federal Mediation and Conciliation Service, and the AEC. These procedures reaffirm in detail the guiding principles stated in the President's Commission Report of 1949.[31] Subject to "the Atomic Energy Commission's responsibility under the law and to the limitations inherent in the critical nature of the atomic energy program," the determination of wages, hours, and working conditions are to be left to collective bargaining free from governmental interference.[32] While informal discussions undoubtedly were held, a renewal of the pledge to conform to the panel procedures was apparently not specifically sought or obtained. The procedures simply state that "it is expected that unions and contractors will continue to abide by"

[28] Wage Stabilization Board or Construction Industry Stabilization Board, National Labor Relations Board, Joint Board for Settlement of Jurisdictional Disputes, or Federal Mediation and Conciliation Service.

[29] *Thirteenth Semiannual Report of AEC*, pp. 179-180.

[30] Members of the panel appointed were: Cyrus S. Ching (chairman), Thomas W. Holland, Peter J. Manno, Arthur M. Ross, Phillip Weiss, and Rev. Leo C. Brown. John E. Dietz of the Federal Mediation and Conciliation Service staff was appointed executive secretary. The present members of the panel are Ching, Brown, O. S. Colclough, Holland, Ross, and Russell A. Smith.

[31] Federal Mediation and Conciliation Service, *Procedures of the Atomic Energy Labor-Management Relations Panel* (1953), also printed in Newsletter, *Labor-Management Relations in the Atomic Energy Industry* (AEC, September 1953), No. 34.

[32] *Procedures of the Atomic Energy Labor-Management Relations Panel*, p. 2.

continuity of production during collective bargaining, mediation, and a reasonable period for referral to the panel.[33]

A change significant in form, though perhaps not so great in fact, is that the panel cannot intervene in disputes except upon referral of the Director of the Federal Mediation and Conciliation Service. The latter, in making a decision on referral, is to consult with the AEC "and other appropriate persons and organizations."[34] While the Davis panel scrupulously required that collective bargaining and mediation be exhausted, the new procedures take from the panel the exercise of judgment, sometimes delicate, as to when that point has been reached. Otherwise the jurisdiction of the panel seems phrased in terms purposely broad and uncertain. Its power is stated to extend to labor-management disputes "in any Government-owned, privately operated atomic energy installation and in any other dispute which threatens to interrupt an essential part of the atomic energy program. . . ."[35]

The Ching panel had handled fourteen disputes when it submitted its first report to the President.[36] Nine disputes concerned operations and the remaining five the construction of facilities.[37] While mediation was undoubtedly used to narrow issues and to an unknown extent in formulating recommendations, the most striking aspect of the panel's report is that recommendations were issued in almost every case. This is to be contrasted with the emphasis on mediation techniques by the Davis panel during the formative period of its existence. If the new panel is viewed as the successor to the original machinery, the explanation for this development is not readily apparent. It may reflect the needs of the parties for more assistance or be an example of the recognized phenomenon that procedures evolve through use. It might even be speculated

[33] *Ibid.*, p. 4.

[34] *Ibid.*, p. 3.

[35] *Ibid.*

[36] *First Annual Report to the President by the Atomic Energy Labor-Management Relations Panel*, July 1, 1953, to June 30, 1954. During the months in early 1953 when no panel was in existence, the Federal Mediation and Conciliation Service made a special effort to resolve atomic energy disputes, including the setting up of two special fact-finding boards. *Sixth Annual Report of the Federal Mediation and Conciliation Service* (1954), pp. 6-7.

[37] The panel's report indicates that seven disputes developed on reopening under an existing agreement, four on renewal, two in connection with initial agreements, and one over troublesome grievances.

that such a mundane factor as the time which panel members find it possible to devote to this part-time service would influence the choice of technique. It could be supposed also that the requirement that the Director of the Federal Mediation and Conciliation Service refer disputes to the panel before it acts would make it more inclined to conclude that all possibilities of settlement by mediation had been exhausted. More fundamentally, the forces of change discussed below may be operating on the disputes-settling process.

Evaluation of the panels' activities

The effectiveness of the panel concept and methods should be measured in the light of the total labor-management relations picture in the atomic energy program. Such a study is not available at the present time. Obviously, even a display of strike statistics or lack thereof would be an incomplete story. Solely from the viewpoint of maintaining production, the efforts of contractors and union officials, the attitude of the workers, and the panel procedures combined to present an impressive record in the operation of government-owned, privately operated installations. The final report of the Davis panel at the end of 1952 stated that no interruptions had occurred in production facilities which were thought by the Commission to be vital to national security.[38] Perplexing stoppage problems occurred in construction, but here also the panel was active both in settling particular disputes and in assisting the parties to develop durable procedures.[39] In the writer's experience, the local prestige of the panel was very great at the Paducah, Kentucky, site.

If one were to search for the essential ingredient in that degree of success which acknowledgedly is to be attributed to the panel idea, perhaps major credit would be assigned to the familiar but some-

[38] *Thirteenth Semiannual Report of AEC*, p. 179.

[39] The percentage of total working time lost in the construction program is customarily given in the Commission's Semiannual Reports. No attempt has been made to compare these figures with national standards. The figures vary greatly according to site. See also Granville M. Read, "The Savannah River Project" (speech released by E. I. du Pont de Nemours & Co., November 18, 1954), p. 13. Since 1952 the Atomic Energy Commission has had an arrangement with the Bureau of Labor Statistics to provide data comparing gross average hourly earnings and hours worked in some of its manufacturing operations with inorganic chemicals and petroleum and coal products industries. Some data on average monthly labor turnover are also supplied. See *Thirteenth Semiannual Report of AEC*, pp. 53-55.

times ignored fact that machinery which the parties themselves have helped to create and agreed to may work because it is their own. There is no real substitute for agreement by the parties. That which comes closest, however, is agreement on the avowed substitute. One would have to put into the equation, moreover, the expertise of the panels. Some of the additional elements which would need to be considered would include an analysis of benefit levels, the skill of the AEC, contractors, and union leaders, the composition and attitude of the work force, and the influence of public opinion. At a minimum it can be stated that adjustments have been achieved to a degree that Congress has not felt compelled to deal legislatively with the problem of strikes in the atomic energy program.

The increased resort to recommendations as distinguished from mediation may be further evidence of the atmosphere of transition which surrounds atomic energy. One of the elements of change which may be operating on the present handling of disputes is the evolving economic status of the program.

THE ATOMIC ENERGY ACT OF 1954

The Atomic Energy Act of 1946 provided for a virtual government monopoly of the development and production of fissionable materials.[40] As we have seen, however, this monopoly in practice was not an absolute one. The Commission interpreted congressional intent and administrative efficiency to require it to utilize private contractors. To that extent the concept of a partnership or cotrustee relationship between the government and private enterprise prevailed.[41] But the pressures for greater industrial participation in the development of the new resource began to be felt.[42] Finally, in

[40] 60 Stat. 755 (1946), as amended, 42 U.S.C. § 1801 et seq. (Supp. 1952). The statute was popularly known as the McMahon Act.

[41] See Oscar M. Ruebhausen and Robert B. von Mehren, "The Atomic Energy Act and the Private Production of Atomic Power," Harvard Law Review, LXVI (1953), pp. 1450, 1459-1462.

[42] The Atomic Energy Commission and a number of utility and chemical organizations joined in an "Industrial Participation Program" from which a number of plans evolved. In 1952 the Joint Committee on Atomic Energy held hearings and released a document compiled by its staff entitled Atomic Power and Private Enterprise. In 1953 the Joint Committee held further hearings on the same subject. See Atomic Power and Private Enterprise, Joint Committee on Atomic Energy, 82d Cong., 2d sess. (December 1952); Atomic Power Development and Private Enterprise, Joint Committee on Atomic Energy, 83d Cong., 1st sess. (June and July 1953).

1954, President Eisenhower proposed revision of the 1946 Act to provide for widened cooperation with our allies, improved procedures for the control and dissemination of information, and broadened participation in the development of peacetime uses of atomic energy. In response, hearings on a proposed amendment were held,[43] and after lengthy debate and great opposition the Atomic Energy Act of 1954 was passed.[44] To a limited extent private enterprise was granted an opportunity to develop the potential of the atom.[45]

In a debate of such proportions one would suppose that attention to the role of the government in labor-management relations would accompany consideration of a change of philosophy toward private industry's assuming a greater role in the production and use of fissionable material. In fact, scant notice was taken of the impact the past or new program might have on traditional patterns in labor relations. At the beginning of the 1954 hearings on the proposed amendment, Representative Holifield of California, the leader of the opposition to the bill in Committee and in the House, inserted into the hearing record two speeches which he had made earlier

[43] See *Atomic Energy*, Hearings on S. 3323 and H.R. 8862 to amend the Atomic Energy Act 1946, Joint Committee on Atomic Energy, 83d Cong., 2d sess. (1954).

[44] 68 Stat. 919 *et seq.*, Pub. L. No. 703, 83d Cong., 2d sess. (August 30, 1954), hereafter referred to by section number only.

[45] While abandoning the governmental monopoly approach of the 1946 Act, Congress adopted what might be termed a system of regulated private enterprise. See David F. Cavers, "The Atomic Energy Act of 1954," *Scientific American*, CXCI (November 1954), p. 31, for a discussion of the role of private industry under the new law. The AEC retains its ownership of all atomic fuel. § 52. However, it is empowered to issue licenses authorizing private industries to own and operate facilities for producing and using nuclear materials. §§ 53, 101-103. Industries which are so licensed can apply for a license to obtain nuclear fuel from the AEC. § 53. The AEC automatically acquires legal title to by-product materials such as plutonium produced as a result of utilizing the nuclear fuel. § 81. Electricity produced from the use of the atomic fuel can be sold by the licensee under normal utility controls. §§ 182, 272. Certain provisions to protect the public interest have been inserted in the bill. See Cavers, *op. cit.*, pp. 32-33. These provisions further limit the freedom of private enterprise to proceed as it might in other businesses. The resulting picture has been described as "a far cry from the world of Adam Smith. It presents a mixed economy, perhaps a mixed-up one." *Ibid.*, p. 35. For the view that the public interest is not protected adequately by the new Act, see Walter Adams, "Atomic Energy: The Congressional Abandonment of Competition," *Columbia Law Review*, LV (February 1955), p. 158.

from the floor.[46] These framed the two problems in the labor relations area which were to be considered briefly by the Committee
and by Congress.

The first issue was the extent of labor representation on the
Atomic Energy Commission or in its councils.[47] Later Representative
Holifield offered on the floor of the house an amendment to the bill
which would have provided for a "Labor-Management Advisory
Committee" to the Commission, but the amendment was defeated.[48]

[46] *Atomic Energy*, Hearings, pp. 14-24.

[47] "Whether or not legislative provisions can be written to alleviate the persistent sore spots in atomic labor management relations, certainly the legislation can at least provide for more effective labor representation in the councils
of the Atomic Energy Commission." *Ibid.*, p. 16. Representatives Holifield and
Price, in their statement of separate views on H. R. 9757, protested the "omis-
sion of labor-management provisions." *Amending the Atomic Energy Act of
1946, as Amended, and for Other Purposes*, Joint Committee on Atomic
Energy, 83d Cong., 2d sess., Rep. No. 2181 (1954), pp. 105, 132-133.
The plan to add to the Atomic Energy Commission some labor representation apparently had its origin in a resolution of the 1953 Convention of the
American Federation of Labor. Andrew J. Biemiller, the AFL representative
who appeared before the Joint Committee's 1953 and 1954 hearings, indicated
that in his view the Atomic Energy Commission was management-oriented.
Atomic Power Development and Private Enterprise, p. 484; *Atomic Energy*,
Hearings, pp. 277-278. He suggested to the Joint Committee that some members of the AEC might be drawn from the ranks of organized labor. Moreover,
he presented the proposal contained in an AFL convention resolution. The
AFL proposed a labor-management advisory committee to aid the Atomic
Energy Commission in a number of matters relating to its labor policy. The
major portion of Biemiller's argument in support of the committee was devoted
to its functions in determining which topics of bargaining were so secret as to
be beyond discussion. *Atomic Power Development and Private Enterprise*,
pp. 484-485; *Atomic Energy*, Hearings, pp. 279, 280, 281. He indicated that
those bargaining on the labor side of the table in atomic energy plants had
felt that management was using secrecy as a means of avoiding bargaining
on certain issues. Another function of the labor-management relations advisory
committee which the AFL proposed would have been to aid in a change-over
from the restricted type of bargaining current in atomic development and
production to normal labor-management relations. *Atomic Power Development
and Private Enterprise*, p. 484.

[48] *Congressional Record*, 83d Cong., 2d sess., 100:135 (July 19, 1954),
10395. For Representative Holifield's statements in support of the amendment,
see *ibid.*, pp. 10398, 10409. The proposed amendment read: "Sec. 27. Labor-
Management Advisory Committee: There shall be a Labor-Management Advisory Committee to advise the Commission on all matters relating to labor-
management relations in atomic energy plants and facilities owned or licensed
by the Commission, including measures to promote collective bargaining and
alleviate industrial strife, health, and safety standards and workmen's compen-

The second question in which Representative Holifield was interested was the impact of private development of atomic energy on collective bargaining.[49]

A number of factors may account for the surprisingly minor role of labor-management relations in the hearings and debates which accompanied this major amendment of the framework of the program. There was much at stake, including the emotional public power issue. There was no apparent interest or pressure from the executive branch for legislative consideration of this matter. While there was some testimony in the hearings on behalf of the AFL on this particular problem,[50] it seems that neither of the major interest groups concerned, management or labor, attempted to mobilize real sentiment on the issue. Moreover, something of a tradition had grown up since 1948 for the more informal route of top-level negotiations among contractors, labor, and experts representing the public, to arrive at procedures. The flexible nonstatutory machinery previously discussed may have been thought to be satisfactory for any immediate problems. It is not clear from the debates whether Congress assumed that the panel machinery for the settlement of

sation provisions and other terms and conditions to be observed by contractors or licensees of the Commission, the application of Federal statutes governing employment and labor standards, personnel security procedures, and the effects of atomic energy enterprises on established industries and occupations. . . ." *Ibid.*, p. 10395.

On the floor of the House the opposition to the proposal was directed to the lack of precision in defining what the committee would do and the lack of showing of any need for such a committee. *Congressional Record*, 83d Cong., 2d sess., 100:139 (July 23, 1954), pp. 11061-11062. One of the members of the Joint Committee on Atomic Energy indicated in the House debate that the Committee had "agreed . . . that it [the amendment] covered such a broad field we should lay it aside until ample time was available to consider it." *Ibid.*, p. 11062.

[49] "Greater freedom of enterprise in atomic energy carries with it the commensurate obligation of insuring the like freedom to labor." *Atomic Energy*, Hearings, p. 23. Biemiller also indicated the view of the AFL on labor-management relations if and when private industry took over atomic energy production and development. "[I]f there is to be free private enterprise in the atomic field so must there be free collective bargaining." *Ibid.*, p. 278. "[O]nce atomic energy is used in the general industrial field, we don't want to see it then considered as a separate kind of an operation so far as labor relations are concerned. We have been willing to do that under a weapons program, but we want to make certain that that does not continue." *Ibid.*

[50] See footnotes 47, 49.

disputes or the more traditional pattern would prevail when private employers commenced production in the atomic energy field. Finally, the degree of private industrial development immediately foreseen may have indicated to the legislators that the problem was one for the future.

EMERGENCY DISPUTES AND NATIONAL POLICY IN ATOMIC ENERGY: 1955

Although no serious debate on the subject of the government's role in the settlement of disputes in the program accompanied the revision of the Act, there would appear to be several questions worthy of current consideration. The special meaning attached to the emergency dispute in the atomic energy field may take on new shadings in the light of technological developments and the changes in national economic policy. It may be found that the panel machinery should be more narrowly limited; that it is no longer valid as national labor policy[51] and should be discarded; or that it should be broadened and strengthened.

As a matter of fact, there have been indications that such an evaluation may be undertaken. One of the most troublesome disputes handled by the Ching panel arose in April 1954, on wage reopenings pursuant to agreements existing between the Carbide and Carbon Chemicals Company operating installations at Paducah, Kentucky, and Oak Ridge, Tennessee, and the Atomic Trades and Labor Council, AFL, and two locals of the United Gas, Coke, and Chemical Workers of America, CIO. The panel's recommendations, issued in June 1954, were rejected by the CIO.[52] This dispute had

[51] While the existing machinery might be characterized as having been established as a voluntary policy of the parties, such an analysis would seem formal and technical. It is suggested that when Congress is induced to inaction by the formulation of machinery by the executive branch of the government with the consent of management and labor, then, broadly conceived, the result, while having the advantage of voluntarism, nevertheless represents "national labor policy" in this area.

[52] The dispute was eventually settled in November 1954, on the basis of the panel's recommendation with the additional provision of a staggered increase in settlement of the January 1955 reopening. A chronology of the dispute may be found in *First Annual Report to the President by the Atomic Energy Labor-Management Relations Panel*, cases 8-11. In the interim President Eisenhower had resorted to the injunctive procedures of the Labor Management Relations Act. See the reports of the board of inquiry pursuant to Executive

ramifications beyond the immediate threat to production. In July 1954, Secretary of Labor James P. Mitchell held a meeting with CIO officials which led to a return to work without resort to an injunction at that time. An understanding was reached at this meeting: (1) that a conference of union leaders would be held with the Atomic Energy Commission to discuss matters of housing, health, and community facilities and other problems affecting workers living in the communities where atomic energy facilities are located; and (2) that a study "to seek to improve labor-management relations and to strengthen collective bargaining in the atomic energy field" would be initiated.[53] A meeting was held among CIO, AFL, and AEC representatives on August 23, 1954. It was reported that in addition to discussing the community relations matters, the union officials expressed the view that "conditions affecting collective bargaining in the atomic energy program are unfavorable" and requested the Commission to consider steps to improve the situation.[54] At the same meeting Walter Reuther, president of the CIO, recommended that the Commission establish a labor advisory committee with representation from among the unions engaged in collective bargaining in the industry.[55]

Later in August 1954, the Secretary of Labor announced the appointment of David L. Cole to head a five-man advisory group on labor-management problems in atomic energy.[56] According to the announcement, this group is to "study the role of government in

---

Orders No. 10542 and No. 10543, July 10, July 19, 1954. The Davis panel had also met with a rejection of a recommendation in a dispute between the Carbide and Carbon Chemicals Company and United Gas, Coke, and Chemical Workers, CIO, representing employees at the Oak Ridge K-25 Plant. In that case the company "sweetened" the panel's recommendations and this offer became the basis for settlement. See *Thirteenth Semiannual Report of AEC*, pp. 185-186. Of course, the question readily occurs whether specialized machinery of this sort can survive even an infrequent rejection of its recommendations.

[53] Newsletter, *Labor-Management Relations in the Atomic Energy Industry*, No. 40, p. 3.

[54] Newsletter No. 41, pp. 3-4.

[55] Reuther also recommended that the President establish a National Advisory Committee to study housing and community policy in atomic energy centers. *Ibid*.

[56] It was stated that the other four members of the group would be appointed by the Labor Department on the recommendation of Cole. *Ibid*. No further steps had been announced early in 1955.

labor relations in atomic plants owned by the government but operated by private firms. The group will recommend improvements in the procedure for settling disputes."[57] During its progress such a study conceivably could inhibit the effectiveness of the panel, but the advisory group can be expected to be sensitive to this relationship. As a matter of form there may be advantages to having such a study made under auspices apart from the panel itself.

Wherever a study is centered, it may be ventured that several lines of inquiry would be helpful as prelude to formulation of sound conclusions. It will be especially important to develop the contemporary setting in which a disputes-settling mechanism must operate.

Collective bargaining in atomic energy

At the time of initial formulation of the "status quo" procedures in 1948-1949, collective bargaining was new to the atomic energy program. No pattern of organization had developed.[58] Only two contractors had union relationships in the program,[59] and there had been multiple contractors at particular installations. The Commission did not furnish the contractors even general standards as a guide to its reimbursement policy. The problem of community facilities in terms of housing, schools, recreation, etc. was then even more than today in the picture at some installations. Patterns traditional in construction might be expected to carry over to some extent to the initial period of operations, particularly when construction and manufacturing overlapped and the same labor force and unions were involved. Competition in the labor movement was bound to be acute during the initial organization period. There have been developments at national union levels which can be expected to have eventual impact on this problem. In new facilities there were supervisory personnel to train. New unions could not always count on experienced leaders at local levels, quite apart from the problem of acquainting the membership with the limita-

[57] *Ibid.*
[58] See *Fortune,* L (November 1954), pp. 80-82, for a discussion of present strength of the major labor federations in the program, with particular emphasis on the structural problems encountered by the Metal Trades Department, AFL, in combining craft affiliation with industrial unit bargaining.
[59] Straus, *op. cit.,* p. 44.

tions as well as the advantages of the union.[60] There were wage policy and grievance administration patterns to evolve.

A collective bargaining study in atomic energy would be especially challenging. As will be discussed, there is no "industry" concept by which it would be readily possible to define the scope of the study. The sites are widely dispersed geographically from Hanford, Washington, to Aiken, South Carolina. There has been a deliberate effort to avoid industrial centers. The contractors are diverse, including such special employers as universities along with established major companies, for example, General Electric and Union Carbide. The usual investigation of historical management policies would be more directed to the relationship of over-all company policies formulated for private operations to those followed in the special environment. On the union side, organization and the initial bargaining phase have been carried out under a unique set of conditions. Interwoven in this situation is not only the peculiar nature of the facilities, but also the difficult and uneasy role of the Atomic Energy Commission, a third party to the bargaining relationship. The composition of the work force would also be of interest. The level of skills and living conditions are brought together in unusual combination.

The proposed collective bargaining analysis should include a detailed study of the operation of the Davis and Ching panels. How many agreements were negotiated or disputes settled without the intervention of the panel? At what stage of negotiations were the panel procedures invoked? By whom? What techniques were employed by the panel and with what results? Have the procedures been modified through use, and, if so, to what extent? What is the relationship of the panel with the parties and with the interested agencies of the government? How do the national emergency injunctive procedures operate in specific disputes in which an extra "layer" of machinery which includes the recommendation technique

[60] For example, the writer was struck by the situation which developed during initial contract negotiations at Paducah. The bargaining committee, some of whom were going through negotiations for the first time, became so convinced of the equity of their initial demands that top-level union negotiators had great difficulty in persuading them to accept a compromise. Perhaps this stemmed not only from inexperience in the ritual of collective bargaining, but also from the fact that they had been oversold during the prior contested election campaign.

is introduced between the parties' efforts and government intervention?

Without attempting to list all the questions which might be considered, such a study should develop whether we have here an example of the well-known phenomenon that many stresses accompany the introduction of collective bargaining. Have these strains been minimized by maturing relationships?[61] It is not intended to imply that the panel procedures were not sound when originally adopted in 1949 or even when recreated in 1953. But it is urged that a pertinent question at this juncture is whether the need to guide the collective bargaining institution in this program is sufficiently great today to justify specialized procedures. Like the child confined to the nursery, there are dangers of inhibiting growth. It is recognized, however, that even if it were found that the need for assistance has been to some or to a large degree satisfied, other factors might influence a determination in the national interest to continue existing arrangements. Presumably policy must be oriented to international as well as domestic considerations.

Present area of emergency

To define the appropriate role of the government in the emergency disputes settlement phase of the atomic energy program it also would be essential to mark out the area of emergency. One of the obstacles to this effort is that there is no atomic energy "industry." The activities of the Commission's contractors vary greatly, including not only construction and manufacturing, but also ore processing, laboratory research, and town maintenance and service.[62] One could seek to distinguish between policy applicable to government-owned, privately constructed and operated facilities on the one hand, and on the other, activities connected with the private industrial development of atomic energy. This is to be contrasted with differentiating between the weapons and the pacifica-

---

[61] A member of the AEC staff has observed in discussing the troubled labor relations at the Paducah site: ". . . the first eighteen months were spent in chaotic efforts to find the answers, the next six months saw the answers emerge, and the last eighteen months have produced productive and effective relationships." Herbert Hubben, Book Review, *Industrial and Labor Relations Review*, 8 (January 1955), p. 305.

[62] *Thirteenth Semiannual Report of AEC*, p. 53.

tion-of-the-atom aspects of the program. The latter distinction perhaps is meaningful only at the fabrication level. It would seem difficult to make a distinction between weapons and industrial uses with respect to mining, processing, transportation, and perhaps even laboratory work. Suggestive of the problem are the power plants projected by the now familiar Dixon-Yates contract, which are to use conventional energy sources, and the plant being built at Shippingport, Pennsylvania, which is to involve commercial production of nuclear power. Disputes at either of these sites might be construed as threatening "to interrupt an essential part of the atomic energy program" and therefore to be within the jurisdiction of the present panel.[63] Or are these plants simply a part of the electric power industry? One would surmise that any collective bargaining for workers engaged in the construction and operation of these plants will fall under traditional concepts of adjustment in which the possibility of use of economic pressure largely uninhibited by governmental intervention remains a useful device.

With respect to the role of the government in disputes settlement at plants which the Atomic Energy Commission owns, but which are operated by private contractors, the essential ingredients of an examination of the problem would include elements which are external to the labor-management relationship in the program, as well as the collective bargaining study suggested above. For example, present secrecy requirements may be quite different from former ones. It is to be remembered, moreover, that at the time of the original formulation of the "status quo" procedures in 1948-1949, it was widely assumed that the United States had a near international monopoly of nuclear weapons. The United States was rushing to stockpile these weapons. The labor relations features were related to the need for continuity of operations which was in turn premised on military considerations. The intervening development of the hydrogen bomb and other weapons may require the military emphasis to be placed elsewhere. For our major problem of national security may be not only the production of weapons but, at least equally, the capacity to deliver and to defend. Superficially, at least, there is something anomalous about specialized procedures for almost all disputes in the atomic energy program

[63] *Procedures of the Atomic Energy Labor-Management Relations Panel*, p. 3.

while primary reliance is placed on collective bargaining in an industry developing and producing, for example, nuclear-powered aircraft.

Obviously, these are questions which can be considered meaningfully only by persons with access to information and an understanding of strategic concepts not possessed by the ordinary citizen. However, to the extent that the public has sensed a changed military equation, underlying group opinion operates in behalf of intervention in labor-management disputes in the atomic energy field in a quite different fashion from six years ago.

With respect to the question of labor policy in the industrial participation sphere, the rate of growth, which was being considered anew in hearings by the Joint Committee on Atomic Energy early in 1955,[64] depends on too many variables of technology and incentive to be estimated now. As a matter of prognosis, it would appear that a corporation which had developed an industrial use for atomic energy which was "practical" would be in a position similar to corporations engaged in less dramatic pursuits as far as its labor-management relations were concerned. The factory or reactor would have to be constructed. The process would involve all the skills and interests of the building trades. In the more distant future workers engaged in building the atomic automobile, manufacturing new plastics, preserving foods, or generating power would for the most part be performing tasks similar to those performed in industry today. Some skills involved in atomic energy production may be unique, but it is likely that the interests in wages, hours, and other conditions of employment would be

---

[64] The AFL proposal for a labor-management advisory committee to the AEC was repeated by Andrew J. Biemiller in the 1955 hearings. The committee would deal with "(1) collective bargaining processes and obligations in an industry so closely linked to the national welfare, (2) the difficulties posed by on-the-job security regulations, (3) the need for retraining and developing an adequate supply of competent and cooperative skilled labor, and (4) the resolution of health and safety problems arising in atomic operations." *Development, Growth, and State of the Atomic Energy Industry*, Joint Committee on Atomic Energy, 84th Cong., 1st sess. (1955), pt. 2, pp. 324-325, 331-332. See also information furnished for the record: Martin P. Durkin, General President, United Association of Journeymen and Apprentices of the Plumbing and Pipefitting Industry, "Labor Meets Problems of the Atomic Age," *ibid*, p. 332; letter from Anthony Matz, International President, International Brotherhood of Firemen and Oilers, *ibid.*, pt. 3, p. 588.

similar to those of workers in occupations elsewhere. The third-party bargaining feature would be removed. Some considerations of secrecy might remain, although these seem speculative. Certainly the threat to national security of a work stoppage would appear more remote than in the weapons phase. If interruptions of production would damage facilities or leave radioactive materials uncontrolled which might result in danger to inhabitants of the surrounding area or to the workers when they resumed their jobs, safeguards would have to be assured. This is not an entirely new problem, as the experience of the basic steel industry amply shows. Management engaged in developing peaceful uses for atomic energy can be expected to desire its usual area of discretion—especially because the implications of settlements reached for conventional operations are even more obvious than is the case with contractors operating plants under government contract. Organized labor will have a natural interest in normal collective bargaining conditions.

It may be a number of years before the construction and maintenance of atomic factories and the production of atomic products will involve sufficient numbers of workers to give rise to serious questions of national labor-management relations policy. However, if the labor disputes role of the government in the atomic energy program is to be reconsidered, some attention should be given to defining the panel's jurisdiction more carefully.[65] A tendency or desire to extend its domain is not to be attributed to the panel. However, the panel can be expected to be more effective within such area of emergency as may justify its long-range existence if the extent of its responsibility is clarified.[66]

[65] On a more general level of policy, it has been reported that Lewis L. Strauss, chairman of the Atomic Energy Commission, feels that because of the common characteristics of fuel and technology in power reactors and weapons it is difficult to separate the two programs administratively. Duncan Norton-Taylor, "The Controversial Mr. Strauss," Fortune, LI (January 1955), pp. 110, 112.

[66] Other nations have commercial atomic energy development programs, but apparently the experience in Great Britain is the only one which rivals that in the United States sufficiently to justify consideration of the effect of the atom on collective bargaining. Differences in the nature of the economies and characteristics of the labor movement may render any analogy suspect. However, the contrast in viewpoint merits some examination.

British atomic energy research and development was assigned in 1945 to the

The "status" of the panel

If an area of emergency is delimited in which it is thought desirable to have the assistance of the panel mechanism for some time to come, it is suggested that consideration be given to the status of

Ministry of Supply with most of the staff and employees covered under civil service protections. Ministry of Supply, *Britain's Atomic Factories* (1954), pp. 4-5. Thus the English pattern of collective bargaining between the government and its civil servants carried over into atomic development. *Parliamentary Debates*, Commons (Hansard), 1953-1954 sess., 524 (1954), pp. 890, 955. In 1953 the Conservative Government proposed a change in the organizational framework for the development and production of atomic materials, and a committee was appointed to study the ways by which control could be shifted from a ministry status to a governmental corporation. Prime Minister, *The Future Organization of the United Kingdom Atomic Energy Project*, Cmd. 8986 (1953), p. 3. The committee reported that the Trade Union Side of the Joint Industrial Council and the Staff Side of the Ministry of Supply Administrative Whitley Council had made a number of recommendations dealing with labor-management problems in atomic energy production and development. The unions felt that the new atomic corporation should recognize appropriate unions, and that consideration should be given to maintaining the civil service benefits which had accrued during the time that atomic development was under the Ministry of Supply. *Ibid.*, p. 8.

The Atomic Energy Authority Bill, apparently proposing the substance of the committee report, was introduced in the House of Commons and considered in the latter part of 1953 and in the early part of 1954, almost contemporaneous with the revision in the United States. (See also Canada: An Act to Amend the Atomic Energy Control Act, 2 & 3 Eliz. II, Ch. 47 [1954].) Such part of the debate as was devoted to labor-management relations under the proposed corporate organization was far more concerned with the loss of civil service benefits which might occur when employees of the Ministry of Supply engaged in atomic work transferred to the new Atomic Energy Authority than with questions of representation or of avoiding strikes in a vital industry. See, for example, *Parliamentary Debates*, pp. 855, 866-867, 879, 890, 907-910. However, there was one question which was raised that is similar to discussions which took place in Congress. Some members of Commons felt that there should be a labor representative on the Board of Authority. *Ibid.*, pp. 855, 887. See footnotes 47, 49, 64.

The United Kingdom Atomic Energy Authority Act of 1954, as finally passed, 2 & 3 Eliz. II, Ch. 32 (1954), set up a government corporation to conduct both research and development in peacetime uses of atomic energy, an organization similar to a British nationalized industry. The Act provides for some degree of collective bargaining and does not in itself ban strikes which might interrupt production. Doubtless it is hoped that alternative procedures will lessen the risk of stoppages. The labor-management relations section of the Act provides in part:

7.—(1) Except so far as the Authority are satisfied that adequate machinery exists for achieving the purposes of this section, it shall be the duty of the

the panel. The Davis panel was serviced by the Atomic Energy Commission. When the Ching panel was appointed by President Eisenhower, it was transferred to the Federal Mediation and Conciliation Service on the ground of administrative consistency. As described by the new panel, it was placed there "for housekeeping purposes only."[67] Presumably the panel maintains liaison with the Atomic Energy Commission and with the White House as well. As noted, the Secretary of Labor also has been involved in negotiations looking toward the settlement of a dispute,[68] and the Labor

---

Authority to seek consultation with any organization appearing to them to be appropriate with a view to the conclusion between the Authority and that organization of such agreements as appear to the parties to be desirable with respect to the establishment and maintenance of machinery for—

(a) the settlement by negotiation of terms and conditions of employment of persons employed by the Authority with provision for reference to arbitration in default of such settlement of such cases as may be determined by or under the agreements; and

(b) the promotion and encouragement of measures affecting the safety, health and welfare of persons employed by the Authority and (so far as in the opinion of the Authority considerations of national security permit) the discussion of other matters of mutual interest to the Authority and such persons, including efficiency in the Authority's work.

As in the United States, organization and collective bargaining are contemplated in the British program. Unlike ourselves, the British have not treated atomic energy as unique by limiting the function of the strike. However, the right to resort to coercive action in industry in general has been much more restricted in Great Britain since early in World War II than in the United States. The former restrictions were modified by the Industrial Disputes Order, 1951, which does not prohibit strikes and lockouts. But when made, an award of the Industrial Disputes Tribunal is legally enforceable. See Ministry of Labour and National Service, *Industrial Relations Handbook* (1953), pp. 130-138; Allan Flanders, "Great Britain," in Walter Galenson, ed., *Comparative Labor Movements* (New York: Prentice-Hall, 1952), esp. pp. 54-70.

[67] *First Annual Report to the President by the Atomic Energy Labor-Management Relations Panel*, p. 1.

[68] The tendency of disputes to gravitate "upward" toward the President's desk is, of course, not new. To the outsider it would appear that Secretary Mitchell is performing some of the functions handled by Steelman in the previous administration. It should be stressed that Mitchell's involvement in mediating the 1954 Oak Ridge-Paducah dispute did not occur until after the application of panel procedures, which in this case appeared at least temporarily to fail to resolve the dispute. When a dispute reaches such proportions that resort is made to the national emergency provisions of the Labor Management Relations Act, the President or his top advisers are necessarily involved. If an appeal procedure from the panel were to develop even as a matter of expectation, however, the implications for the usefulness of the panel are obvious.

Department is the sponsor of a study of labor-management problems in the field including an evaluation of dispute settling procedures.

Aside from a transitory appearance of some confusion or, perhaps more accurately stated, diffusion of responsibility for disputes settlement in the atomic energy field, two questions occur.

First, with full recognition of the experience and contribution of the Federal Mediation and Conciliation Service in aiding labor and management generally to adjust their differences, is it sound to have the case load of a disputes settlement agency concentrating in the atomic energy field controlled by the Director of the Service? The risk would be that the Service might either hold cases too long before referring them to the panel or send them too quickly. Much depends, of course, on the day-to-day relationship of the Service to the panel. Admittedly mediation should be exhausted. The panel has and should continue to accommodate its function to the Service's customary area of responsibility. It is a legitimate query, nevertheless, whether the determination on accepting a particular case, and the timing, should not be made from the panel's perspective of not only avoiding work stoppages in the industry, but also promoting the growth of sound relationships. The panel has particularized experience with the parties, issues, and trends in the labor relations phase of the atomic energy program. While the Service's trained mediators assigned and cleared for this work would be able to duplicate this experience at a local or regional level, they could not be expected to have a total picture. On balance it would appear that the question of control of the panel's case load might be re-examined along with broader questions relating to the panel's status.

There is a second and related question of a "home" for the panel within the executive branch of the government. Since the continued emergency nature of the atomic energy program presumably accounts for the panel's existence, an argument could be made either for returning the panel to the cover of the Atomic Energy Commission or for placing it within the Office of Defense Mobilization.

It is probably less important that these questions be settled right than that they be settled. Ambiguity as to the panel's status and future is perhaps reflective of the air of transition which surrounds the industry. Nevertheless, doubt on these matters is likely to be cumulative, and to that extent the panel's role is made more difficult. The present panel is, of course, mindful of the problem. As it expressed this delicate matter in its recent Report to the President:

Status of Panel. As the situation has developed in the atomic energy program, . . . it has become increasingly clear that the status of the Panel needs to be kept under continual study. Status assumes importance because of its effect upon the attitudes of labor, management, the governmental agencies concerned, and the public towards the work of the Panel. Discussions have been had concerning clarification of the Panel's status, and it is hoped that these may lead to a proper solution in the near future.[69]

SIGNIFICANCE OF PANEL IDEA FOR OTHER INDUSTRIES

The panel machinery devised to assist disputes settlement in the atomic energy program may be thought to hold interest for other industries with similar problems. For example, John T. Dunlop has noted that of the areas of the economy in which national emergency disputes are most likely to occur—coal, maritime, steel, railroad, and atomic energy—two, the railroads and atomic energy, have specialized machinery designed to prevent work stoppages of an emergency nature.[70] Dunlop proposes that the parties in the other industries be encouraged, perhaps by Congress and with the assistance of the Federal Mediation and Conciliation Service, to develop private or quasi-public machinery which would operate between the resort to economic pressure by the parties and the induced resort to injunctive procedures by the government.

I have great confidence in the ingenuity of the parties to develop such procedures. They can develop their own conciliation steps; they may decide to limit stoppages to some fraction of the total production of the industry; they may mutually select new wage leaders more apt to reach agreement; they may declare in advance their willingness to handle any vital cargo or production. In brief, the subject of emergency disputes should itself become a subject of bargaining between the parties in the

[69] *First Annual Report,* p. 2.

[70] John T. Dunlop, "The Settlement of Emergency Disputes," *in* L. Reed Tripp, ed., *Proceedings of the Fifth Annual Meeting* (Madison: Industrial Relations Research Association, 1953) pp. 117, 122.

particular industries in which these issues arise at the request of the government.[71]

If the panel is to serve in any sense as a "model" for other industries, it is elementary that account must be taken of its origins and the circumstances under which it has operated. As previously discussed, the panel came into a program in which labor-management relations were not past the organization phase, except, of course, in construction. The nature of the jobs was to some extent undetermined. There was a peculiar structure of bargaining with the Atomic Energy Commission exercising an ambiguous veto power over settlements. Both the government and, if memory be sound, the general public considered the slightest stoppage to hold grave peril to the country and hence to be unthinkable. The contractors, while experienced in operations elsewhere, were new to the program, were uncertain of the relationship of this activity to their private operations, and were uneasy as to the role of a government contractor. The unions were concentrating on establishing themselves in the field and developing leadership and structural patterns.

The significance of the panel idea in atomic energy, therefore, is limited by its genealogy. Here, as elsewhere, heredity and environment are important, as Dunlop would, of course, recognize. Indeed, it is fundamental to his view that any machinery applicable to other industries be shaped by the parties themselves, who would have a natural awareness of the traditions and context of their own industry.[72]

CONCLUSION

The panel concept was daring in its origins. At the time the temptation was to resort to stronger measures. The public and

[71] *Ibid.*, pp. 122-123. This proposal may be supposed to parallel to some extent Dunlop's thesis that the formulation of the legal framework for collective bargaining should be removed from the arena of partisan politics. He suggests that in order to avoid the instability of the election returns, union and management groups should engage in what amounts to national collective bargaining on the subject of legislation and share the responsibility for submitting the result to the political process. *Ibid.*, pp. 121-122. For an exploration of the relationship between government and these major interest groups at the state level, see Gilbert Y. Steiner, *Legislation by Collective Bargaining* (Champaign: University of Illinois, Institute of Labor and Industrial Relations, 1951).

[72] Dunlop, *op. cit.*, p. 123.

congressional reaction to serious strikes would have been immediate. There was an almost irresistible tendency to throw out any solution which did not assure continuity of production in the program.

In the face of such distinctive conditions, there was no resort to the extension of abstract principles. The "voluntary" indefinite procedures, supplementing collective bargaining, represented our characteristic adaptation of previous habits of action. Nevertheless, the "formula" for collective bargaining in atomic energy was directly influenced to the extent that only the transportation industry occurs as an analogy. In most cases, that "formula" was expected to be an alternative to the use of the national emergency provisions of the Labor Management Relations Act applicable to basic industries. Thus government intervention in the collective bargaining process in atomic energy, although of a lower magnitude, is more constant than the pragmatic response to individual disputes characteristic of generalized national labor policy. The panel idea and its execution undoubtedly have made enduring contributions to the establishment of sound bargaining relationships in the atomic energy program.

Today one senses that the panel is an institution in transition. It operates in a setting in which profound changes have occurred since the time of its conception and are daily taking place.[73] New weapons have been produced and presumably stockpiled. International tension has, if anything, become aggravated. But the resultant stresses on the economy are at least distributed to other segments than the production of atomic and thermonuclear weapons. Industry, agriculture, and medicine have caught the vision of peacetime uses of the atom. While research continues apace, there is much for industry to digest. On the pacification-of-the-atom side, therefore, if we have not moved from the research to the engineering phase, at least the latter occupies a place of greater prominence. The very changes implied in the Atomic Energy Act of 1954 reflect the dynamic nature of the field.

[73] A good summary of the "changing perspectives in atomic energy" is contained in *Amending the Atomic Energy Act of 1946, as Amended, and for Other Purposes,* to accompany H. R. 9757, which eventuated in the Atomic Energy Act of 1954. The purpose stated was to make our "legislative controls better conform with the scientific, technical, economic, and political facts of atomic energy as they exist today." *Ibid.,* p. 1.

What, then, of a disputes settlement "formula" for the future?
It is possible that the present procedures are the best that can
be devised and are needed to meet the problems created by the
entrance of private industry on the stage. Perhaps the older technique might be applied in some instances but not in others.[74] On
the other hand, perhaps a complete revision of policy is justified
by the recent significant developments.

Certainly there will be problems of coverage of the "formula,"
if such there is to be. It must be recognized that to look only to the
disputes which arise in the atomic energy field is not enough. Not
all disputes which will occur will be within an area of emergency
justifying the application of special procedures. The occasion will
arise when the scope of the panel idea must be defined more narrowly and sharply.

Beyond the problem of coverage, there are considerations of
method. Although recommendations have lately been the fashion,
as a plan it would seem impossible to improve on the uncertain and
flexible techniques inherent in the panel procedures. The format
of the panel recognizes that no single concept of disputes will
suffice. Disputes arise of varying scope, issues, and attitudes—
each with its peculiarities. It is reasonable to suppose that as disputes are various in character, so should be the tools for their
resolution.

It is proposed that it would be well to evaluate periodically
restrictions placed on labor and management in the light of the
evolving status of the atomic energy program and that the present
is an especially appropriate time. Though the conclusions conceivably may differ, the point of departure is the same as in 1948.
There are times when we need "education in the obvious more than
investigation of the obscure." We may be reminded that self-determination of the terms and conditions of employment by the parties
themselves has been thought to be the basic value of the collective
bargaining institution.

Moreover, it may be supposed that there is an organic relation

[74] This approach would be analogous to the treatment Congress gave to the
problem of secrecy and security in the program under the 1954 Act. The approach there was to authorize the AEC to vary security investigation requirements depending upon the class of work and degree of defense importance of
the information to which access would be permitted. § 145.

in a society between its political, social, and economic institutions, and the administration of the employer-employee relationship. Industrial democracy is in a sense both a derivative and a correlative of political democracy. Breathing room for collective bargaining—the greatest technique yet devised for inducing agreement—is thought to be in the interest of management, of labor, and of the public. Restrictions on the freedom of labor and management carry their own label: "Caution—May Be Habit Forming."

The boundaries of the atomic energy field are tenuous. While the eventual impact is not foreseeable, even a conservative estimate would anticipate considerable spread of the art into related areas of the economy. In this context, our approach toward labor-management conflicts which arise in atomic energy bears both present and potential implications for national labor policy. Limitations imposed on labor-management relationships in this sphere may hold germs of contagion for which there is no ready immunization. Exceptions have a way of becoming rules, and rules, exceptions. If such be true, it is momentarily, at least, puzzling why this problem has not created more concern. The explanation would seem to be that it is subordinate to a larger, more troubling challenge. For the central problem with which we are confronted is not under what institutional pattern atomic products are to be produced, but to what use we are to put the product. Our new heroes, the scientists, worry too. They tell us that sources are now ours which hold both peril and promise. There seems at least a chance that these science fiction developments will eventually be used to fry our breakfast eggs rather than to create new desolate landscapes. Meanwhile we would do well to be about integrating the new field with the basic structure of our society. For though we may influence the range of the odds, we cannot choose but to gamble. We may be in sight of posterity in our own time, but we are ever past the point of no return.[75]

[75] It is a conventional observation that our understanding of ways of accommodation between man and man and nation and nation seriously lags behind the discoveries of the physical sciences. Yet it may be that the lasting significance of these advances to the Mt. Everest of invention is not to be found even in that appealing phrase "Atoms for Peace." Rather one may "pray with faith believing" that the awesome proportions of the atomic revolution may supply the imperative for a "crash" program in the ordering of human and world affairs. We have nothing to lose but everything.

THE SEARCH FOR A FORMULA

BY R. W. FLEMING
University of Illinois

This chapter examines some of the better-known proposals for dealing with emergency strikes—including that hardy perennial, compulsory arbitration.

Any attempt to categorize the proposals which have been made for handling emergency strikes is well-nigh impossible unless one resorts to the label "miscellaneous." By using that device, however, it can be said that the proposals fall into three general groups: (1) ingenious suggestions for a so-called "statutory strike" to replace the actual work stoppage; (2) compulsory arbitration with its frank abandonment of the principle of voluntarism; and (3) a miscellaneous category which here includes the Virginia and Massachusetts laws as well as a proposal for special emergency panels by industry. Partial production as a possible solution to the emergency strike is deliberately omitted. Voluntary resort to the shortened workweek in the coal industry, which is not uncommon, has in no way obviated the necessity for a strike. Plans for partial production could not be implemented by the parties during the 1952 steel strike despite their agreement with the government on the principle. The mechanical difficulties of such a solution in public utilities seem almost insurmountable.

Since the statutory strike is both unconventional and provocative, it is perhaps entitled to first consideration.

THE STATUTORY STRIKE

The statutory strike was first proposed in print in 1949, when Marceau and Musgrave published their plan in the *Harvard Business Review*. Their basic idea is summarized as follows: "Under conditions of a statutory strike, the union could not call a work stoppage, and the company could not stop making work available, but the terms of operation would be such as to place upon both parties the same economic burden which would be incurred under an actual work stoppage."[1]

Goble suggested a similar scheme in 1950. His theory was that it would (1) substitute a new sanction (method of inflicting injury) for the traditional strike and lockout, (2) neutralize or eliminate the stop-work or lockout procedure as a factor in collective bargaining, (3) preserve the established balance in economic bargaining power as between management and labor, and (4) stabilize the national economy.[2]

Chamberlain seems to be the most recent advocate of the statutory strike,[3] though others have admittedly advanced the idea.[4] The proposals vary in important detail, but the essential idea behind all of them is the same. Marceau and Musgrave would require the company to pay for all work performed at a rate so high that it would stand in the same profit and loss position as it would have if the strike had ensued. On the other hand, workers would be paid so little that they would be under the same economic pressure that a strike would generate. The difference would be deposited in a public trust fund. Receipts from the trust fund would be paid to the U. S. Treasury. The money could then be used for the general needs of the government or some special public services. It could also be used as the parties wished after the conclusion of the statutory strike. They might even decide to divide it between them-

---

[1] LeRoy Marceau and Richard A. Musgrave, "Strikes in Essential Industries: A Way Out," *Harvard Business Review*, XXVII (May 1949), p. 287.

[2] George W. Goble, "The Non-Stoppage Strike," *Current Economic Comment*, XII (August 1950), pp. 3-12.

[3] Neil W. Chamberlain, assisted by Jane Metzger Schilling, *Social Responsibility and Strikes* (New York: Harper, 1953), pp. 279-286.

[4] Cf., for instance, Charles O. Gregory, "Injunctions, Seizure, and Compulsory Arbitration," *Temple Law Quarterly*, XXVI (Spring 1953), pp. 397-405.

selves, though the authors differed on the advisability of permitting this step.

Goble would permit either labor or management to apply voluntarily to the National Labor Relations Board for a nonstoppage strike order. The company would then be required to supply information to the NLRB, from which the Board would determine its current net earnings. Thereafter, the Board would issue an order requiring the company to segregate a pro rata part of the earnings and deposit the amount in a designated bank to the credit of the Board. At the same time, all wages and salaries, of both production workers and executives, would be cut 25 per cent, and this amount would likewise be deposited in a segregated bank account. The company could neither pay dividends nor add to its surplus during the period of the controversy, and no strike benefits could be paid by either labor or management. Bargaining would continue between the parties, and if no agreement were reached within ninety days the segregated funds would be forfeited to the government. This procedure would continue until an agreement was reached, with funds being forfeited at ninety-day intervals. Some additional refinements designed to resolve various technical difficulties and objections are added.

Where public hardship would result, Chamberlain would have the government issue an order directing employees to remain on their jobs unless, as individuals, they chose to resign their employment and all attaching rights. At the same time, he would direct management to continue production to fill all incoming orders, maintaining the schedule of prices then in effect. Wages for production employees would be reduced 50 per cent, and the returns of the company limited to actual out-of-pocket or variable expenses plus one-half of fixed costs. Excess funds would be forfeited into the public treasury.

There is always a strong temptation to dismiss novel ideas of this kind as ingenious "gadgets" designed, unfortunately, for a field in which "gadgets" do not fit. But they warrant more serious consideration, both because they are the reasoned products of serious scholars and because they suggest a method of preserving voluntarism while at the same time protecting the health and safety of the public.

It may not be fair to lump the statutory-strike proposals together for analysis, since they do differ. Some examples come to mind immediately.

Marceau and Musgrave assign to a court the unenviable task of deciding what is a "living wage," and therefore the extent to which wages shall be cut during the life of the dispute. Aside from the enormous administrative difficulty of determining such a level under explosive conditions, the process would seem to offer almost limitless possibilities for propaganda which would do little to enhance the settlement of the dispute. Goble and Chamberlain avoid this problem by simply cutting wages by a fixed percentage during the strike.

Goble makes the law applicable only by choice of the parties, thereby certainly avoiding possible legal difficulties which await the others who impose the procedure at the instance of the government. But in relying on the free choice of the parties, he renders less protection to public health and safety.

Only Goble calls for a reduction in executive salaries during the course of the dispute. This seems to be a two-edged sword. Executive salaries are not ordinarily reduced during strikes. Therefore, when Goble proposes that executive salaries be cut and at the same time applies the procedure only by choice, it is difficult to see what incentive there will be for executives (who are usually not owners) to invoke the plan. On the other hand, it does impose a burden on executives which the other plans do not.

Chamberlain limits the return of the company to actual out-of-pocket or variable expenses plus one-half of fixed costs. In so far as receipts exceed outlays, the difference will be paid into the public treasury. Lawyers will certainly be concerned with the legality of these proposals. Can the government order management to continue production on a basis which permits recovery of only half of the fixed costs and forfeits the difference between income and outgo into the public treasury? Is this "just compensation"? Can the procedure be validated even by accompanying seizure, which the author finds undesirable?

Differences of the kind cited above are, however, largely procedural. It may therefore be quite possible to devise modifications which will satisfy most critics. The more serious problems are substantive and apply to all the schemes which have been proposed.

In the first place, each of the proposals proceeds on the assumption that the strike is primarily an expression of economic force between contending parties, and that what is wanted is a procedure which will exert economic pressure while, at the same time, maintaining production. Thus Chamberlain says:

The solution required is one under which the strike substitute comes into play while production continues. We need a procedure which enables each party to "swing the ax" against the other in demonstration of its economic power in the institutional order, as a means of making disagreement on its terms costly to the other party, but which permits a continued flow of goods and services to consumers and other producers.[5]

It is this basic assumption which gives rise to serious question. From the coldly logical and rational point of view, the strike may be little more than the application of economic pressure. But is this all there is to it? Does anyone who has watched a John L. Lewis or a Sewell Avery parade across the national stage in the last twenty years think that such colorful and complex personalities regard the strike as nothing more than an economic device to be used under "business as usual" conditions? Does not Chamberlain's detailed account of the critical Duquesne Light Company utility strike in the fall of 1946 illustrate the fact that the strike is much more than the exertion of economic pressure?[6]

A major strike is normally preceded by lengthy negotiations which are unavoidably tinged with emotion. As the critical date approaches, the tension increases. Attention is focused on the leaders (especially on the union side), and no matter how responsible they are, they cannot escape a sense of power. The union, like the family, tends to close ranks under attack. It is then a part of a "movement," not simply an agency motivated by economic ends.

J. R. Hicks once said, "A union which never strikes may lose the ability to organize a formidable strike, so that its threats become less effective."[7]

Norman J. Ware has pointed out that "among the young, the

[5] Chamberlain, *op. cit.*, p. 279.
[6] *Ibid.*, pp. 191-229.
[7] J. R. Hicks, *The Theory of Wages* (London: Macmillan, 1935), p. 146.

emotional value of strike experience is often a clear gain, and it is perhaps not much of an exaggeration to say that, unless we can control and limit the discipline of machine labor and adjust it to human needs, the strike is a necessary emotional release from mechanization."[8]

In any event, whether one agrees with either Hicks or Ware, is it not apparent that any major strike is something more than the exercise of economic force? The statutory-strike proposal seems to take no account of these other aspects. Can it succeed without doing so?

Secondly, within the realm of economic force, the statutory-strike proposals all assume that the most serious damage inflicted on management by the strike is the immediate loss of profits. Is this so?

The coal industry has certainly given rise to more alleged national "emergencies" than any other. It is common knowledge that the coal industry is plagued with overproduction. Thus, when a strike occurs, there is invariably a sizable amount of coal above ground. Often the miners' workweek has already been reduced for this very reason. Neither management nor the union is anxious to have coal glut the market, and the public suffers no inconvenience in the early days of a coal strike because there is no shortage of coal. By the time stocks have been reduced so that the strike is being felt, the strike may have been in effect sixty to ninety days. Against this background, which seems unavoidable if any real economic pressure is to be exerted on either side, what chance is there for a statutory strike to be imposed?

The transit industry, which at the local level is often regarded in the "emergency" strike category, is another example of a different problem. Profits are seldom high and often nonexistent. Transport executives have apparently been much more worried about the long-run loss of business which would follow a stoppage than they have about a temporary loss of profits. Yet for this industry the statutory strike will maintain service, thus removing the main economic pressure.

Thirdly, is there any escape from the fact that the statutory strike encourages the maintenance of the status quo? The 1949 steel strike

[8] Norman J. Ware, *Labor in Modern Industrial Society* (Boston: Heath, 1935), p. 116.

illustrates the point. In that case, the union wanted pensions provided through unilateral company contributions. The companies felt strongly enough about the issue to resist to the point of a strike. An "emergency" fact-finding board was appointed. A strike occurred, and eventually a settlement was reached.

In the steel case, the companies were ready to sacrifice not only their profits but other economic advantages which flow from continued production in return for a principle. The statutory strike would have diminished the loss imposed upon the steel companies. True, it would also have lightened the load which the workers had to bear, but the decrease in burden would not seem proportionate where management feels a strong institutional urge to resist.

When basic changes in the status quo are concerned—a "look at the books," the guaranteed annual wage, codetermination—it is submitted that the statutory strike will inevitably strengthen the company's resistance.

Finally, is there any reason to believe that the statutory strike is politically realistic? The proposal has been public property now for five years. During that time, there seems to be no evidence that it has attracted any real interest or support from labor, management, or legislators. Congressman Velde of Illinois did introduce the Goble plan in the Eighty-second Congress. His bill, H.R. 5449, was referred to the Committee on Education and Labor but was never reported out.

The opposition of labor and management to such a law would not necessarily be fatal, although, as the original authors admit, there is "no reason to believe that the public is ready to adopt a law which both labor and management are against."[9] It is also possible that the views of labor and management will change. Certainly, a noticeable change has come over both labor and management with respect to the way in which great strikes are conducted today as compared with thirty years ago.

The impetus for statutory-strike legislation will have to come from somewhere, and the source of that pressure is not apparent. The related groups have shown no interest, and the legislative process is such that existing machinery is hardly likely to be supplanted with so novel an idea in time of crisis.

[9] Marceau and Musgrave, *op. cit.*, p. 290.

In summary, it is difficult to avoid a conclusion that the statutory strike, as so far suggested by its proponents, is inadequate. It under-estimates the noneconomic factors in a strike, overemphasizes the short-run restriction of profits while at the same time minimizing the value of other factors such as continued production, inevitably bal-ances the scale in favor of the status quo, and is politically unreal-istic.

There are, of course, other criticisms which some students con-sider even more serious than the points made above. Chief among these is the question of whether workers will put forth any real effort when their wages are substantially reduced. This leads to the ultimate query of whether it is the appearance or the effect of a strike which one is interested in avoiding.

COMPULSORY ARBITRATION

Actual experience with compulsory arbitration is limited in the United States. Until after World War II, only Kansas had passed such a statute, and this was in the wake of the first world war. Some seven hundred coal strikes are alleged to have taken place in that state in the years 1915-1919. A prolonged strike in the winter of 1919 led to serious shortages of coal. The state attempted to apply the antitrust laws and appointed a receiver for the mines. Against this background, the legislature passed a compulsory arbitration law.[10] The constitutionality of the law was under steady attack, and after a stormy administrative history it was finally declared uncon-stitutional by the U.S. Supreme Court in 1923.[11] The Court ruled that the authority given the agency contravened the due process clause of the Fourteenth Amendment in that it curtailed the right of an employer, on the one hand, and of the employee, on the other hand, to contract about his affairs. Thereafter, Kansas abolished the industrial court, although the statute still remains on the books.

Only after World War II and the record number of strikes in 1946 was further legislative interest in compulsory arbitration shown in this country, and then it was restricted to the public utility field. In 1947, seven states passed variations of a public utility compulsory

[10] Harold S. Roberts, "Compulsory Arbitration of Labor Disputes in Public Utilities," *Labor Law Journal,* I (June 1950), pp. 694-704.

[11] *Wolff Packing Co. v. Court of Industrial Relations,* 262 U. S. 522 (1923).

arbitration statute.[12] The experience under the New Jersey and Pennsylvania laws has been examined by several students, and their findings may be read elsewhere.[13] In February 1951, the U.S. Supreme Court held the Wisconsin law unconstitutional on the ground that it abrogated the right to strike, which was protected for workers in interstate commerce by the Taft-Hartley Act.[14] This decision cast a serious shadow over the constitutionality of other state compulsory arbitration laws and slowed to a walk the experience being gained thereunder.

The principal experience with compulsory arbitration under peacetime conditions and in the free world has been in Australia and New Zealand. It has been popular in America to point out that, since these countries still publish strike statistics, compulsory arbitration obviously does not work. But in his excellent series of lectures at Massachusetts Institute of Technology in the spring of 1953, Justice Arthur Tyndall of the Court of Arbitration in New Zealand suggested that it was difficult to reconcile the American concept of compulsory arbitration with the system which operated in New Zealand.[15]

Among other things, he points out that the invocation of the New Zealand industrial court process is *voluntary* with the parties, and that not all industries have chosen to be covered. Thus he argues that strike statistics are deceptive, since they include important industries such as coal mining and the waterfront industry which have not invoked the Act.

[12] The number varies according to how one defines "compulsory." Generally the seven states are said to be Florida, Indiana, Michigan, Nebraska, New Jersey, Pennsylvania, and Wisconsin.

[13] Lois MacDonald, *Compulsory Arbitration in New Jersey* (New York: New York University, Institute of Labor Relations and Social Security, September, 1949); Robert R. France and Richard Lester, *Compulsory Arbitration of Utility Disputes in New Jersey and Pennsylvania* (Princeton: Princeton University, Industrial Relations Section, 1951); Thomas Kennedy, "The Handling of Emergency Disputes," in *Proceedings of Second Annual Meeting* (Madison: Industrial Relations Research Association, 1949).

[14] *Amalgamated Association of Street, Electric Railway and Motor Coach Employees of America, Division 998, et al. v. Wisconsin Employment Relations Board,* 340 U. S. 383 (1951).

[15] Arthur Tyndall, *The Settlement of Labor Disputes in New Zealand* (Cambridge: Massachusetts Institute of Technology, Industrial Relations Section, Department of Economics and Social Science, 1953), p. 49.

The main arguments for and against compulsory arbitration can perhaps best be stated through a series of questions with brief comments on each:

1. In a free-enterprise economy, is the strike peril sufficiently serious to warrant the imposition of a compulsory settlement?

David Cole, whose first-hand experience with national emergency disputes is unsurpassed, is perhaps the leading exponent of the view that special legislation for dealing either with national or local emergency disputes is unnecessary. He points out that on the national level we have thrived for over a century and a half without specific laws,[16] and that in the states, strikes in public utilities have not presented greater problems nor been as frequent in industrial states like New York, Illinois, Ohio, and California, which do not have antistrike legislation, as in states like New Jersey, Pennsylvania, Indiana, Michigan, and Wisconsin, which do have such legislation.[17]

Cole's views on the impact of the national emergency strike are documented to a large extent in Chapter I, "An Economic Definition of the National Emergency Dispute," and Chapter II, "The Economic Impact of Strikes in Key Industries" in this volume. In brief, those chapters suggest that under present conditions the range and frequency of national emergency strikes are small, and their economic impact exaggerated.

Strikes in public utilities do, of course, raise some special problems, for their products are essential and they cannot be stockpiled.[18] This perhaps explains why, when the American Institute of Public Opinion has asked, "Should laws be passed to forbid all strikes in public service industries such as electric, gas, telephone, and local transportation companies?" majorities of from 58 to 64 per cent have supported such legislation in three different polls.[19]

Academicians and even practitioners, who oppose compulsory

[16] David Cole, "The Role of Government in Emergency Disputes," *Temple Law Quarterly*, XXVI (Spring 1953), p. 382.

[17] The Governor's Committee on Legislation Relating to Public Utility Labor Disputes, *Report to Governor Robert B. Meyner* (New Jersey 1954), p. 18.

[18] Cf. Edgar L. Warren, *The Settlement of Labor-Management Disputes* (Rio Piedras: University of Puerto Rico Press, 1951), p. 72.

[19] AIPO Poll (February 27, 1946), "Should Laws be Passed to Forbid All Strikes in Public Service Industries," in Hadley Cantril and Mildred Strunk, eds., *Public Opinion, 1935-46* (Princeton: Princeton University Press, 1951), p. 826.

arbitration on the ground that emergency strikes are few and far between and create few actual—as distinguished from potential—emergencies, may be barking up the wrong tree so far as the general populace is concerned. For, as Robert France noted in his examination of the working of the Virginia law:

The attitude of the Virginia Governor has not differed from that of other executives and administrators in invoking statutes dealing with emergency labor disputes. *It is safer to use the laws and be criticized by some representatives of labor and management, and a few academicians, than to risk some injury to the public.* (italics added) [20]

2. Are emergency labor disputes amenable to resolution through a quasi-judicial proceeding?

Proponents of compulsory settlements through labor courts (many of them lawyers—and one must remember that legislatures are often composed predominantly of lawyers) usually profess an inability to see any difference between the resolution of labor disputes and any other kind of dispute before a judicial tribunal.[21] Though conscious of the difficulty of providing specific legislative criteria for the resolution of such disputes, they note that the same general proposition is true, for instance, in the case of public utility commissions set up to pass on utility rates. From this they argue that since utility rates are controlled by a public commission, there is no reason why wages and conditions of work should not be similarly controlled.

Few observers of the industrial relations scene will dispute the fact that there is an analogy between a typical court proceeding and the interpretation of a collective bargaining contract through an arbitration proceeding. But the situation is quite different where the terms of a new contract are concerned. There are, for example, no universally agreed upon economic principles which will automatically guide the arbitrators to a decision. Compulsory arbitration statutes have tended to resolve this dilemma by establishing criteria in terms of standards prevailing in the operating area. Such

[20] Robert R. France, "Seizure in Emergency Labor Disputes in Virginia," *Industrial and Labor Relations Review*, VII (April 1954), pp. 361-362.

[21] "Should the Federal Government Require Arbitration of Labor Disputes in All Basic Industries?" *The Congressional Digest*, XXVI (August-September 1947), pp. 202-224.

criteria are invariably resisted by public utility unions on the ground that it means they must always be followers and can never be leaders. This may cause arbitration boards to seek other ways of relieving the pressure, with the possible result that areas not previously within the scope of collective bargaining will be invaded.[22]

A conclusion that labor disputes differ from ordinary disputes submitted to our courts is surely entirely warranted. On the other hand, courts and administrative tribunals do handle difficult substantive and procedural problems. Utility rate regulation, condemnation proceedings, fair trade practices, and food and drug regulation are examples which come to mind immediately. Thus if the only serious objection to compulsory arbitration is the one of establishing satisfactory legislative or administrative criteria, one suspects that the problem can be solved.

3. Will compulsory arbitration impair free collective bargaining?

Representatives of both management and labor generally answer this question in the affirmative.[23] Many observers agree with them.[24] In sum and substance, they take the position that management will fear making an offer in bargaining lest the offer become a floor in a later arbitration proceeding, that labor will fear offering a compromise lest the compromise become the ceiling in a later arbitration proceeding, and that in any event wages cannot be controlled without the same authority ultimately extending to prices, profits, and other areas of the economy.

[22] Cf. Nathan P. Feinsinger in *To Repeal Compulsory Arbitration,* Hearing on Bill 87-8 62-A, and 94-A, Joint Senate and Assembly Labor Committee, February 23, 1949 (Milwaukee: Wisconsin State Federation of Labor Transcript), p. 30.

[23] Chamber of Commerce of the United States, *Compulsory Arbitration: Opposed* (Washington: The Chamber, September 1947); National Association of Manufacturers, *Compulsory Arbitration: A Manual for Secondary School Debates* (New York: The Association, 1949); Boris Shishkin, "Should the Federal Government Require Arbitration of Labor Disputes in All Basic American Industries?" *American Federationist,* LIV (February, 1947), pp. 18-20; Arthur J. Goldberg, "Statement of Arthur J. Goldberg, General Counsel, Congress of Industrial Organizations and the United Steelworkers of America, CIO, Before the Governor's Commission on Labor, Commonwealth of Pennsylvania," unpublished (April 8, 1953).

[24] Herbert R. Northrup, *Strike Controls in Essential Industries,* Studies in Business Economics, No. 30 (New York: National Industrial Conference Board, 1951); Harold S. Roberts, *Compulsory Arbitration of Labor Disputes* (Honolulu: University of Hawaii, 1949).

There is insufficient American experience on which to base a judgment as to the inevitability of further economic controls once wages come under control through compulsory arbitration. Justice Tyndall, of the New Zealand Court of Arbitration, seemed to feel that there is no necessary connection.[25] But Mark Perlman thought from his Australian studies that the arbitration courts had become a regular partner with the employers and the unions in framing socioeconomic policy.[26]

In so far as America is concerned, both MacDonald and Kennedy were convinced from their examination of the New Jersey experience that the law had impaired collective bargaining. Their findings have recently been confirmed by a nearly unanimous tripartite committee in its report to Governor Robert B. Meyner on legislation relating to public utility labor disputes.[27] Kennedy concluded: (a) both sides feared to suggest a reasonable basis for settlement lest the other party use it as a springboard for securing a better settlement through compulsory arbitration; (b) negotiators feared assuming responsibility for a settlement when better terms might be arrived at through compulsory arbitration; (c) unessential bargaining demands were harder to settle, since the parties were inclined to leave them in on the chance that the board might give a favorable settlement; (d) compulsory arbitration encouraged the growth of professional advocates on both sides who argued the cases, thus tending to take the settlement out of the hands of local people; and (e) where the company would be concerned with rate increases before a public utility commission, it might feel that its case was fortified if a wage increase was ordered by a compulsory arbitration board.[28]

France and Lester seemed a little less sure that the effect of the law on collective bargaining could be stated so categorically. Basing their opinion on a study of the New Jersey and Pennsylvania laws, they were inclined to feel that bargaining relationships which were functioning successfully before the enactment of the laws were not disrupted greatly by the statutes.[29]

[25] Tyndall, op. cit., p. 53.
[26] Mark Perlman, The Australian Arbitration System, Occasional Paper 57 (Honolulu: University of Hawaii, August 1951), p. 9.
[27] Report to Governor Robert B. Meyner, p. 18.
[28] Kennedy, op. cit., pp. 21-23.
[29] France and Lester, op. cit., p. 87.

The chairman of the Wisconsin Employment Relations Board, who administers the Wisconsin law, has said that he finds no evidence that collective bargaining has been discouraged by the compulsory arbitration law in his state. A leading utility lawyer agrees with him, though various union representatives dissent.[30]

Justice Tyndall feels that the New Zealand practice of disallowing references in court to any offers or counteroffers made in the course of negotiations takes care of the fear which the parties might otherwise feel with respect to normal negotiations.[31]

From all this, it would seem to be a fair conclusion that most observers believe compulsory arbitration has an adverse effect on collective bargaining. The critical question is how serious the effect is and also whether it is inevitable. Where the attitude of the parties toward the law is one of dissatisfaction from the outset, it is reasonable to suppose that the effect will be more serious. On the other hand, it is possible that experience would diminish, though not erase, the impact of the law upon normal collective bargaining.

4. Will "politics" inevitably affect the operation of a compulsory arbitration system?

Gagliardo, in relating the Kansas experience after World War I, says that Judge Higgins, a member of the Kansas Industrial Court, wrote the following statement in 1924:

I contend that, because of the constant political influence brought to bear upon the Court of Industrial Relations beginning early in the first year, it has never had a fair chance. . . . such a law cannot be successfully administered by a political committee or by any tribunal dependent upon a politician in the governor's office.[32]

MacDonald, Kennedy, Lester, and France all agreed, from their examination of the New Jersey experience, that the issue of compulsory arbitration had become a party issue (though not a vital one) and that there were charges of "politics" in its administration.

Maclaurin, in his study of compulsory arbitration in Australia, points out that both labor and management in Australia favor retention of the present law, but that there is some opposition in the

[30] To Repeal Compulsory Arbitration, p. 43.

[31] Tyndall, op. cit., p. 51.

[32] Domenico Gagliardo, The Kansas Industrial Court: An Experiment in Compulsory Arbitration (Lawrence, Kans.: Kansas University Press, 1941), pp. 227-228.

ranks of labor which "has taken the form of agitation for a change in the personnel of the federal court and for legislative amendments which would provide emphasis on conciliation and reduce legalism rather than for any drastic change in the system as such."[33]

It would appear to be the unanimous judgment of those who have studied arbitration experience, both in the United States and abroad, that "politics," primarily in terms of seeking favorable amendments to or abolition of the statute, will play a definite part in the life cycle of a compulsory arbitration law. In the United States, it is the common experience that one political party sponsors the act and the other opposes it. Under those circumstances, it is hard to see how "politics" can be kept away from the problem.

Attempts by pressure groups to amend or change the administration of a law are not unique in a democracy. Indeed, it would be strange if they did not do so. The difficulty in connection with compulsory arbitration arises because such conduct is incompatible with free collective bargaining to which we claim to be committed.

5. Will labor disputes be eliminated by enactment of a compulsory arbitration act?

No one argues that strikes will disappear after the enactment of a compulsory arbitration law. Everyone agrees that there have been strikes despite such legislation in every jurisdiction in which it has ever been tried. Thus the question becomes not whether compulsory arbitration legislation will eliminate strikes, but whether it will improve the present record.

Justice Tyndall admits that the New Zealand system has not eliminated strikes, but he gives as his opinion "that if the present system were abolished there would be a large increase in strikes."[34] Maclaurin reports that the Australian experience has been "somewhat disappointing" in this respect.[35]

Kennedy and MacDonald, in their studies of the New Jersey Act, found little basis for expressing a judgment as to the effect of the statute on strikes. They noted that there had been strikes, but thought it debatable whether there were more or fewer than would

[33] W. Rupert Maclaurin, "Compulsory Arbitration in Australia," *American Economic Review,* XXVIII (March 1938), p. 77.
[34] Tyndall, *op. cit.,* p. 53.
[35] Maclaurin, *op. cit.,* p. 67.

have occurred without legislation.[36] Lester and France agreed that, with respect to New Jersey, services had been largely maintained, but they thought perhaps "the record would have been almost as good without the Act."[37] However, with respect to the Pennsylvania law, they found that "in a few instances, the Act apparently prevented strikes that would have occurred otherwise."[38]

In Wisconsin, at the time the chairman of the Wisconsin Employment Relations Board testified before the legislative committee in 1949, nineteen cases had come before the Board in one way or another, and there had been only one utility strike in the state since the enactment of the law.[39] However, there was no way of comparing what would have happened without the law, and strikes in public utilities in that state prior to the passage of the law had been most infrequent.

6. Are compulsory arbitration awards enforceable?

Students and practitioners alike are in agreement that one of the great problems of compulsory arbitration is the question of enforcement. However, some feel that the merits of such a system cannot be allowed to depend upon enforceability. In this connection, Chamberlain has said:

It has often been argued that a decision unpopular with the union members cannot be enforced, since thousands of strikers cannot be jailed. Criminal penalties are not the only means of enforcement, however. To honor such an argument would be to admit that no legislation controlling unions but opposed by bodies of workers could ever be sustained, since by the simple act of striking they could make it a nullity or force its rescission. The same line of argument would make equally unworkable the fact-finding, injunction and seizure approaches, since in all such cases refusal of the striking employees to return to their jobs would be equally possible. Any strike-control legislation must inescapably rely on compliance by the striking employees, a reliance which does not appear to be unrealistic. If any major groups in a society are above the law, we have a more serious problem than strike control on our hands.[40]

[36] Kennedy, *op. cit.*, p. 27; MacDonald, *op. cit.*, p. 76.
[37] France and Lester, *op. cit.*, p. 60.
[38] *Ibid.*, p. 80.
[39] *To Repeal Compulsory Arbitration, op. cit.*, p. 39.
[40] Chamberlain, *op. cit.*, p. 24.

The trouble with Chamberlain's argument is that it is the universal experience, both here and abroad, that it is difficult to enforce compulsory arbitration awards. Jail sentences are both impractical and impolitic.[41] New Jersey switched from penal to monetary penalties, but never found it expedient to enforce either, despite a number of violations.[42] Penal provisions in New Zealand have not been invoked in thirteen years, despite the fact that many illegal strikes have occurred.[43] And in Australia if the parties are strong enough to flout the court's authority and won't need its benefits shortly afterward, there is little the court can do to punish recalcitrance.[44]

Whether we like it or not, compulsory arbitration awards are hard to enforce. And if major groups in our society cannot be above the law, neither—in the words of Disraeli—can government afford to display its impotence.

To summarize, with respect to compulsory arbitration: (1) There are in fact not many "emergency" disputes which can be said to endanger the public health and safety sufficiently to warrant the imposition of compulsory controls in a free society; yet public sentiment favors enactment of legislation designed to resolve such disputes. (2) Resolving labor disputes through a quasi-judicial procedure is not as analogous to our civilian court disputes as some would argue, but it is sufficiently like the work of existing administrative agencies to be feasible. (3) Compulsory arbitration will unquestionably adversely affect collective bargaining, though in varying degrees, and perhaps never to the point of bringing the whole economy under regulation. (4) "Politics" in connection with the act cannot be avoided in the United States, and there will always be a tendency to seek both favorable legislation and administration, which will in turn impair collective bargaining. (5) Compulsory arbitration will not eliminate labor disputes, but it may reduce them. (6) Enforcement of an award which is unacceptable to labor will be extremely difficult no matter what the sanctions are.

In weighing the arguments, the writer concludes that compulsory arbitration is undesirable. Nevertheless, he thinks the staff report

---

[41] Kennedy, *op. cit.*, p. 24.
[42] *Ibid.*, p. 25.
[43] Tyndall, *op. cit.*, p. 56.
[44] Perlman, *op. cit.*, p. 11.

on emergency disputes to the Subcommittee on Labor of the Eighty-second Congress summed up the situation well when it said:

While enthusiasm for compulsory arbitration of disputes in public utilities is thus restrained, a growing number of observers seem to think that one form or another of compulsory settlement—that is, settlement without work stoppages—will have to be supported in situations where the national health and safety are directly jeopardized by a work stoppage. This support is developing despite the known inadequacies of compulsory arbitration and its adverse effects on genuine bargaining by the parties. The maintenance of unhindered collective bargaining in the preponderant sector of the economy, where there would be no interference with the freedom to strike or lock-out, gives some assurance that the results of free bargaining would continue greatly to influence, if not actually determine, the arbitration awards. It has been observed that many settlements have finally been made after prolonged strikes, which are not markedly different from fact-finding proposals made before the stoppage occurred. Where other devices, like seizure and injunction, were used to gain continued production, these added nothing substantial to the final settlement and as a practical matter only put off the time of settlement.[45]

MISCELLANEOUS PROPOSALS

Most emergency strike proposals, other than the statutory strike and compulsory arbitration, involve some combination or variation of mediation, fact finding, seizure, and the injunction. Thus, in one way or another, they are dealt with elsewhere in this volume. Moreover, there are so many of them that a detailed examination of each would be impossible. There are, however, two situations which seem to deserve mention in this chapter. The first is the pattern called for under the Virginia and Massachusetts laws for dealing with emergency disputes, and the second is the proposal for emergency panels in specific industries.

A detailed account of the Virginia experience is already on the record,[46] but little has been said about the Massachusetts law.

The Virginia Act was originally passed in 1947 and then replaced in 1952 with two other statutes—largely in an attempt to avoid the

---

[45] *Emergency Disputes Settlement,* Staff Report to the Subcommittee on Labor and Labor-Management Relations of the Senate Committee on Labor and Public Welfare, 82d Cong., 2d sess. (December 1952), p. 46.

[46] France, *op. cit.*

effects of the U.S. Supreme Court decision invalidating the Wisconsin compulsory arbitration law.

Under the 1947 Act, the parties to a public utility dispute had to give notice, and the governor or his representative could then attempt to mediate. If this failed, the governor could request them to submit to arbitration, and if one or both refused, they could then give a strike notice to be effective not less than five weeks after the date of the notice. If the governor decided that a strike would threaten the public health, safety, or welfare, he could seize the facilities. Prior to the stoppage, the governor ascertained which employees were essential to continued operations and then polled them as to their willingness to work for the state. The status of an employee was unaffected by his unwillingness to work for the state, but he could not change his mind about working once the stoppage started. The governor could recruit replacements. Once seizure took place, the status quo was maintained as far as wages and working conditions were concerned. Settlement of the controversy was left to private negotiation. The state compensated the utility by turning over 85 per cent of the net income of the operations after deducting all expenses.

The Virginia legislature repealed the original Act in 1952, and replaced it with two new statutes—the Public Utility Seizure Act and the Public Utility Labor Relations Act, which omitted most of the procedures preliminary to seizure found in the old law. Two changes were made in the seizure act. One permits the utility to refuse to turn over its facilities to the governor if it believes his judgment is wrong with respect to the results of a stoppage. The governor may meet this challenge by asking the courts for an order to show cause why the utility should not be seized. The other amendment is with respect to compensation and provides, in addition to the 85-15 per cent split mentioned above, that this "shall in no wise control the amount of just compensation to be allowed to the utility."[47]

As of December 31, 1952, the governor had resorted to seizure nine times, there had been two strikes where the governor took no

[47] "Public Utility Seizure Act," *Code of Virginia 1950*, Article 56-509 et seq.; "Public Utility Labor Relations Act," *Code of Virginia 1950* (1953 Replacement Volume), Article 40-95.

action other than attempted mediation, and in one reported lockout the governor had also refused to seize. France's findings with respect to the Virginia law may be summarized as follows: There is no strong evidence that the Act has interfered with collective bargaining, but there are indications that it may in the future. There is often no incentive to management to settle, since the cost of a wage increase may in some cases balance with the loss from seizure. The Act will apply unevenly in different industries; for example, bus companies are often on a slim or nonexistent profit margin where seizure will entail no loss and may help get a rate increase. Partial operation (resulting from employee refusal to work) will put more pressure on some managements, but is likely to be opposed by the state because of the potential financial liability involved; some success in terms of maintaining services can be claimed for the Act. Enforcement is difficult even in a state where labor is weak. Administrative officers will be inclined to err on the safe side in finding whether or not an emergency exists.[48]

To the outside observer, it would seem that the Virginia law has too few alternatives. Following mediation, there is only seizure. Seizure means the status quo for labor and an economic formula for management which is not necessarily unfavorable. Thus there is little incentive for settlement. Even from the state's point of view, the merits of the law seem dubious, for it involves potential financial liability, a problem in conflict of interest with respect to rates, and the political hazard of seizure. The device for replacing employees who refuse to work for the state seems destructive of morale in the state service. More than once, in bus strikes, the state has apparently brought in drivers from the Highway Department. Finally, enforcement will, in all likelihood, become increasingly difficult as the inequities of the law become more apparent.

The Massachusetts law was enacted in 1947 and amended in 1954. It provides that where the Commissioner of Labor and Industries finds that a labor dispute "imminently threatens a substantial interruption in the production or distribution of essential goods or services he shall certify the dispute to the Governor."[49] The gov-

[48] France, *op. cit.*
[49] *Acts and Resolves, The Commonwealth of Massachusetts* (1954), Chapter 557, Section 1.

ernor then undertakes an investigation which may include an informal hearing before the governor, the Commissioner of Labor and Industries, and the Commissioner of Public Safety, at which the parties are heard on the sole question of whether an interruption is imminent and will curtail essential goods and services to such an extent as to endanger the health and safety of any community. If the governor makes an affirmative finding, he may then require the parties to appear before a moderator to show cause why they should not submit the dispute to arbitration. The moderator may also mediate. If he is ultimately unsuccessful in getting the parties into agreement or in persuading them to arbitrate, he is required to make public his findings as to the responsibility of either or both for the failure. He may not comment on the merits of the dispute in his report.

A second alternative is for the governor to request the parties voluntarily to submit the dispute to an emergency board of inquiry of three members empowered to recommend settlement terms. The board may be tripartite in character.

If the governor finds the above procedures inappropriate for a given dispute, or if the dispute remains unsettled in spite of having utilized the procedure, he declares an emergency, during which period he either makes arrangements with the parties for partial production to protect the health and safety or seizes the plant. During seizure, the governor may, in his discretion, put into effect the recommendation of the board of inquiry (assuming there has been one) or appoint a special commission to make findings. The latter may also, in the discretion of the governor, be put into effect. "The special commission shall base its recommendations on such of the factors normally taken into account in collective bargaining or voluntary arbitration as it deems material, including the conditions in existence in the industry affected."[50]

If the governor decides that the intervention of the state is no longer necessary, he may terminate the emergency without regard to whether the dispute is settled.

There has been only limited experience with the law. Four cases occurred in 1953, but prior to the 1954 amendments the moderator could not conciliate. In three cases, the moderators were successful

[50] *Ibid.*, Section 4(B)(2).

in defining the issues and in thus contributing to the arbitration which followed.

The Massachusetts law represents the "arsenal of weapons" approach which so many distinguished experts have recommended in the emergency field. It makes available to the governor almost every known approach to the emergency dispute and then relies upon his discretion for appropriate use. Ultimate protection to the public is provided through what amounts to compulsory arbitration, but innumerable loopholes and incentives to voluntarism are provided along the way.

In the judgment of the writer, the Massachusetts law comes about as close as it is possible to come, in our present state of knowledge, to a satisfactory emergency disputes law. Only time, and the freedom to operate without conflict with the federal law, will tell whether the law works. Both its strength and its vulnerability may lie in the vast discretion lodged in the governor. Any hint of favoritism in its administration, or perhaps even an error in judgment, can discredit the law. Parenthetically, one might note that enactment of the Massachusetts formula on a national scale would require a degree of confidence between the legislature and the executive which has not always existed. The Eightieth Congress would likely have shown little enthusiasm for giving President Truman so wide a choice in preference to the present provisions of the Taft-Hartley Act.

Finally, there are proposals for establishing specialized emergency machinery on an industry-by-industry basis. These proposals have taken different forms. Dunlop has suggested that, since it seems certain we are going to have emergency strike legislation on the books, Congress should simply pass a law "requesting the parties in these industries to submit to the Congress in a year their suggestions for mitigating emergency dispute stoppages in these industries."[51] This approach is suggested by Dunlop's conclusion that emergency disputes have been best handled in the railroad and atomic energy areas where the parties substantially designed their own procedures.

[51] John T. Dunlop, "The Settlement of Emergency Disputes," in *Proceedings of Fifth Annual Meeting* (Madison: Industrial Relations Research Association, 1953), p. 122.

Mayer had earlier suggested a scheme similar only in that it pursued an industry-by-industry approach.[52] He would, however, have the government establish full-time permanent panels in various fields directly affecting the public interest. These panels would serve largely an educational function in that they would collect and disseminate data, including studies of the underlying causes of dispute in the particular field. In actual emergencies, the panels would conduct hearings and then make public recommendations for settlement. Mayer believes that such an over-all procedure would lead to knowledge and reason taking the place of emotion and passion in national emergency situations.

It may be a commentary on the cynicism of our times, but there are probably few observers (least of all those in the educational world!) who share Mayer's belief that education and reason will replace emotion and passion once the "facts" are known. Moreover, the creation of full-time panels under government auspices would certainly give rise to suspicion of government meddling with the affairs of the parties.

The Dunlop proposal, on the other hand, would presumably be acceptable to everyone and welcome to most. The hitch comes in its implementation. Emergency dispute provisions are now enmeshed in the Taft-Hartley political controversy. Congress is notoriously difficult to interest in the long-run approach. Few Presidents have had the kind of rapport with both industry and labor which would be conducive to success in offering leadership to such a venture. Labor and management have shown no initiative of their own. The road to self-government is rough, and at this stage in our national history, neither the parties nor the government are showing any disposition in the emergency dispute field to follow it.

CONCLUSION

Short of that happy day when there are no more critical labor disputes, the perfect emergency disputes law will presumably be worked out in a cool, calm, nonpolitical atmosphere and be acceptable to both labor and management, preserve voluntarism and still

[52] Henry Mayer, "Issues and Solutions in Public Emergency Strikes," in *Proceedings of New York University Second Annual Conference on Labor* (Albany: Matthew Bender, 1949), pp. 573-585.

protect the public health and safety, apply uniformly and still give the parties equal incentive to settle their differences, and provide a strike substitute which takes into account not only the economic but all the other aspects of the strike. And then, when this perfect law is written, we are likely to find that "no machinery to settle disputes can remain the same over time. Use changes it. All three parties in these emergency disputes are continuously adapting their positions to the move of the other parties."[53]

Realistically, the perfect law isn't going to be written. Unfortunately, we aren't even likely to consider a "better" law until an emergency forces us to do so. In that connection, it is regrettable that the present conflict between state and federal jurisdiction in this area impairs the kind of experimentation which our federal system might otherwise provide.

One final comment—a blend of cynicism and idealism—seems in order. We have apparently abandoned hope that the affairs of labor and management can be so administered that there will be no emergencies. Yet for every emergency dispute there are a hundredfold settlements reached through bargaining. Why? Is it accidental, or have we as yet simply not found the answer? William L. Leiserson, one of the nation's wisest and most seasoned observers of labor-management problems over a long period of years, has often observed to the writer that in his experience emergencies don't "just happen." More often they grow out of a long period of mutual dissatisfaction. Is there no hope that we can eventually develop the art of administration to the point where there will be no emergency disputes?

[53] Dunlop, *op. cit.*, p. 119.

· XII ·

SEIZURE IN EMERGENCY DISPUTES

BY ARCHIBALD COX
Harvard University

The haphazard evolution of "seizure" as a technique for dealing with national emergency disputes makes it appropriate to review what has been done in the name of seizure before turning to appraisal of its future uses and, finally, to a short analysis of the legal problems.[1]

THE HISTORY OF SEIZURE

In May 1941, North American Aviation and UAW-CIO locked horns in a labor dispute. Despite their agreement to continue production while the National Defense Mediation Board endeavored to arrange a settlement, pickets were posted about the plant in Inglewood, California. The Communist party line still called for impeding rearmament, and there was reason to believe that the picketing stemmed from Communist activities and that once the workers entered, the pickets would be removed. For the government to seek an injunction would provoke hostility, even if the Norris-LaGuardia Act were not an insuperable barrier. Use of troops to break the picket lines for a private employer would recall bloodshed reaching back to the Pullman strike of 1894. President Wilson's seizures of industrial property during World War I fur-

[1] For helpful and more detailed discussions of seizure, see Ludwig Teller, "Government Seizure in Labor Disputes," *Harvard Law Review*, LX (1947), p. 1017; Bertram F. Willcox and Elizabeth S. Landis, "Government Seizures in Labor Disputes," *Cornell Law Quarterly*, XXXIV (1948), p. 155.

nished a happier example, for if the flag were raised over the premises and the workers were called upon to serve their government, a military squad might march through the picket line without reviving such bitter memories. Accordingly, the President directed the Secretary of War to take possession of the North American plant. Soldiers entered the plant, the flag was raised, and production was resumed immediately. The North American management continued to operate the business, and when the seizure ended thereafter, the government and company exchanged mutual releases. No one was concerned at that stage with the effect of seizure upon the parties' negotiations.

Several months later the National Defense Mediation Board recommended that Federal Shipbuilding and Dry Dock Company and Industrial Union of Marine and Shipbuilding Workers, CIO, include a maintenance-of-membership clause in their collective bargaining agreement. When the company refused, the union called a strike. After the company offered the shipyard to the Navy Department for immediate possession and operation, the President directed the Secretary of the Navy to take possession. The strike ended, and a little later the NDMB recommendation was put into effect. As at North American, events marched too fast for precise analysis of legal problems concerning the status of workers and the rights and obligations of the government.

The Federal Shipbuilding seizure set a pattern followed throughout the war. Authority for the early seizures was found in the President's powers as Chief Executive and Commander-in-Chief of the Army and Navy. Later the War Labor Disputes Act[2] provided statutory power to take possession of and operate for the government any "plant, mine or facility equipped for the manufacture, production, or mining of any articles or materials which may be required for the war effort or which may be useful in connection therewith." Existing terms and conditions of employment were preserved except that the War Labor Board was authorized to order changes upon application of the agency operating the seized establishment.

During World War II the primary goal of the national labor policy was maximum production of military equipment and essen-

[2] 57 Stat. 163 (1943).

tial civilian supplies. The chief instrument was the tripartite War Labor Board established pursuant to a voluntary "no strike" pledge given by organized labor in exchange for a promise to submit unsettled disputes to the Board. When a strike occurred, the major aims became (a) to bring about the prompt resumption of work and (b) to build up the authority and prestige of the War Labor Board. Seizure was a remarkably effective technique for accomplishing these all-important but limited purposes. In appraising the value of seizure in peacetime emergency disputes, however, three peculiarities deserve attention:

1. The wartime atmosphere, especially the desperate sense of urgency during the early years of World War II, contributed greatly to the effectiveness of seizure. Few men are so lacking in patriotism as to join a wartime strike against the government. Few organizations are strong enough to defy the public outcry against a deliberate challenge to the nation.

2. Seizure or the threat of seizure was not used to bring about a negotiated settlement of the underlying labor dispute. If issues were open when a plant was seized, the WLB was available and charged with the duty of establishing appropriate terms and conditions of employment. In most cases the WLB had made a decision, and although the parties were nominally free to negotiate a different settlement, seizure was in reality a sanction for commanding the obedience of the recalcitrant party.

3. There was scant need for concern about the effect of the seizure upon free collective bargaining. Wage stabilization and WLB policies narrowed negotiations. The establishment of a tribunal with power to decide unsettled labor disputes, although it preserved all possible voluntarism, presupposed willingness to substitute government determination in place of free negotiation of terms and conditions of employment. In the Montgomery Ward case,[3] for example, the President seized not to halt the strike but to preserve the effectiveness of WLB decisions.

Some of the inadequacies of seizure began to appear even before the war ended. In 1943 the United Mine Workers refused to order its members to resume work despite seizure, and the produc-

[3] *United States v. Montgomery Ward & Co.*, 150 F. 2d 369 (7th Cir. 1945), *vacated and dismissed as moot*, 326 U. S. 690 (1945).

tion of bituminous coal was not resumed until the government evolved a devious exception to wage stabilization standards which awarded the miners a large wage increase. In 1944 seizure of San Francisco Bay shipyards failed to terminate a machinists' strike.

The termination of hostilities in 1945 reduced the need for government intervention, but intensified the difficulties when intervention was required. The call to serve the nation no longer stirred the same patriotic impulses, partly because of the postwar let-down but also, I suspect, because it was becoming apparent that plant seizures really left men working for the same private employer. Between 1945 and 1953 seizure proved ineffective to prevent a stoppage on numerous occasions. In January 1946 the Secretary of Agriculture secured the strikers' return to work in meat-packing plants only by promising to ask the National Wage Stabilization Board for authority to put into effect whatever wage increase a fact-finding board might recommend. When the New York harbor tugboats were seized in February, the strikers refused to go back to work until the companies and union agreed to arbitration a week later, thereby forcing the military and naval authorities to furnish tugboats under armed protection. In May, seizure checked for a few days but did not prevent a railroad strike. In November 1946 the bituminous coal miners went on strike during a period of government operation.

The coal strike introduced a new element into the machinery of seizure. The government obtained an injunction against continuance of the strike and when UMW disobeyed the decree, it instituted contempt proceedings against UMW and John L. Lewis.[4] In later disputes between rail carriers and railway labor organizations, seizure seemed to be simply the formal preliminary to an injunction.[5] Such measures have different connotations and involve different consequences than the seizures during World War II.

The lack of an agency empowered to adjudicate the underlying dispute also raised questions concerning the relationship between seizure and the settlement of disputes. In some postwar cases the

[4] *United States v. United Mine Workers of America*, 330 U.S. 258 (1947).

[5] *United States v. Switchmen's Union*, 97 F.Supp. 97 (W.D. N.Y. 1950); *United States v. Brotherhood of Locomotive Firemen and Enginemen*, 104 F. Supp. 741 (N.D. Ohio 1952), *vacated and dismissed as moot*, 343 U.S. 971 (1952).

government virtually dictated the settlement, as in the meat-packing seizure when the strikers were promised that the recommendations to be made by a fact-finding board would be put into effect, and in the seizure of the coal mines in 1946 when the Secretary of the Interior negotiated an agreement with UMW fixing wages and other terms and conditions of employment which the government hoped, albeit mistakenly, the employers would adopt. Other seizures were followed by collective bargaining which led sometimes to private agreement on the terms of a contract, with or without the aid of fact finding, and occasionally to voluntary arbitration. After the 1951 rail seizure, there was so little progress in negotiations that nominal government operation continued for more than fifteen months. Thus, no pattern evolved out of the postwar seizures, and only those who were intimately associated with each controversy can appraise factually the extent to which seizure helped or handicapped negotiations. But it became plain that the effect of seizure upon bargaining could be ignored no longer.

THE LEGAL PROBLEMS OF SEIZURE

Power to seize

Under the Constitution, the federal government has power to "seize" industrial property involved in a labor dispute in order to assure the supply of goods and services essential to the national defense, safety, and health. The conventional rationale finds the authority in the power of eminent domain. Eminent domain extends to temporary takings. A government which can take land to improve navigable waterways, provide electric energy, or promote urban redevelopment surely has power to take the temporary use of industrial facilities, upon payment of just compensation, in order to preserve the public health and safety or even to prevent serious damage to the economy. If one looks to the reality rather than the words, the requisite constitutional authority resides in the commerce clause. Seizure is rarely more than (1) a prohibition against disruption of the employment relation and (2) direct prescription of terms and conditions of employment. Neither regulation curtails civil liberty or property rights in violation of the Constitution.[6] The

[6] *Youngstown Sheet & Tube Co. v. Sawyer*, 343 U.S. 579, 588, 603-604, 631, 667 (1952). See also *State v. Traffic Telephone Workers Fed.*, 2 N.J. 335, 66 A.2d 616 (1949) and cases cited.

choice between direct regulation and "seizure" is a matter of legislative preference.

Most executive seizures have been based upon statutory authority delegated by Congress. Wilson and Franklin Roosevelt asserted presidential power to seize during wartime emergencies without legislative sanction. President Truman exercised similar authority during the steel crisis of 1952, but the Supreme Court of the United States ruled the seizure unlawful.[7]

In the steel case there was considerable diversity in the opinions of the six justices in the majority. The opinion of the Court, which was delivered by Mr. Justice Black, seems to hold flatly that seizure is an exercise of lawmaking power vested exclusively in Congress. Mr. Justice Douglas stated the argument even more specifically:

The seizure of the plant is a taking in the constitutional sense. . . . The branch of the government that has the power to pay compensation for a seizure is the only one able to authorize a seizure or make lawful one that the President has effected.[8]

Four justices were more cautious. Their opinions, with differences in emphasis and nuance, rest heavily upon the fact that Congress, in the Taft-Hartley Act, had established a legislative policy for dealing with emergency disputes quite different from the President's course of action. Mr. Justice Jackson held that the case raised only the question whether the Constitution permitted an executive seizure "incompatible with the expressed or implied will of Congress."[9] Mr. Justice Frankfurter found the President's action unlawful because "the authoritatively expressed purpose of Congress to disallow such power to the President and to require him, when in his mind the occasion arose for such a seizure, to put the matter to Congress and ask for specific authority from it, could not be more decisive if it had been written into §206-210 of the Labor Management Relations Act of 1947."[10] Mr. Justice Burton and Mr. Justice Clark dealt with the question in much the same fashion. All four opinions are consistent with the possibility that their authors would have joined the three dissenters in upholding the presidential seizure if Congress had not provided an alternative in the Taft-Hartley Act.

[7] *Youngstown Sheet & Tube Co. v. Sawyer,* 343 U.S. 579 (1952).
[8] 343 U.S. at 631-632.
[9] 343 U.S. at 637-640.
[10] 343 U.S. at 602.

In short, the lawyer can give the legislator only this vague advice: (1) There is no executive power to seize industrial property while the national emergency disputes provisions of the Taft-Hartley Act are in force, certainly not until its procedures have been exhausted and almost surely not then. (2) It is uncertain whether the President might lawfully exercise this power if the Taft-Hartley provisions were repealed and no substitute measure adopted, or whether he can seize the railroads after exhausting the procedures of the Railway Labor Act.[11] Perhaps the legislator would reply that he would be glad to perpetuate the uncertainty.[12]

Legal consequences of seizure

Many of the legal questions raised by a lawful seizure remain unanswered because the essential nature of the action is ill defined. The semantics and trappings of seizure are those of government possession and operation of property taken for public use. The military march in. The flag is raised. Orders are issued in the name of the United States. Below the surface the arrangement usually looks quite different. The same executives run the business as before. Production is not limited to articles required by the government. Business is transacted as if by a private concern rather than public authority; indeed there is often an agreement by which the company undertakes to operate the properties as the government's agent for its own risk and account. To the best of my knowledge, no important business decision has ever been made by the government rather than the management. Workers are treated as employees in private industry under statutes clearly inapplicable to government employees save that they may be prohibited from striking. Should the façade determine the legal consequences and thereby gradually shape the practice, or should the law regard the practice as determinative of the true nature of the arrangement?

The question arose first in *United States v. United Mine Workers*[13] where the Supreme Court of the United States was required to rule upon the legal effectiveness of an injunction obtained by the government to prevent a coal strike while the mines were being op-

[11] The latest seizures of the railroads were based upon the Act of August 29, 1914, 39 Stat. 645, which applies only "in time of war."
[12] See p. 240.
[13] 330 U.S. 258 (1947).

erated under a seizure order. A majority of five justices concluded that the Norris-LaGuardia Act did not bar issuance of the injunction. The opinion which Mr. Chief Justice Vinson delivered on behalf of himself and Justices Reed and Burton assumed that the Act forbade "the Government's seeking an injunction for the benefit of private employers," but held that for the purposes of the case "the incidents of the relationship existing between the Government and the workers are those of governmental employer and employee." Justices Black and Douglas concurred in the ruling, but with the explicit statement that the Norris-LaGuardia Act is applicable to "anything less than full and complete Government operation for its own account."[14] It has not always been noticed that these two votes necessary to make up a majority might not be available to sustain an injunction in seizures where the government has agreed that the operation would be for the account of the employer. And the practice has seldom, if ever, conformed to their supposition.

The financial consequences of seizure were considered in *United States v. Peewee Coal Company*.[15] The owners of an unprofitable coal mine seized in 1943 recovered judgment in the Court of Claims for the additional losses resulting from wage increases granted by the government to comply with a War Labor Board decision. The Court of Claims held that there was no legal or business justification for the payment since WLB directives were only advisory. The Supreme Court affirmed the judgment by a divided vote. The opinion delivered by Mr. Justice Black on behalf of four justices who voted to affirm rests upon the theory that the United States became the proprietor of the business and therefore was "entitled to the profits from, and must bear the losses of, business operations which it conducts."[16] The four dissenters agreed that there was technically a taking but denied that it made the United States the proprietor entitled to the gains and subject to the losses. "Nothing was recoverable as just compensation, because nothing of value was taken from the company; and it was not subjected by the Government to pecuniary loss." The opinion went on to point out that there was no proof that the mine could have operated without government intervention and the payment of higher wages.

[14] 330 U.S. at 329.
[15] 341 U.S. 114 (1951).
[16] 341 U.S. at 117.

Mr. Justice Reed, who cast the deciding vote, apparently felt that he was bound by the finding that there was no legal or business justification for the wage increase, but on the more fundamental issue he sided with the dissenters. In his view the seizure of industrial property in a labor dispute, like the operation of the railroads in World War I, was a special kind of taking which ought not to place upon the government the burden of losses incurred during its "supervision" of the business unless the supervision added to the losses.

Although the case involved an unprofitable mine, it seems apparent that the Court was more concerned with the rule applicable to profits. The opinion of Mr. Justice Black explicitly declared that profits during seizure would go to the government. Under such a rule, the threat to seize or continue a seizure would put tremendous pressure upon an employer to make concessions to the union, although an administration friendly to business might relieve the pressure by entering into a contractual arrangement by which the company would operate the property in exchange for the profits.[17] But the four dissenters and Mr. Justice Reed seem to reject this conclusion and to lay the ground for a decision that unless the owner is ousted—obviously an impractical step—he continues to operate the business for his own account.

Seizure proliferates a myriad of lesser questions of law, the most important of which may be the status of employees under social and labor legislation. Since no definitive answers are available, lack of space prevents their discussion.[18]

THE FUTURE OF SEIZURE

Seizure is an instrument of public labor policy, not an end in itself. Providing instruments for the effectuation of policy requires an understanding of what a people, through its government, wishes to do; thereafter we may look for the means of accomplishment.

[17] Under this approach the company may recover "just compensation"—a right which Mr. Justice Black regarded as "conceptually distinct" from the right to have the government bear the losses. For this reason it was unnecessary for him to discuss the proper measure of compensation. In the only ruling on this issue, the Supreme Court of Virginia held that it was proper to take into consideration the fact that the property was strike-bound. *Anderson v. Chesapeake Ferry Co.*, 186 Va. 481, 43 S.E.2d 10 (1947).

[18] Some of these problems are discussed in Willcox and Landis, *op. cit.*

One major goal of labor policy is to preserve a large measure of free enterprise by eschewing government dictation of wages, hours, and other terms and conditions of employment. Wage and hour laws narrow the range of bargaining. Fiscal policies influence price and wage levels. A vigorous administration may exert informal pressures, subtle or hard-fisted. But with allowance for these forces, our essential purpose is still to preserve a system for fixing terms of employment without direct government regulation. In an industrial society this ideal of economic self-determination requires collective bargaining through strong labor unions.

The weight of the government is felt not only when it speaks on substantive issues but also when it determines bargaining procedures or alters the courses of conduct open to either party. Is it unduly cynical to ask whether organized business supported the eighty-day injunction authorized by the Taft-Hartley Act unmindful of the effect inability to strike would have upon the bargaining power of unions? Was organized labor's preference for executive action quite oblivious to what unions gained through fact-finding boards and seizure? Furthermore, no administration can be wholly indifferent to the bargains struck in key industries affecting the national level of wages and prices.

One who is not committed to the interests of business, right or wrong, but who holds no belief in the constant, eternal purity of labor, is likely to conclude, therefore, that ideal legislation dealing with national emergency disputes would avoid any built-in bias affecting the relative bargaining power of the parties, but would nevertheless allow the administration to preserve neutrality or exert limited pressure in either direction according to economic conditions and the merits of the issues, while at the same time securing an essentially private voluntary settlement.

A second important goal is to prevent or terminate strikes threatening an emergency. In wartime we cannot tolerate even a brief strike or lockout. In peacetime it may well be true that no strike outside an atomic energy plant seriously threatens a public catastrophe; and perhaps the hardships, economic loss, and reprisals of a major nationwide strike, even on the railroads, would build antibodies carrying an immunity against recurrence of the disease far more effective than governmental prescriptions for its cure. But this, I fear, is largely the outlook of theoreticians. Government administrators have little doubt of the need for strong measures to prevent strikes from interrupting the supply of essential goods and services.

In the last analysis the two goals may well be inconsistent because of the nature of collective bargaining. Prolonged negotiations tend to bring about agreement, or at least to narrow the area of disagreement. Persuasion may produce consent. Weariness, exhaustion, the desire to get on with other business, lead to compromise. But often the bargain is not struck until one minute before midnight when there is no possible escape from choosing between compromise and battle. In such instances, collective bargaining works because both sides conclude that the risks of losses through a strike are so great that compromise is cheaper than economic battle. When a strike occurs, the controversy may be settled only when both parties become convinced that continuing the struggle will cost more than acceptance of the terms the other offers. Without the strike or the fear of a strike there would be few risks in disagreement. For this reason those who ask complete security against strikes would *pro tanto* abolish collective bargaining and substitute government regulation of wages, hours, and other terms and conditions of employment. Those who wish to preserve free collective bargaining in essential industries must be prepared to pay for their freedom in the currency of strikes, economic loss, and human suffering.

In concrete cases, the dimensions of quantity and time are added. Government dictation of the terms of settlement of a wage dispute involving pipefitters on an AEC construction project has different implications in terms of preserving a free economy than government determination of the wages paid in basic steel. A sixty-day strike in the bituminous coal fields would normally do less damage than a five-day tie-up of railroad transportation. Assuming that each national emergency dispute required a choice between the competing objectives of (a) preserving free collective bargaining and (b) protecting the public from the cost of a potentially catastrophic strike, we might accept in each case what appeared to be the lesser evil in the circumstances then existing and thus, by the very variety of choices, could approach closer to both goals than through an advance commitment to either.

The dimension of time introduces another important factor. The longer the government avoids a commitment to settle the dispute or prevent the strike, the less likely it is that the government will have to take action. While some danger of a strike remains, while there is the chance, but only a chance, of government intervention, the risks may furnish the motive power to bring about agreement.

May we not say, therefore, that the value of any method for dealing with emergency disputes can be measured by three tests: (1) It must lead to continued (or renewed) production of essential goods and services. (2) It must look to a settlement of the underlying dispute without government influence being confined by the economic philosophy of the administration. (3) It must preserve and delay, if it does not avoid, the necessity for choosing between the first two objectives. Finally, we must inquire whether any advantages which seizure offers over other forms of government intervention in these respects are outweighed by collateral demerits.

Seizure as a means of preventing or terminating strikes

In a limited number of situations, seizure alone may be sufficient to postpone, if not prevent, a strike or lockout. Collective negotiations sometimes reach an impasse in which both management and union wish to avoid interrupting production while they continue negotiations, but they may find that strike deadlines have been fixed so firmly that neither party can back away from the conflict without dramatic government intervention. Similarly, the technique may furnish a line of retreat to the union which cannot back down from its strike talk without outside assistance. And a summons to work for the government may tip the scale when both sides, or either, are hesitating over the choice between an immediate strike and a makeshift solution.

Possibly management and union negotiators, like children, must sometimes be forced to suffer the consequences of their own mistakes in order to educate them for the future. Such considerations are pertinent in deciding whether seizure is warranted in a particular case, but they have only trifling relevance to deciding whether this method of preventing a stoppage is sometimes so valuable that it ought to be available. By hypothesis we are dealing with disputes which may lead to a public catastrophe too serious to permit standing aside to teach the parties a lesson.

A more serious defect is that resort to seizure gradually destroys its psychological values, thereby making it progressively less effective. Each seizure has made it more apparent that the employer carries on business in the same manner as before. Certainly railroad employees noticed no change in status during the long period of nominal government operation between the issuance of the executive order on February 8, 1951, and the ultimate settlement on May 23, 1952. The more sophisticated union officials and lawyers must also have been aware that the executive order, the subsequent directions of the Secretary of Defense, and the operating agreement required the Army not to interfere with the normal operation of the railroads by their regular management. The net profit went to the carriers just as if no seizure had occurred. Perhaps the cure for this inherent weakness is seizing and operating struck businesses for the actual rather than nominal account of the government.[19]

Seizure is sometimes essential to invoking any legal sanction against a disastrous strike. The Taft-Hartley Act authorizes an eighty-day injunction where a dispute affecting a substantial part of an industry engaged in interstate commerce imperils the national health or safety, but this provision is not applicable to railroads or airlines subject to the Railway Labor Act. Consequently, after Taft-Hartley or Railway Labor Act procedures have been exhausted, the Norris-LaGuardia Act would bar the government from further legal remedies unless it seized the properties so as to bring the situation under the United Mine Workers case.

One may well ask why it should be necessary to go through the forms of seizure if it is only a step toward the eventual and indispensable issuance of an injunction. Three answers may be offered: First, seizure may result in the resumption or continuance of production without the need for legal coercion. Second, where an injunction is necessary, the command to work for the government, even under a token seizure, still has somewhat different connotations than the old equity procedure that left bitter scars on the mind and soul of organized labor. Third, as suggested below, the

[19] See p. 239.

difficulties attendant upon seizure may deter the government from rushing too hastily into a suit for an injunction.

Effect of seizure upon settlement of underlying dispute

To achieve the goal of privately negotiated terms and conditions of employment, we rely primarily upon collective bargaining backed by mediation and the pressures of government and public opinion. Here time is an important factor because the processes of persuasion (and of exhaustion) are often time-consuming.

Seizure's effectiveness in gaining time for negotiation and mediation is the same as its value in preventing or terminating a stoppage. Probably it also increases the force with which the government can demand a settlement in the name of the public. The flag and the presence of government officials are constant reminders of the need for action. When a high official requests a settlement in order to terminate government occupation, his words imply an "or else" which is highly effective so long as there is uncertainty concerning the powers of the government and the rights and liabilities of the parties. Conversely, the desire to be free of an undefined responsibility for managing a private business may increase the vigor of government mediation.

When persuasion fails, the risks of disagreement may force the parties to accept some compromise which both deem preferable to battle. For the union, seizure or the threat of seizure poses three hazards:

1. The government may forbid a strike but make no change in existing wages or conditions of employment. In a period of rising wage rates, the union might find time passing while it sought to bargain without the aid of the strike, a weapon for which the employer's desire to get back his property would be scarcely a substitute.

2. The government may establish what it considers just and equitable wages at a level below what the union could obtain from the employer in an immediate compromise. The wages set would nevertheless tend to control the ultimate bargain.[20]

3. Seizure may adversely affect the status of both the employees and the union. Apparently the unions have given little thought to

[20] See p. 239.

the danger, but if the government becomes the employer in any substantial sense, legal complexities multiply. May the government properly grant a union the right to be the exclusive representative of government employees? Are the employees still subject to state workmen's compensation laws? Does their status change under social security and unemployment compensation? What of grievance arbitration?

Too many variables enter the calculus in any given situation to permit precise generalization, but it seems fair to conclude that (a) the risk of seizure puts less pressure on a union to compromise than the fear of a bare injunction against a strike; (b) there are occasions on which a union would prefer seizure to either a strike or the best compromise available; but (c) seizure *may* be managed in such fashion that the pressure on the union is even more than under an injunction.

Upon some employers the fear of seizure appears to weigh heavily. Even nominal government operation violates cherished concepts. The presence of potential busybodies nosing about the industry is distasteful, and the negotiations necessary to restore normal conditions may lead to prying questions. One cannot foretell the extent to which the government will interfere with the management of the enterprise—especially an administration unfriendly to business. The businessman's lawyers are unable to give him firm advice concerning his right to recover compensation, the incidence of added costs, his tort or contract rights and liabilities, the status of his employees, his duties toward the union, and a thousand other worrisome questions. At best there will be additional strain on executives and the expenditure of time and money. In the end the government may put into effect a wage scale so favorable to the employees that the company can secure exclusive control only by much larger concessions than the union would currently accept as a settlement.

It is harder to appraise whether the risks facing an employer balance the hazards which seizure presents for a labor union. In the past, unions have been able to negotiate rather favorable contracts in industries seized by the states as well as the federal government, and this has been the method of handling emergency disputes favored by organized labor. But former federal seizures took place under an administration generally friendly to labor, and all occurred during an inflationary period. In the long run, two other factors seem likely to alter the balance of risks, and perhaps to reduce them, to such an extent as to destroy the value of seizure as a means of achieving negotiated settlements.

1. Many of the risks which the average employer sees in seizure are only vague imaginings, and the questions the lawyers cannot answer are usually compromised or avoided. Government operation of the railroads in 1951-1952 cost the carriers only the time and trouble which the dispute would have occasioned however handled. The only losses which companies suffered as a result of the wartime or immediate postwar seizures were the costs of government-dictated settlements. The typical seizure order leaves the management in full control of the business, and, despite the views of several Supreme Court justices, the ultimate financial settlements have regularly treated the entire operation as carried for the account of the company just as if there had been no seizure. Thus personal or vicarious experience may dissipate many of the fears which generate pressure for settlements. Continued use of seizure would also lead to court decisions clarifying doubtful points of law and thereby substituting calculable costs for speculation.

2. Seizure puts heavy pressure on the government to determine the substantive issues. The government can scarcely defend taking possession and requiring men to work as its employees without accepting some responsibility for the fairness of the conditions of employment; yet if it accepts the responsibility, its determinations are likely to control the final settlement. A satisfied employer can refuse further compromise and thereby force the government to remain in possession and compel the men to work under an injunction until the union backs down, at least to the point where settlement is possible with the aid of a face-saving gesture. If the union is content, it can stand pat, leaving the employer to face the Hobson's choice of settling on the terms the government has established or else managing his business for his own account but with the government in nominal possession.

A possible solution is for the government to maintain existing conditions of employment and also keep the profits of the enterprise during government possession.[21] In times of rising wage levels, both the union and the management of a profitable enterprise would then feel pressure to compromise their dispute. The chief objection is that just compensation for the possession of strike-bound property pending the settlement of the labor dispute may be so small a sum that retaining the profits would too often tip the scales heavily in favor of the union, with a resulting reduction in the proportion of disputes settled prior to seizure. The Virginia seizure law, which provides for retention of 15 per cent of the profits, is subject to the criticism that neither this percentage nor any other predetermined figure has a rational foundation.

After federal seizure, the government and the employer usually agree that the employer will operate the property in behalf of the government and pay any losses in exchange for the profits of the operation. Whenever the employer takes the seizure too lightly, the best course would seem to be for the government to enter the bargaining with a threat to reduce the fee paid management under the operating agreement unless something is done to settle the dispute.[22] This would draw the government into the determination of the underlying dispute, but such an impasse cannot be broken without some form of government pressure. Since the government itself would not have unlimited bargaining power (it would be helpless if management withdrew entirely), this form of interference leaves more room for self-determination and creates a lesser precedent than compulsory arbitration or even direct negotiation between the government and the union.

Seizure as a means of preserving uncertainty

Even though a seizure may end in government dictation of the terms and conditions of employment, it preserves the risks which produce private agreement longer than any other procedure for dealing with emergency disputes. This is true for two reasons:

1. Seizure is more flexible than any other single method of dealing with emergency disputes. The government may move one step at a time, and each step opens new alternatives. It is therefore harder

[21] See pp. 231-232 with respect to the government's power to keep the profits.
[22] The right to renegotiate the fee should therefore be reserved in the original operating agreement.

for the parties to calculate the consequences of continued disagreement.

2. Seizure raises so many problems for the government that it reduces the likelihood of government intervention and preserves more risks of a strike. In a national emergency dispute, the immediate pressures on the government are calculated to hasten intervention. The costs are long-range implications easily underestimated in an apparent crisis. Filing a bill for an injunction to enjoin a strike presents few hazards. It is too easy to appoint a fact-finding board. Under the necessary enabling legislation the process of compelling arbitration would have irresistible attraction whenever there was an emergency dispute. But seizure is distasteful to any administration. The same legal problems which worry corporation lawyers disturb government attorneys. In the absence of a statute, the President's power to seize industrial property is questionable. Even if he has constitutional power, he may face political reprisals in consequence of a reaction against "executive dictatorship." Once the government takes possession claiming to be employer, it becomes harder to evade a moral responsibility for the terms or conditions of employment. Thus the difficulties which seizure raises for the government are a useful counterpoise to public pressure. A basic program which forced the government to face them before acting on the cry of "National Emergency!" might contribute more effectively than any other to the objective of preserving private determination of terms and conditions of employment.

Collateral objections to seizure

A major objection to the use of seizure in national emergency disputes is the alleged threat to private property. Many people regard seizure as executive dictatorship, marking a further step down the road to government ownership. This view is often held sincerely, and the blaring headlines during the seizure of the steel mills in 1952 and the solemnity of the Supreme Court's special session attest its hold upon much of the public. But if one looks to the substance instead of the tyrannical words of a seizure order, it becomes apparent that there may be scant difference between an executive seizure in a labor dispute and the appointment of a receiver in equity or trustee in bankruptcy. In the latter instances, government intervenes for the purpose of protecting financial creditors, and the property is administered under the cloak of judicial protection. In the former case, the need for intervention is the greater because it is the public interest which requires protection. If the manner of government operation were regularized, the financial consequences defined, and the resulting legal relationships clarified, the principal difference between executive seizure and a judicial receivership would lie in nomenclature. The lack of established legal restraints gives seizure an appearance of uncontrolled executive power which would soon be dispelled once litigation in the courts produced decisions upon the legal consequences. Unfortunately, the very uncertainties which furnish ground for fear and criticism also give seizure its chief advantages. To cure the fault would impair the value.

CONCLUSION

Seizure alone would seldom be an effective solution for national emergency disputes. As an available alternative, or in conjunction with other measures, it appears to have considerable psychological value both in emphasizing to the employees the public need for continued work and in making it difficult for both parties to calculate the cost of disagreement.

But seizure is a wasting asset because experience and the development of legal principles would tend to dissipate the peculiar risks involved. A statute supplying a legal foundation for executive action, unless limited to a bare delegation of authority, would also substitute calculable costs for uncertainty. Accordingly, sound policy would seem to dictate resort to seizure only in those rare crises where executive action may be justified without an established legislative policy.

THE LOCUS OF FEDERAL AUTHORITY

IN NATIONAL EMERGENCY DISPUTES

BY MURRAY EDELMAN

University of Illinois

Separation of powers is justified, or condemned, on the ground that it furnishes checks on unilateral action by any one branch of government. One branch checks another, however, only to the extent that it represents the values of different groups of the population: in the degree that it is designed to receive and reflect different information as to factual situations and people's reactions. If the branches reflected the same values, they would consistently reinforce, not check, each other's policies.

Because of significant differences in the extent and character of their constituencies, in their facilities for gathering information, and in the acts they are able to perform, the executive, legislative, and judicial branches of the national government may often represent varying, even conflicting, points of view in a controversial policy area such as labor relations, at least for the duration of a strike. This chapter will try to identify that allocation of federal authority to deal with disputes that will maximize the chance of early settlement and of avoiding future strikes in those relatively few industries in which interruptions in production may create emergencies.

It would be pointless to devise a set of maxims advising administrators, congressmen, and judges in what order or under what conditions they *should* intervene in disputes. Each of them must act when enough pressure to do so builds up as the result of a strike, or face political sanctions. What can be done is to examine what forms of advance congressional authorization to the President and the courts make it most probable that the values of early settlement and avoiding future emergencies will be paramount in the formulation of policy. The executive and judicial branches are guided to some extent as to timing and flexibility of action by legislative enactments, and their activities may influence Congress in turn.

Specifically, Congress may grant the courts authority to issue injunctions in labor disputes upon application of the Attorney General or upon application of a private party, or both; or it may deny to the courts authority to issue such injunctions under specified conditions. Congress may grant or withhold authority from the executive to intervene in specific ways, notably by seizure; and it may encourage executive intervention by joint or concurrent resolution. It is unlikely that it may deprive the executive of authority to intervene by moral suasion, mediation, voluntary arbitration, or the use of troops. The specific questions to be answered, then, are these: (1) Under what conditions are the respective branches likely to intervene? (2) What form of congressional exercise of discretion in the matters listed here will best serve the causes of industrial peace and continuing good industrial relations in the critical industries?

The data which explain whether and when a government agency will intervene in a dispute and what it will do if it does intervene may be classified for convenience of discussion into two types:

1. Economic data and social context, including current and long-term comparisons with other unions and companies, internal relationships within the union and management groups, relative bargaining positions and strengths, priorities among the bargaining demands, economic impact on other industries and groups, and impact on other governmental programs.

2. Public reactions and political effects.

Recognizing that no one of the branches is homogeneous or monolithic, it is nevertheless true that there are institutional[1] rea-

[1] References to "institutional" characteristics in this paper designate those features of the executive, legislative, or judical branches which can be expected

sons why they consistently differ from each other in access and sensitivity to these data more than they differ internally. In inexact fashion the reasons can be catalogued.

ECONOMIC DATA AND SOCIAL CONTEXT

So far as the first type of data is concerned, the information can come only from experts in the field of industrial relations who have made a careful study of the background of the specific dispute. Recent empirical studies have emphasized the wide diversity of immediate causes of disputes, the complexity of their economic ramifications, and the profundity and subtlety of analysis that must be brought to bear to understand them. This is not a field for the dilettante or the novice. Only the executive branch includes agencies skilled in gathering the statistical and qualitative information that permits an informed judgment as to whether government action is called for and what measures are most likely to end the dispute quickly and in such a manner as to promote a continuing and productive relationship. Often as important as these matters is the effect of the strike on government programs, especially those involving foreign policy or defense. Because these programs are administered in the executive and the President is responsible for their success, he is in the most strategic position to weigh the dangers of their interruption against other considerations. The President may also appoint fact-finding boards of outsiders to supplement the work of the Bureau of Labor Statistics, Federal Mediation and Conciliation Service, Council of Economic Advisers, and other informed agencies.

Not only is the executive branch staffed to gather this type of information, but it has compelling reasons to pay some attention to it. The President's moral and political prestige depends ultimately on his ability to administer concrete programs successfully. Unlike any one congressman, he is blamed if an atomic energy program or an economic stabilization program bogs down. He cannot ignore empirical facts and expert judgment of their long-run implications, even when these are not widely appreciated by lay onlookers.

There is nothing to prevent congressional committees from re-

to persist and to influence policy regardless of the individuals currently in office. It is these institutional factors which permit the student to make tentative generalizations about differences among the branches.

ceiving testimony as to the matters included in this category of data, and they sometimes do so. The most objective and complete information is likely to be developed in the executive agencies, however; and, for the reason already suggested, most of the 531 members of Congress will feel less pressure to be influenced by it than the President does. In Congress the second category of data is relatively more significant.

Since the advent of the Brandeis brief, courts have regularly taken note of the economic and social implications of cases that come before them. As compared with the executive, however, court reliance upon such data is qualified in some important ways. The information is supplied to the court by attorneys employed to advocate a partisan point of view. There is little assurance that adversary argument about a situation will develop either all the relevant data or judgments more considerate of all affected groups than either of the partisan judgments. This danger is enhanced by the fact that no particular court is responsible for dealing with the consequences of a bad decision, and this is an important function of the executive. The multiplicity of courts, the varied backgrounds of judges, the arbitrariness of judicial notice,[2] and restrictions on admissibility of evidence are other institutional reasons for doubting that the data in the first category will consistently play as important a role in judicial decisions as in executive ones.

With respect to most strikes, careful study of the economic and social context is likely to raise grave doubts about the advisability of intervention. So far as the relations of the parties themselves are concerned, the case for letting the parties work out their problems for themselves is well known. So far as economic impact on other groups is concerned, careful studies by Warren,[3] Bernstein and Lovell,[4] and Chamberlain and Schilling[5] indicate that it is only

[2] *Black's Law Dictionary* defines "judicial notice" as "the act by which a court, in . . . framing its decision, will, of its own motion, and without the production of evidence, recognize the existence and truth of certain facts, having a bearing on the controversy at bar, which, from their nature, are not properly the subject of testimony, or which are universally regarded as established by common notoriety."

[3] Edgar L. Warren, "Thirty-Six Years of 'National Emergency' Strikes," *Industrial and Labor Relations Review*, V (October 1951), pp. 3-19.

[4] Irving Bernstein and Hugh G. Lovell, "Are Coal Strikes National Emergencies?" *Industrial and Labor Relations Review*, VI (April 1953), pp. 352-367.

[5] Neil W. Chamberlain and Jane M. Schilling, *The Impact of Strikes* (New York: Harper, 1954).

rarely as serious as a casual newspaper reader might be led to believe, although Chamberlain is more inclined than the others to classify some leading strikes of recent years as emergencies. In any case, the expert is usually less willing than others to concede a case for intervention in a particular instance. The executive branch is therefore likely to be slower to intervene drastically and to do so in fewer cases.

PUBLIC REACTIONS AND POLITICAL SANCTIONS

The fact remains, nonetheless, that governmental agencies do and must respond to public reactions. It is accordingly necessary, if we are to understand what government will do, to consider the influence in the respective branches of the various groups that are affected by the dispute as well as the influence in government of expert judgments.

Public reaction to disputes and their effects on political fortunes are of intimate concern to every congressman. If his constituents or those who help him in campaigns include angry suppliers of the struck industry, disgruntled consumers of its scarce products, or sympathetic relatives of strikers, the congressman will make an effort to know it. He will also know it if his rural constituents, without a close economic nexus, are nonetheless aroused by what they regard as the effrontery of urban radicals; and he will probably know it if his constituents really don't care very much in spite of alarmist newspaper headlines. Congressional voting patterns are rarely simple expressions of these political ties, but they are complicated expressions of them. Although we know altogether too little about the complications, we know enough to suggest something about their bearing on congressional intervention in emergency disputes. The congressional process differs from that of the other two branches in this connection chiefly in three respects: the election of congressmen from single-member districts, the probability of logrolling, and the underrepresentation of urban areas in Congress.

The first means that there are marked differences in the sensitivity of the respective members of Congress to groups seeking intervention in strikes. Under present governmental arrangements, none of these groups is likely to be strong enough to produce formal congressional action during the strike itself. This is true not only because Congress may not be in session or because congressional action on controversial matters is slow. It is also true because most congressmen have some constituents on each side and many who are apathetic, and because execution of any policy involves executive and judicial action, usually of a kind these branches are already authorized to perform and may already be performing. That formal congressional action in the course of a strike is rare is not chance.

Congressional action during a national emergency strike would doubtless occur despite these facts if the strike threatened to continue and the executive and judicial branches were prohibited by legislation from intervening effectively first. A crisis severe enough that most congressmen assume their constituents are concerned spurs even the Congress to prompt action, as in a declaration of war. It has occasionally been suggested that Congress might "trigger" government intervention by determining its timing and perhaps its general character, while leaving it to the executive or judicial branches to carry out the directive by appropriate administrative or judicial process. This could be accomplished easily and constitutionally by the device of a joint congressional resolution or by concurrent House and Senate resolutions; and in the absence of other governmental action, groups with a strong interest in ending the strike would make every effort to overcome congressional inertia by persuading sensitive congressmen that the injury to the economy and to their constituents was substantial.

It is predictable, however, that this arrangement would not result in intervention calculated to produce healthy industrial relations, maximum production, or adequate protection of vital public programs. The timing of government intervention is an ideal instance of the kind of question that should be influenced by careful investigation of the dispute by all the most rigorous methods, inadequate as they are, of the slowly progressing disciplines of industrial relations and labor economics. The total picture involves a history of negotiation and of frictions, economic impacts susceptible of analysis only by complicated statistical and economic techniques, and strong and weak reactions by various groups that vary considerably in their facility for making a public outcry, off Capitol Hill and on it. The last-named feature is highly relevant, but it clearly ought not to be the only "trigger."

It is, in fact, highly probable that congressional action in the heat of a dispute does not even reflect this feature adequately. When there are strongly held positions in Congress, the possibility of logrolling exerts a constant temptation for moderate positions to be sacrificed to them in return for favors on other bills. If and when a dispute received wide and alarmist attention, the strongly held position would be increasingly in favor of precipitate action to end the strike on any terms, whether this were necessary to preserve widely held values or not. In the congressional arena of interest conflict, quick action without opportunity for groups with a less immediate interest to be heard usually means that maximum influence is accorded economic minorities which can persuade even a minority of congressmen that they are being hurt.

This phenomenon is sufficiently important to the subject of the present chapter that it deserves careful attention, even though our knowledge of the congressional process is regrettably slight. In Congress the number of men who strongly favor hasty action to end a strike on any terms and in any atmosphere may be relatively small. A much larger group whose constituents are not immediately affected and who are relatively apathetic may favor alternative policies, such as appointment of a fact-finding board. As the strike continues, the first group's views are likely to grow more intense; and throughout the strike it is likely to feel more strongly on this issue than the second group—strongly enough, probably, to be willing to trade a vote on other, unrelated issues for more support on this one. A considerable number of congressmen in the second group may very well yield to logrolling pressure of this kind, for each of them is sure to be eager to get support for some unrelated favorite bill or possibly to appease business groups that might be a source of future campaign funds. In the heat of the dispute, convictions as to long-term impacts on their constituents and others are not developed because there is no time for the necessary study of the dispute's context and ramifications. There is accordingly an institutional reason why positions held strongly by relatively few congressmen are likely to triumph over those with milder support from a larger number of congressmen. In the heat of a strike this would probably mean congressional "triggering" that is based upon (a) the views of that segment of the population most immediately

excited about the strike and not necessarily those most fundamentally affected by it, and (b) the pattern of support for unrelated
issues concurrently on the congressional calendar.

This result is especially likely when issues are not easily understood by many people or when legislative action is quick, with
relatively little publicized discussion. Marked underrepresentation
of urban areas in Congress means that most members will have
little comprehension of the actual long- or short-range impact of
the strike and will feel free to engage in logrolling or to yield to
those with an alarmist view without fear of sanctions by urban
workers. In short, there is likely to be a built-in insensitivity to labor
needs as compared with the Chief Executive.

Although the fact that Congress has not often intervened in emergency strikes in the past prevents us from acquiring adequate evidence of the accuracy of this theory of the dynamics of logrolling,
consistent differences in presidential and congressional positions on
tariffs and on price controls in emergencies suggest that it is highly
likely. In both these areas, logrolling has meant that widely held
interests are likely to lose in the legislative arena when pitted against
interests held strongly by relatively few congressmen.[6]

The President, as an elective officer and because of his responsibility for all policy areas, is also sensitive to public reactions and
political sanctions; but his interest in them is likely to be somewhat
weaker than that of most congressmen for several reasons. First,
his constituency is national, which means that group interests that
dominate a considerable number of congressional constituencies
may still be small minorities from his perspective and that urban
groups as a whole may loom larger. Second, and more important,
he has to administer concrete programs successfully, which means
he must give considerable attention to the empirical facts and to
expert judgment as to their long-run implications, for his political
appeal depends in the last analysis on the voters' satisfaction with

[6] Bentley suggests that logrolling is the "most characteristic" legislative
activity. Its importance and relevance justify inclusion here of a theory of its
dynamics which is admittedly speculative in part. Cf. Arthur F. Bentley,
The Process of Government (Bloomington: The Principia Press, 1908), pp. 370-
372, for a provocative discussion of the interplay of group interests in logrolling and a suggestion of the distinction emphasized here between wide,
weak interests and narrow, strong ones

economic conditions as well as on his ability to make popular gestures.[7]

Less directly than either of the other branches and with a greater time lag, courts follow election returns; but this is an imprecise way of saying that within the important limits fixed by their training and economic status, the values of judges change with the same events which influence the values of other people. Federal judges are not in peril of direct sanctions at the polls, as are congressmen and the President. With respect to this category of data, then, the judicial branch is likely to be less sensitive than the other two.

A significant institutional characteristic of the judiciary in this connection is the fact that fewer persons are involved in decisions in any one court than is the case in either the executive or in Congress. This is particularly true in the issuance of injunctions, the most common form of judicial intervention in emergency strikes. In the executive and legislative branches, certain consistencies already noted in methods of selection of officeholders and of gathering information make possible comparative statements about their respective policies that are likely to hold true regardless of the current incumbents. The probability is always far from a certainty because the personal attachments and friendships of a particular incumbent may better explain his group interest affiliations than those institutional factors. When a large number of people are involved in the decision, however, the uncertainty arising from this source is reduced. In the case of the federal judiciary, the uncertainty is all the greater, not only because the sources of information are more haphazard and the factor of election is absent, but also because fewer persons (often only one) are involved in the decision.

It must be emphasized that these differences among the branches are at their greatest when action must be quick and must occur during a dispute. Emergency strikes, more obviously than most governmental problems, require quick decisions, and the differences in question are of correspondingly greater significance.

[7] The analysis of the President's position illustrates the fact that the distinction suggested here between empirical data and political reactions is an academic one, useful only for analysis. Both types of information are indexes of group reactions. The distinction does make it easier, however, to clarify the correlation between differences in executive, legislative, and judicial policy on the one hand and differences in their structure and procedures on the other.

It would be foolish to pretend that political science is in a position to predict the character of public policy in any specific situation. The institutional facts mentioned here make a few statements possible, however. (1) Congressional action is likely to be influenced more than that of the other branches by the reactions of differentiated publics, although these are in turn strengthened or weakened by the complex pattern of relations inside Congress and by the nature of other congressional business. (2) Executive action is likely to be influenced more than that of the other branches by the economic and social milieu and by expert judgment of the implications of these data, but political reactions are also important. (3) The bases for judicial policy are less predictable or uniform, especially in view of the restrictions on admissibility of evidence, the arbitrariness of judicial notice, the multiplicity of courts, the varied backgrounds of judges, and the smaller number of persons involved in judicial decision making.

FORMS OF ACTION AVAILABLE TO THE RESPECTIVE BRANCHES

When the forms of action available to the respective branches are considered, the result also favors the executive as the most appropriate agency to which to entrust responsibility to intervene in a national emergency dispute.

The courts are inhibited by their inability to do much more than enjoin specified types of action or the strike itself and to impose fines or imprisonment for contempt.

Under the Taft-Hartley Act, an injunction may be issued only upon application of the Attorney General at the direction of the President or upon application of the NLRB. In the former case, which is applicable to national emergency disputes, there must be a presidential finding that continuance of the strike will imperil the national health or safety.[8] In the latter case there must be reason to believe that an unfair labor practice has been committed.[9] The equity jurisdiction of the courts to issue injunctions upon application of an employer is sharply limited by the Norris-LaGuardia Act, although the fact that the Act itself is subject to interpretation by

[8] Sections 206-208.
[9] Sections 10(c), 10(j), and 10(l).

the courts renders the exact scope of the limitation questionable.[10]

Congress may at any time change either the statutory or the equity jurisdiction of the courts to issue injunctions. To the extent that it permits issuance of injunctions upon application of private parties, Congress allows the courts to determine for themselves the timing of their intervention in emergency disputes. The trend of congressional action in the last twenty-five years has consistently been in the direction of encouraging executive determination of the timing of judicial intervention; and in view of the considerations already discussed, this is a desirable policy. If the grievances underlying a dispute are complicated, the bludgeon of an injunction may aggravate them, and the executive is in the best position to judge the impact of the various factors on affected groups.[11]

The Congress may lay down rules of general and future applicability, but may have difficulty in fashioning a remedy for the case at hand without unintentionally muddying distant waters. To apply sanctions to one of the parties which are clearly without wider or later applicability is to run the risk of enacting a bill of attainder.[12] By resolution, it may call upon the executive to intervene, as suggested above.

The executive enjoys wide freedom of action. Its arsenal of weapons permits it to proffer its good offices; to persuade, cajole, explain, or threaten, behind the scenes or in public; to impose mild or severe sanctions on either party or both; and to set either the courts or the Congress in motion in order to gain the advantages of their legal powers. The specific forms of action potentially available to the executive branch include informal discussion, mediation, voluntary arbitration, fact finding with publicity for recommenda-

[10] The dictum of the Supreme Court in *United States v. United Mine Workers of America*, 330 U. S. 258 (1947), suggests that there may still be considerable discretion in the courts based upon their authority to issue a temporary restraining order even if it should later be determined that they were without jurisdiction in view of the facts of the particular case.

[11] The executive wields some controls even over the injunctive process, for the President enjoys the power to pardon for criminal contempt of court. See *ex parte Grossman*, 267 U. S. 87 (1925). Corwin observes that "the practical significance of the Grossman Case is that it clearly recognizes a pardoning power which is able to cope with 'government by injunction'," and which is important in the field of labor law. Cf. Edward S. Corwin, *The President, Office and Powers* (New York: New York University Press, 1948), p. 199.

[12] Cf. *United States v. Lovett*, 328 U. S. 303 (1946).

tions, direct appeals to the parties and to the public, seizure (with a variety of fiscal and managerial arrangements), application for a court injunction, recommendations to Congress for legislation, the dispatch of troops, and indirect sanctions. The last-named may include zealous enforcement of the draft, the income tax laws, or the wage and hour act, discretion in the award of government contracts, or reliance on any other current legislation which offers scope for the exercise of administrative discretion. In any particular dispute, some of these remedies will favor labor and others management. They offer opportunity to encourage private discussion between the disputants, moral pressure from the immediately interested public or from a larger public created by a presidential statement or a fact-finding report, maintenance of the status quo pending a settlement, a change in the status quo in line with official recommendations, or a direct order to resume work. Probably most important of all, they permit the President to try mild and informal remedies if he thinks the situation calls for them before more drastic ones are needed.[13]

Most of these actions may be employed by the executive branch at any time without specific congressional authorization and involve no constitutional issue. All of them, in fact, except seizure and possibly the dispatch of troops, fall into this category. Indirect sanctions fall into an interesting special category.

In the 1952 steel seizure case[14] the Supreme Court held that the President enjoys no inherent power to seize a plant in order to end a national emergency strike, at least in the context in which that strike occurred. Although a future Court may well permit a future seizure, advance congressional authorization for the President to seize would remove uncertainty. In the past, Presidents have sometimes based seizure action upon a claim of inherent powers. President Roosevelt's seizures of seven plants between January 1942 and the enactment of the War Labor Disputes Act in June 1943 as well as President Truman's seizure of the steel plants in 1952 were justified on this ground, and in the latter instance the Supreme Court held it an insufficient one. Other seizures have been based on wartime acts granting emergency powers to the executive, including

[13] More detailed discussions of their impact on disputes are found in other chapters. Although judges and individual congressmen may also try informal intervention, they enjoy neither the facilities nor the influence on public opinion that the Chief Executive commands.

[14] *Youngstown Sheet & Tube Co. v. Sawyer,* 343 U. S. 579 (1952).

the power to seize in order to maintain production for war. It is hardly open to doubt, however, that Congress may constitutionally grant seizure power to the President in the absence of a wartime emergency, to be invoked upon a finding that the flow of commerce is being interrupted, the national defense is being impaired, or any other evil exists with which Congress may constitutionally deal. If there is to be seizure, the authority to determine when it should be invoked should be vested in the executive for the reasons already discussed. Actual administration of a seized industry is an executive function by definition.

Indirect sanctions have doubtless been employed by governments since prehistoric times as a means of exerting extralegal pressure upon a party when more direct penalties would be invalid, inconvenient, or slow. In World War II they served as a major means of accomplishing the objectives of the War Labor Board, the War Production Board, the War Manpower Commission, and the Office of Price Administration, even after all but the first of these agencies had been authorized by Congress to impose certain direct penalties for violations of their orders. Withholding of government contracts, denial of the use of public employment office facilities, priority referrals of manpower, and "suspension orders" which prohibited an offender from receiving necessary supplies were all utilized without direct legislative authorization. In an important test case, the Supreme Court refused to enjoin the Price Administrator from denying oil to a retail fuel oil dealer for a year for violation of a rationing order. The Court took the view that the suspension order was valid as a direct aid in promoting a purpose which Congress had sought to encourage by creation of OPA.[15] The chances are that indirect sanctions will not be held unconstitutional so long as the Court can be persuaded that they are instrumental in promoting an end sought by valid legislation.

Like mediation or attempts to bring public pressure to bear, indirect sanctions are likely to be applied by the executive whenever it feels enough pressure to do so whether or not Congress or the courts intervene first. On the other hand, they are almost always capable of reversal by judicial or legislative action, and their application in defiance of strong group values would unquestionably bring a quick remedy from one or both of these organs. In an

[15] *Steuart and Bros., Inc., v. Bowles,* 322 U.S. 598 (1944).

emergency dispute there would invariably be the necessary publicity to bring about this result.

A frequent method of presidential intervention in earlier years was the dispatch of troops to maintain order, with or without a request from the governor of the state in which violence allegedly threatened. In case a serious threat to public order should really arise in connection with a dispute, only the executive branch is in a position to resort to this remedy. The device is unlikely to be used short of dire emergency because of the stigma resulting from its abuse in the past to terrorize workers and break strikes. Legal challenges to the President's authority to dispatch troops have been resolved in his favor in the past,[16] and no other holding is likely today.

Taken together, these possibilities constitute an impressive array of presidential remedies, clinical and cathartic. Although their misuse can have serious effects upon private parties, the bases of executive action make misuse much less likely than is the case with the other branches; and executive remedies for the most part are less drastic and therefore more easily changed if they prove unsatisfactory.

Even if there should be a majority in Congress so distrustful of the President as to wish to displace him entirely from any role in handling emergency disputes, it is difficult to see how it might be accomplished. Most forms of presidential action do not require congressional authorization, and a congressional resolution declaring the President without authority to resort to them would almost certainly be held unconstitutional as impinging on the prerogatives of a coordinate branch of government. There is also the practical consideration that Congress may not be in session. These influences probably help explain the failure of the Eightieth Congress to try to reduce Truman's role in national emergency strikes even though that Congress obviously disliked his labor policies.

PUBLIC LABOR-RELATIONS POLICY AND DISPUTES

Although these considerations suggest that the executive is the appropriate branch both to "trigger" intervention and to determine its immediate character during a dispute, the same considerations

[16] *In re Debs,* 158 U.S. 564 (1895).

emphasize the inadequacy of any discussion of government intervention which assumes that either a dispute or an instance of governmental action is an incident complete in itself, with a definite beginning and end. The myriad governmental acts which influence labor-management power relationships and collective bargaining also influence the occurrence of disputes, which are an extension and an integral part of bargaining. Governmental action to change bargaining relations is therefore a phase and major determinant of intervention in disputes.

The contemporary history of industrial relations is a history of changes in wage levels, hours, and conditions of employment through which workers have shared in some degree in the nation's economic progress. Apart from their short-term timing, these changes have not occurred piecemeal as the result of unique conditions in particular plants, but generally over most of the economy and especially in the major industries in which national emergency strikes are likely to occur. The most dramatic recent examples of the phenomenon have been the postwar series of "rounds" of wage rises and advances in fringe benefits. Outstanding illustrations from an earlier day are the eight-hour day movement, the secular rise in money wages and, to some extent, in real wages, and the development of union security in the thirties and forties.

In the case of each of these changes, economic bargaining, government influence, and strikes played major roles, with variations as to their respective significance by issue, by industry, and by political climate. With changes in the values of interested groups of the population regarding appropriate distributive shares of the national product, government intervention was inevitable if direct negotiation did not produce the changes, and strikes were inevitable if nothing else produced them. Government intervention in railway labor relations and strikes in coal are cases in point. Ross has demonstrated that trade union wage policy is not determined by absolute standards in the minds of particular union officials but rather is significantly influenced by comparisons with the achievements of other unions.[17] Similarly, labor's dissatisfaction with its distributive share in general is a function of the climate of values among

[17] Arthur M. Ross, *Trade Union Wage Policy* (Berkeley and Los Angeles: University of California Press, 1948), pp. 49-52.

the interested public, just as public policy is a function of this same climate. This is not to say that unions ask no more than a Gallup poll would concede them, but only that their demands change as evidence appears that there will be some public support for them and a minimum of outraged shock. *In this sense, therefore, government intervention, economic bargaining, and strikes are alternative channels through which dominant public values are tested and finally realized in labor policy.* And it behooves us in critical industries to substitute an acceptable channel for an unacceptable one.

The Congress can give such values their sharpest institutional expression when the legislature is concerned with long-term, generally applicable rules and can act in leisurely tempo with widespread discussion in Congress and among the interested public. There is needed in this process the clearest possible expression of the needs of all relevant economic groups and of the impact of labor policy on each of them as well as on labor and management themselves. In Congress each group with enough support to be of concern to one or more members will find forceful expression if the debate is widely publicized and understood. In the executive branch all groups do not find equally clear expression if only because the decision-making process is not conducted in public to anything like the same degree, and because the President must accommodate conflicting interests to each other before he takes a public stand. In the executive, then, there cannot be that useful period of public interplay between representatives of conflicting groups and interested citizens which is characteristic of congressional action on controversial matters. In the courts the opportunity for expression of those who have not suffered legal injury or are not personally acquainted with the judge is, of course, still more limited.

The chronic reluctance of congressmen to deal with a controversial problem when it can be postponed may be counted on to prevent too frequent congressional action of the kind contemplated here. It would nevertheless be well for Congress to become sensitive to those occasional waves of restiveness accompanying general movements for advances in some phase of social security or in wages after a period of controls. These are recognizable by the astute and careful observer before they become general, and they are predictable to a considerable extent.

We do know something of the times and conditions in which

disputes in critical industries are likely to occur and in which legislation might therefore be considered. In his study of "Thirty-Six Years of 'National Emergency' Strikes," Warren found "significant increases in the number during the two postwar periods—1919-1922 and 1945-1949" and a large number as well in the years between emergence from the depression and the imposition of wartime controls in 1942.[18] He found few during the two world wars, during the open-shop era of 1923 to 1929, and at the bottom of the depression. These findings suggest that disputes are most likely to occur when economic conditions are improving and labor is able and free to seek a larger share of the national income through pressure on management, especially if economic controls have diminished its share in the immediate past. They are less likely to occur when depression, union weakness, or governmental controls make concession from management unlikely or impossible. It is also true that factionalism within a union or rivalry between unions may help produce labor-management disputes, but union factionalism and rivalry are most likely to occur when there is widespread discontent with wages, hours, or conditions of work. Even these disputes are therefore ultimately related to the conformance of labor standards with effective public values.

That congressional attention to the needs of labor and management in critical industries mitigates the chance of national emergency strikes finds its most persuasive evidence in railroad labor history, although, as usual, the social scientist would wish the control situation to be a great deal less clouded. Probably because the impact of railroad strikes is so immediate and obvious to so many economic groups with political influence, a significant number of congressmen and senators have watched the industry warily and usually reacted sensitively. Mediation and arbitration machinery, the eight-hour day, the right to organize and bargain collectively, a retirement plan, and unemployment compensation were all granted by legislation before comparable benefits were enacted for other industries.[19] Warren found that no important rail strike occurred in the twenty years between 1923 and 1943 and that "the number of

[18] Warren, *op. cit.*, p. 6.
[19] That the railroads were the first industry to be granted the dubious attentions of an independent regulatory commission with respect to rates and services is further evidence for the hypothesis.

serious railroad strikes has decreased materially as compared with other industries."[20]

If it is a correct assumption that government action is influenced by the information available to the agency that acts, there are institutional methods of increasing congressional sensitivity to the needs of the industries in which national emergency disputes are most likely to occur. Possibly the most effective such method is enlargement of the congressional committees concerned with labor to include experts on these industries, with an assignment of continuous surveillance over their needs, the state of their industrial relations, and, above all, the impact of strikes in these industries on affected groups of the population.[21] Such studies should be supplemented with regular reports from the executive agencies with information to offer. In the Council of Economic Advisers we already have a rough model of the kind of analytical and preparatory operation which is suggested here for the specific problem of national emergency disputes. That the council is part of the executive office of the President and reports through the President may help explain the frequent lack of congressional enthusiasm for its recommendations. As part of the legislative process, a congressional committee staff would probably be more potent.

This discussion suggests that the executive should be recognized as having paramount responsibility for determining the timing and character of government intervention in the course of national emergency strikes, and that Congress should be encouraged to make sure that strong and widely held public values are realized in labor policy before unions in key industries attempt to effectuate them through strikes. Judicial powers may sometimes be useful in ending emergency strikes, but the decision whether to apply for an injunction should be made by the executive and not by a party to the dispute.

[20] Warren, *op. cit.*, p. 8.
[21] One plan for analyzing the impact of strikes on affected groups has been suggested by Chamberlain. Chamberlain and Schilling, *op. cit.*, Chaps. 2, 3.

APPENDIX A

THE OPERATION OF THE

NATIONAL EMERGENCY PROVISIONS, 1947-1954

BY CHARLES M. REHMUS

Federal Mediation and Conciliation Service

The national emergency machinery has been invoked on twelve occasions since the passage of the Labor-Management Relations Act on June 23, 1947. The first dispute in which the President intervened involved the atomic energy installation at Oak Ridge. Subsequently, the provisions have been applied to the meat-packing industry, telephone industry, maritime industry, Atlantic coast longshoring industry (on two occasions), bituminous coal industry (on three occasions), nonferrous metals industry, a single pipe-manufacturing plant in the steel fabricating industry, and the Oak Ridge-Paducah atomic energy installations.

Work stoppages were involved in nine of the twelve cases: the exceptions were the first atomic energy dispute, the telephone dispute, and the 1948 contract dispute in the bituminous coal industry. In six of the disputes a work stoppage was in progress (or about to start) when the board of inquiry was appointed. In three others, the Pacific coast maritime and both Atlantic coast longshore disputes, a work stoppage began after all the procedures of the Act had been completed and the eighty-day injunction had expired.

The boards of inquiry have all been composed of three members, with the exception of the board in the maritime dispute which was composed of five members in order that it could hold simultaneous

261

(Text continued on p. 268.)

TABLE 2. SUMMARY OF THE TWELVE CASES OF RESORT

Dispute	Parties to the Dispute	Major Issues
1. Atomic Energy Dispute March-June 1948	Atomic Trades and Labor Council (AFL) and Carbide and Carbon Chemicals Corp.	Wages, sick leave
2. Meat-packing Dispute March-June 1948	United Packinghouse Workers (CIO) and five major meat-packing companies	Wages
3. Bituminous Coal Pension Dispute March-June 1948	United Mine Workers of America (Ind.) and bituminous coal mine operators	Beginning and operation of miners' pension plan
4. Telephone Dispute May-June 1948	American Union of Telephone Workers (CIO) and American Telephone & Telegraph Co.	Wages, working conditions
5. Maritime Industry Dispute June-November 1948	Seven maritime unions (primarily CIO) and shipping companies	Hiring hall retention, wages
6. Bituminous Coal Contract Dispute June 1948	United Mine Workers of America (Ind.) and bituminous coal mine operators	Wages, operation of pension plan, union security
7. Atlantic Coast Longshore Dispute August-November 1948	International Longshoremen's Association (AFL) and shipping companies	Wages, overtime rates
8. Bituminous Coal Contract Dispute September 1949-March 1950	United Mine Workers of America (Ind.) and bituminous coal mine operators	Wages, working conditions, pension and welfare funds
9. Nonferrous Metals Dispute August-November 1951	Mine, Mill & Smelter Workers (Ind.) and copper and zinc mine and smelter operators	Wages
10. American Locomotive Dispute October 1952-March 1953	United Steelworkers of America (CIO) and American Locomotive Co.	Wages, union security
11. Atlantic Coast Longshore Dispute October 1953-April 1954	International Longshoremen's Association (Ind.) and shipping companies	Wages, working conditions, appropriate bargaining agent
12. Atomic Energy Dispute July-November 1954	United Gas, Coke and Chemical Workers (CIO) and Carbide and Carbon Chemicals Corp.	Wages

Work Stoppage Data	Date of Appointment and Members of Board of Inquiry

Threatened strike.	March 5, 1948
	  John Lord O'Brien, Chm.
	  C. Canby Balderston
	  Stanley F. Teele

Strike involving 83,000 workers in 20 states began March 16, 1948.	March 15, 1948
	  Nathan P. Feinsinger, Chm.
	  Pearce Davis
	  Walter V. Schaefer

Work stoppage involving 320,000 workers began March 15, 1948.	March 23, 1948
	  Sherman Minton, Chm.
	  Mark Ethridge
	  George W. Taylor

Threatened strike.	May 18, 1948
	  Sumner H. Slichter, Chm.
	  Charles A. Horsky
	  Aaron Horvitz

Threatened strike, Atlantic and Gulf coasts and Great Lakes. Strike involving 28,000 Pacific coast workers began on September 3, after dissolution of injunction.	June 3, 1948
	  Harry Shulman, Chm.
	  Arthur P. Allen
	  George Cheney
	  Jesse Freidin
	  Andrew Jackson

Threatened strike in commercial mines. A 10-day strike involving 42,000 "captive" mine workers occurred during July 1948.	June 19, 1948
	  David L. Cole, Chm.
	  E. Wight Bakke
	  Waldo E. Fisher

A strike involving 48,000 workers began November 12, 1948, after dissolution of the injunction.	August 17, 1948
	  Saul Wallen, Chm.
	  Julius Kass
	  Joseph L. Miller

A strike involving 320,000 workers began September 19, 1949, and continued sporadically through February 1950.	February 6, 1950
	  David L. Cole, Chm.
	  John T. Dunlop
	  W. Willard Wirtz

A strike involving 40,000 workers in 10 western states began August 27, 1951.	August 30, 1951
	  Ralph T. Seward, Chm.
	  G. Allen Dash
	  Joseph L. Miller

A strike involving 1,400 workers producing goods for Atomic Energy Commission contracts began October 20, 1952.	December 3, 1952
	  Abraham J. Harris, Chm.
	  George Cheney
	  Phillip Levy

A strike involving 65,000 Atlantic coast dockworkers began October 1, 1953, and ended after October 5 injunction. An unauthorized strike of 14,000 Port of New York workers began March 5, 1954.	October 1, 1953
	  David L. Cole, Chm.
	  Harry J. Carmen
	  Dennis J. Comey, S.J.

Strike July 7 through July 10, 1954. Resumption of strike scheduled for August 12.	July 6, 1954
	  Thomas K. Glennan, Chm.
	  John L. Floberg
	  Paul H. Sanders

TABLE 2. SUMMARY OF THE TWELVE CASES OF RESORT

Dispute	Date Board Reported to the President	Date Injunction Issued
1. Atomic Energy Dispute March-June 1948	March 15, 1948	March 19, 1948
2. Meat-packing Dispute March-June 1948	April 8, 1948	None requested.
3. Bituminous Coal Pension Dispute March-June 1948	March 31, 1948	Temporary restraining order, April 3, 1948. Permanent 80-day injunction April 21, 1948.
4. Telephone Dispute May-June 1948	None made.	None requested.
5. Maritime Industry Dispute June-November 1948	June 11, 1948	Temporary restraining orders, June 14 and 22, 1948. Permanent 80-day injunction: Atlantic and Gulf, June 23, 1948; Great Lake, June 30, 1948; Pacific, July 2, 1948.
6. Bituminous Coal Contract Dispute June 1948	June 26, 1948	None requested.
7. Atlantic Coast Longshore Dispute August-November 1948	August 20, 1948	August 24, 1948
8. Bituminous Coal Contract Dispute September 1949-March 1950	February 11, 1950	February 11, 1950
9. Nonferrous Metals Dispute August-November 1951	September 4, 1951	September 5, 1951
10. American Locomotive Dispute October 1952-March 1953	December 11, 1952	December 12, 1952
11. Atlantic Coast Longshore Dispute October 1953-April 1954	October 5, 1953	October 5, 1953
12. Atomic Energy Dispute July-November 1954	July 10, 1954	August 11, 1954

Date of Final Report	"Final Offer" Ballot
May 18, 1948	June 1-2, 1948. Employer's "final offer" rejected 771-26.
None made.	Not held.
None made.	Not held.
None made.	Not held.
August 14, 1948	Held on Pacific coast only. Election boycotted by ILWU (CIO) and no votes were cast. Other unions rejected.
None made.	Not held.
October 21, 1948	November 4-5, 1948. Rejected 26,646-1,083.
None made.	Not held.
November 5, 1951	Elections held in a few small plants November 10-11, 1951. Rejected.
February 10, 1953, reporting "no last offer." Supplemented February 11, 1953.	On February 15, 1953, the NLRB postponed election "indefinitely."
December 4, 1953	Not held on recommendation of board of inquiry.
About October 12, 1954	October 21-22, 1954. Rejected 3,480-745.

TABLE 2. SUMMARY OF THE TWELVE CASES OF RESORT

Dispute	Date of Dissolution of Injunction
1. Atomic Energy Dispute March-June 1948	June 11, 1948
2. Meat-packing Dispute March-June 1948	
3. Bituminous Coal Pension Dispute March-June 1948	June 23, 1948
4. Telephone Dispute May-June 1948	
5. Maritime Industry Dispute June-November 1948	September 1-2, 1948
6. Bituminous Coal Contract Dispute June 1948	
7. Atlantic Coast Longshore Dispute August-November 1948	November 9, 1948
8. Bituminous Coal Contract Dispute September 1949-March 1950	April 30, 1950
9. Nonferrous Metals Dispute August-November 1951	November 25, 1951
10. American Locomotive Dispute October 1952-March 1953	March 3, 1953
11. Atlantic Coast Longshore Dispute October 1953-April 1954	December 24, 1953
12. Atomic Energy Dispute July-November 1954	October 30, 1954

Final Resolution of Dispute

Agreement reached on all issues on June 15, 1948, after 50 hours of mediation and negotiations. On June 18, 1948, the President reported to Congress, recommended that a study be undertaken to suggest special methods for handling atomic energy disputes.

Strike at plants of four companies ended on May 21 and at the fifth on June 5, 1948, following union's acceptance of employer's original offer.

Compromise agreement for beginning pension plan reached on April 12, 1948. The union and its president, John L. Lewis, were found guilty of contempt for violation of the temporary order of April 3 and received heavy fines.

Board of inquiry hearings scheduled to begin May 25 were postponed until June 8, 1948. On June 14 in mediation sessions the parties reached agreement on all issues.

Agreements on wages and temporary retention of hiring halls were reached on September 1 for Atlantic and Gulf coasts. Pacific coast strikes were settled on same basis on November 25-30, 1948.

On June 22 a court decision settled pension dispute. On June 24 agreement was reached on all issues with commercial mines. The "captive" mine strike over the union shop was settled during July 1948.

Agreement on all issues was reached and strike concluded in mediation sessions on November 25, 1948.

Strike continued after issuance of injunction, but union was found not guilty of contempt of court. On March 3 the President asked power to seize mines, following which dispute was settled on March 5, 1950.

The union and the largest copper producer reached agreement on September 2, while board was meeting. This was pattern for remaining agreements reached during September-November 1951.

Agreement on all issues reached in mediation sessions, February 21, 1953.

Dispute was fundamentally jurisdictional between ILA (Ind.) and ILA (AFL) as to representation of Atlantic coast dockworkers. New York waterfront strike ended April 2, 1954, so that ILA (Ind.) could participate in second representation election. Contract dispute in other Atlantic ports settled between operators and ILA (Ind.) on February 12, 1954.

Agreement on wage increase reached in mediation sessions, about November 7, 1954.

hearings on both the east and west coasts. All boards filed an initial report with the President except that appointed to serve in the telephone dispute.

Injunctions were requested and obtained in all cases except the meat-packing, telephone, and 1948 bituminous coal contract disputes.[1] The injunction was effective to halt or prevent a work stoppage in every case except the bituminous coal contract dispute of 1950. In this case the work stoppage continued after the issuance of the injunction, and the union and its president were absolved of responsibility for the continuance of the stoppage in a trial for contempt of court.

The boards of inquiry submitted final reports to the President in seven of the disputes, but "final offer" ballots were held in only five of these situations: the two atomic disputes, the maritime dispute, the longshore dispute of 1948, and the nonferrous metals dispute. In each of these ballots the employer's "final offer" was rejected. In the maritime dispute the ILWU boycotted the election and not a single ballot was cast by members of that union.

In only two of the disputes where an injunction was issued was the dispute settled during the statutory eighty-day period; these were the bituminous coal pension dispute and the American Locomotive dispute. As was noted earlier, in three disputes the dissolution of the injunction was followed by a serious work stoppage.

Table 2 summarizes the basic information concerning each dispute, including the parties concerned, work stoppage data, the members and pertinent dates concerning the board of inquiry and the other steps in the national emergency machinery, and the basis for final resolution of each dispute.

[1] Three injunctions were obtained in the maritime dispute: for the Atlantic and Gulf coasts, Great Lakes, and Pacific coast areas, respectively. This, along with the fact that it involved seven unions only some of which participated in the work stoppages, has led some authorities to consider this three different disputes. However, the board of inquiry and the official government records dealt with it as a single dispute involving the same basic issues on all coasts.

APPENDIX B

LABOR MANAGEMENT RELATIONS

(TAFT-HARTLEY) ACT, 1947

TITLE II—NATIONAL EMERGENCY PROVISIONS

Sec. 206. Whenever in the opinion of the President of the United States, a threatened or actual strike or lock-out affecting an entire industry or a substantial part thereof engaged in trade, commerce, transportation, transmission, or communication among the several States or with foreign nations, or engaged in the production of goods for commerce, will, if permitted to occur or to continue, imperil the national health or safety, he may appoint a board of inquiry to inquire into the issues involved in the dispute and to make a written report to him within such time as he shall prescribe. Such report shall include a statement of the facts with respect to the dispute, including each party's statement of its position but shall not contain any recommendations. The President shall file a copy of such report with the Service and shall make its contents available to the public.

Sec. 207. (a) A board of inquiry shall be composed of a chairman and such other members as the President shall determine, and shall have power to sit and act in any place within the United States and to conduct such hearings either in public or in private, as it may deem necessary or proper, to ascertain the facts with respect to the causes and circumstances of the dispute.

(b) Members of a board of inquiry shall receive compensation at the rate of $50 for each day actually spent by them in the work of the board, together with necessary travel and subsistence expenses.

(c) For the purpose of any hearing or inquiry conducted by any board appointed under this title, the provisions of sections 9 and 10 (relating to the attendance of witnesses and the production of books, papers, and documents) of the Federal Trade Commission Act of September 16, 1914, as amended (U. S. C. 19, title 15, secs. 49 and 50, as amended), are hereby made applicable to the powers and duties of such board.

Sec. 208. (a) Upon receiving a report from a board of inquiry the President may direct the Attorney General to petition any district court of the United States having jurisdiction of the parties to enjoin such strike or lock-out or the continuing thereof, and if the court finds that such threatened or actual strike or lock-out—

(i) affects an entire industry or a substantial part thereof engaged in trade, commerce, transportation, transmission, or communication among the several States or with foreign nations, or engaged in the production of goods for commerce; and

(ii) if permitted to occur or to continue, will imperil the national health or safety, it shall have jurisdiction to enjoin any such strike or lock-out, or the continuing thereof, and to make such other orders as may be appropriate.

(b) In any case, the provisions of the Act of March 23, 1932, entitled "An Act to amend the Judicial Code and to define and limit the jurisdiction of courts sitting in equity, and for other purposes," shall not be applicable.

(c) The order or orders of the court shall be subject to review by the appropriate circuit court of appeals and by the Supreme Court upon writ of certiorari or certification as provided in sections 239 and 240 of the Judicial Code, as amended (U. S. C., title 29, secs. 346 and 347).

Sec. 209. (a) Whenever a district court has issued an order under section 208 enjoining acts or practices which imperil or threaten to imperil the national health or safety, it shall be the duty of the parties to the labor dispute giving rise to such order to make every effort to adjust and settle their differences, with the assistance of the Service created by this Act. Neither party shall be under any duty to accept, in whole or in part, any proposal of settlement made by the Service.

(b) Upon the issuance of such order, the President shall reconvene the board of inquiry which has previously reported with respect to the dispute. At the end of a sixty-day period (unless the dispute has been settled by that time), the board of inquiry shall report to the President the current position of the parties and the efforts which have been made for settlement, and shall include a statement by each party of its position and a statement of the employer's last offer of settlement. The President shall make such report available to the public. The National Labor Relations Board, within the succeeding fifteen days, shall take a secret ballot of the employees of each employer involved in the dispute on the question of whether they wish to accept the final offer of settlement made by their employer as stated by him and shall certify the results thereof to the Attorney General within five days thereafter.

Sec. 210. Upon the certification of the results of such ballot or upon a settlement being reached, whichever happens sooner, the Attorney General shall move the court to discharge the injunction, which motion shall then be granted and the injunction discharged. When such motion is granted, the President shall submit to the Congress a full and comprehensive report of the proceedings, including the findings of the board of inquiry and the ballot taken by the National Labor Relations Board, together with such recommendations as he may see fit to make for consideration and appropriate action.

BARD COLLEGE LIBRARY

Main
HD 5324 .I5
Emergency disputes and nationa

35131000903478

WITHDRAWN

BARD COLLEGE LIBRARY
ANNANDALE-ON-HUDSON, N.Y.